Summer in the City

Summer in the City

John Lindsay, New York, and the American Dream

Edited by
JOSEPH P. VITERITTI

Johns Hopkins University Press
Baltimore

Johns Hopkins University Press
2715 North Charles Street
Baltimore, Maryland 21218-4363
www.press.jhu.edu

Library of Congress Cataloging-in-Publication Data

Summer in the city : John Lindsay, New York, and the American dream / edited by
Joseph P. Viteritti.
pages cm
Includes index.
ISBN-13: 978-1-4214-1261-0 (hardcover : acid-free paper)
ISBN-13: 978-1-4214-1262-7 (paperback : acid-free paper)
ISBN-13: 978-1-4214-1263-4 (electronic)
ISBN-10: 1-4214-1261-6 (hardcover : acid-free paper)
1. Lindsay, John V. (John Vliet)—Political and social views.   2. Lindsay,
John V. (John Vliet)—Influence.   3. New York (N.Y.)—Politics and
government—1951–1954. New York (N.Y.)—Social policy. 5. United States—Politics
and government—1963–1969.   6. United States—Social policy.   7. Mayors—New
York (State)—New York—Biography.   I. Viteritti, Joseph P., 1946–
F128.52.S86 2014
974.7'043092—dc23   2013022696

A catalog record for this book is available from the British Library.

*Special discounts are available for bulk purchases of this book. For more information,
please contact Special Sales at 410-516-6936 or specialsales@press.jhu.edu.*

Johns Hopkins University Press uses environmentally friendly book materials,
including recycled text paper that is composed of at least 30 percent post-consumer
waste, whenever possible.

CONTENTS

NYC, Then and Now

Many people involved saw the "occupation" of Wall Street that erupted in 2011 as a Western offshoot of the Arab spring, where popular demands for democracy and justice could lead to regime changes and a redirection of politics. But it is more akin to another time in New York City, when the streets teemed with rebellious energy, when politics were turbulent, when newcomers demanded a voice, and when poor people asked for help. It was a time of dramatic changes in government, economics, demographics, and law. It was a time of antiwar protests and sexual liberation, of black power and flower power. It was a period of progress and reaction. It was the national decade of civil rights and social justice, of race riots and crumbling cities. It was a time when the city government asserted itself, only to be followed in the next decade by a harsh fall, when New York stood on the brink of bankruptcy. It was the moment before the big correction, when the state stepped in and told the city to lower its sights, get its house in order, and live within its means. It was the time when a young progressive Republican Congressman ran for mayor in a stubbornly Democratic city and won.

John V. Lindsay served as mayor from 1966 to 1973. He was a controversial figure, angering conservative Republicans and regular Democrats alike by aligning himself with racial minorities and poor people who had been left on the sidelines of politics. Although he was an outspoken critic of the Vietnam War, Lindsay responded to President Lyndon Johnson's Great Society agenda with more enthusiasm than any other mayor in the country. In visibly leading New York peacefully through the racial turmoil that racked other cities, and as vice chair of the National Commission on Civil Disorders appointed by Johnson, Lindsay became a national spokesman for cities and the people who lived in them. At a time when urban crime and the fear it engendered was becoming a national epidemic, Lindsay embraced public space as a natural treasure. At a time when the middle class continued to flee cities for the suburbs, Lindsay understood that arts and culture were unique components of urban life that could anchor development and be enjoyed by all.

History has not been kind to Lindsay. He has justifiably taken his share of blame for the discrepancy between revenues and expenditures that led to the 1975 fiscal crisis and the gimmicks that went along with it as well. But the practices that fomented the crisis predated Lindsay and even escalated after he left City Hall. Urban decline was a national phenomenon. As chief executive Lindsay attracted the most impressive array of talent that had ever been assembled in the city. Their influence has continued through every subsequent mayoral administration, in New York State, and in other governments. They implemented some of the most innovative management reforms in the history of local government. They approached economic development in a way that distributed its benefits widely, among ambitious businessmen threatening to leave and unemployed workers hoping to stay, among struggling artists and destitute single mothers. Most important of all, they set priorities that advanced the movement toward political and economic equality that has been reversed today.

John Lindsay is more relevant now than at any time since he left City Hall. We need to consider whether the post–fiscal crisis priorities that sent us in a new direction sent us too far off a more just path, whether the winter frost that settled over the post-crisis city left too many of its most vulnerable exposed.

Existing Literature

There is a short, uneven body of literature on Lindsay. *The Ungovernable City* by Vincent Cannato is the most extensive book treatment of the former mayor.[1] Writing from a strong right-of-center perspective, Cannato deals with Lindsay as a proxy for American liberalism and its failed mission. It is a serious book that raised legitimate questions about the way business was conducted in New York and other cities. It questioned the role that government was playing in resolving social conflict and deprivation and especially the city's part in that role. But the central premise of the book is now open to question. Though not entirely successful, the Great Society agenda that Lindsay embraced and extended brought poverty and unemployment down to levels that even the most ambitious policy makers in the city today would deem unrealistic. By 1970, the city unemployment rate was 4.9 percent, compared with 10.5 percent in 2010.[2] In 1969, the poverty rate was 11.9 percent, compared with 20.1 percent in 2010.[3]

Martin Shefter's *Political Crisis / Fiscal Crisis: The Collapse and Revival of New York City* is a well-regarded, historically informed study of the fiscal crisis.[4] He attributes much of the city's overspending and poor accounting to Lindsay. Shefter, like other scholars of the period, however, explains Lindsay's support of poor people and minorities as an opportunistic response to "interest group liberalism." He doesn't account for the political risks or liabilities involved when an elected official embraces the cause of those who are weak. Nor does he acknowledge that Lindsay's politics were rooted in a strong philosophical commitment to equality and civil rights that was evident early on in Lindsay's congressional career.

Charles R. Morris's *The Cost of Good Intentions: New York City and the Liberal Experiment, 1960–1975* is the most even-handed assessment of Lindsay to date.[5] It explained the causes of the fiscal crisis of the 1970s and was pivotal in emphasizing that American cities could not continue to conduct their affairs the way they had. At the same time Morris was not unsympathetic to the compassionate goals that contributed to fiscal collapse. Morris's book marked the beginning of the post-liberal era. It reflected a growing body of literature that emphasized the limits of cities and their capacity to solve deeply rooted social problems.[6] It marked a retreat from the activist governmental role characterized by the Great Society. This volume asks two important questions: whether we have moved too far in the other direction since the fiscal crisis and what can be learned from the Lindsay period that preceded it.

Lindsay's Relevance

There has been a recent flurry of interest in John Lindsay. In 2010, the Museum for the City of New York sponsored a special exhibit on his mayoralty. Simultaneously, New York's public television station WNET produced a documentary film featuring Lindsay's years at City Hall. As part of the same project, Sam Roberts of the *New York Times* edited *America's Mayor*.[7] This glossy, photo-rich collection contains essays from a cross-section of journalists, academicians, and government practitioners who knew, studied, or remembered Lindsay and the years he served as mayor. It is an entertaining and informative book that should be read alongside this one.

While the mortgage crisis and the consequential financial meltdown were in full bloom when the Roberts book was published, the political reaction to it was still nascent. Today polls show that most Americans believe that political and economic inequality is among the most serious problems facing the country. They have lost faith in institutions.[8] Civic participation, a hallmark of the Great Society / Lindsay agenda, is at an all-time low. It is time for a new conversation about national priorities, and cities must be part of the discussion.

American local government has played a special role in the civic project. It is the place where individuals learn to be citizens, where they acquire a sense of responsibility toward one another. Because of its historic role as the gateway to America for a vast flood of immigrants entering the country in the nineteenth and early twentieth centuries, New York City has played a unique part in that epic story, as a place of opportunity where lives were reborn. It turned generations of immigrants into Americans. It built a generous system of public services. It tried to take care of its poor.

By the time John Lindsay became mayor, however, the newcomers started to look different. They were black and brown and were not well received by those who ruled. Their needs were greater than the needs of those who preceded them; but the city was no longer growing. Middle-class residents and corporations had begun to move out; the loss of tax dollars meant that the municipality could not even afford to give newcomers the services and benefits that were made available to previous generations. Eventually, as resources disappeared, the high aspirations of the past were confronted with the harsh realities of finance, resistance, and injustice. The city was forced to reorder its priorities. The city has prospered since the reforms imposed after the fiscal crisis, but not everybody has benefitted. We need to look back. We need to reassess the balance sheet diagnostics that informed the post-liberal thinking of the past four decades.

The so-called economic recovery that has occurred since the 1975 fiscal crisis notwithstanding, one out of five New Yorkers lives in poverty. Voting in city elections has dropped 20 percent in the past four decades.[9] At a time when poverty levels are high and participation in elections is low, there is much to be learned by reexamining the agenda John Lindsay set for New York in the context of larger political and economic trends. Beyond his focus on a redistribution of benefits to help those most in need, Lindsay created institutions that incorporated underrepresented minorities into the lifeblood of politics. He tried to move government closer to the people. He tried to make the city a more livable place for all people. This book suggests that the policies produced by the combustion of politics that emanated during Lindsay's mayoralty can inform contemporary decision making. If Lindsay's tenure revealed much of what was wrong with the liberal agenda, he is also emblematic of what was right; and that story has yet to be told. More than any mayor since Fiorello LaGuardia, John Lindsay understood and fostered the civic project that has been lost as the city became absorbed in sustaining its fiscal solvency.

What Follows

In order to assess the record of any mayor, one needs to understand the time in which he served and the challenges it posed. In the first chapter, I set the stage for the remainder of the book by describing the political, social, and economic context in which Lindsay governed, including demographic changes, racial tensions, the civil rights movement, the black power movement, the welfare rights movement, the Great Society agenda, local partisanship (Democratic and Republican), the post-

Wagner labor movement, and the economic recession. The important elements of this context are both national and local. Drawing on his speeches, public statements, and early policy initiatives, I will outline the vision for the city that Lindsay brought to the job.

In the second chapter, Geoffrey Kabaservice reminds us of a time when the term "progressive Republican" was not an oxymoron, shedding further light on the historical context. He introduces us to Lindsay the man and the politician. He traces the evolution of Lindsay's career as a progressive in the Republican Party and as a politician in a city controlled by Democrats, explaining how deep-seated principles exhibited early on informed the way he governed. Kabaservice insists that there are real differences between progressives and liberals and explains the implications these differences have in the policy realm. While generally favorable to Lindsay, Kabaservice is somewhat disappointed in the former mayor's occasional retreat from bedrock progressive Republican principles.

Clarence Taylor plunges us more deeply into the turbulent topic of race relations in chapter 3. Taylor understands Lindsay's approach to race as an extension of values that were evident during his time in Congress, where Lindsay had a strong record pertaining to civil rights and social justice. Taylor looks closely at several key issues that define the record, including the civilian complaint review board controversy in the police department, the battle over community control of schools in Ocean Hill–Brownsville, and the scatter-site housing debate in Forest Hills, Queens. He explains how the creation of the Urban Action Task Force was part of Lindsay's larger attempt to establish lines of communication in troubled neighborhoods and gives an account of how Lindsay succeeded in incorporating a new generation of black and Latino leaders into the politics of New York City.

In chapter 4, Charles R. Morris presents an analysis of spending, borrowing, and taxation polices both before and after the 1975 fiscal crisis. He reviews the historical record in the context of major demographic changes, national policies, and economic trends. He explains how flawed accounting practices that led to faulty revenue projections led to default on accumulated debt. He believes that Lindsay deserves part of the blame for spending money the city did not have, but he also finds that there was plenty of blame to go around. He closes his economic portrait of the city with a candid description of the rise of "plutocracy" since the fiscal crisis.

In the fifth chapter, David Rogers illuminates the culture clash that ensued when Lindsay brought in a group of star managers led by Frederick Hayes to overhaul the byzantine bureaucracy responsible for delivering city services. Rogers conducts a detailed evaluation of the innovations they implemented, including the creation of superagencies, program planning and budgeting systems (PPBS), the role of the project management office, the productivity program, the work of the RAND Corporation, and the Office of Neighborhood Government that was created to bring government closer to the people. Some of these initiatives were more successful than others. He also introduces us to some of the key officials that Lindsay brought into his administration.

Paul Goldberger writes on Lindsay's approach to planning, design, architecture, and the use of physical space in chapter 6. He considers the distinct changes Lindsay made to the cityscape and his legacy with regard to planning practices and policy. He tells us how Lindsay blurred the boundaries between the public and private realms through incentive zoning, recruited celebrity architects to incorporate design considerations in planning, effectively opposed Robert Moses' approach to urban renewal, put political muscle behind preservation, and rethought the use of public space and public housing—all the while being less enamored with the practice of participatory planning than is generally understood and never quite succeeding at what he tried to achieve.

In chapter 7, Lizabeth Cohen and Brian Goldstein describe Lindsay's efforts to promote economic development as an upstream fight against inevitable transition from an industrial to a service-based economy. Although the transformation was national and global in scope, Lindsay argued that local government had a responsibility to blunt the adverse effects it would have on all New Yorkers, whether they be blue chip executives of major corporations or blue-collar workers in the local shipyards and factories. They tell how he formed partnerships with the private sector to retain corporate headquarters in Manhattan and sought to create new opportunities for working people in the outer boroughs. And, according to Cohen and Goldstein, he was the first chief executive to appreciate how the cultural assets of the city could fuel the declining economy.

Mariana Mogilevich elaborates on Lindsay's policies in the areas of arts and culture in the eighth chapter. As she explains it, Lindsay's practices in these areas reflect his overall understanding that cities are at the center of civilization and that arts and culture must be made available to all people, from the grand halls of the Metropolitan Museum of Art to the streets and playgrounds of every neighborhood in the outer boroughs. In sum, arts and culture would contribute to individual personal development, the expansion of democracy, and the economic health of the city as well.

With the benefit of the analyses presented in the previous chapters, I will conclude by assessing the Lindsay legacy, its relevance to contemporary policy, and its implications for the future. This is not to suggest full agreement among the contributors concerning the issues at hand, nor complete accord between them and me.

I am well aware of those differences and in order to honor them I have allowed for a certain amount of overlap in the forthcoming chapters so that each author could provide his or her own perspective on key episodes that have defined the Lindsay record. And while I will draw on the original research and insights provided by my coauthors, I would not pretend to speak for them when drawing my own conclusions.

—J.P.V.

NOTES

1. Vincent J. Cannato, *The Ungovernable City: John Lindsay and His Struggle to Save New York* (New York: Basic Books, 2001).

2. Unemployment data are drawn from U.S. Census published rates. See also Patrick McGeehan, "Jobless Rate in June Rose to 10 Percent in City, Despite Hiring," *New York Times,* July 20, 2012, p. A15.

3. Poverty data are drawn from U.S. Census published rates. By 2012, the poverty rate was 21.2%.

4. Martin Shefter, *Political Crisis / Fiscal Crisis: The Collapse and Revival of New York City* (New York: Basic Books, 1985).

5. Charles R. Morris, *The Cost of Good Intentions: New York City and the Liberal Experiment, 1960–1975* (New York: Norton, 1980).

6. See, for example, Paul E. Peterson, *City Limits* (Chicago: University of Chicago Press, 1981).

7. Sam Roberts, *America's Mayor: John V. Lindsay and the Reinvention of New York* (New York: Columbia University Press, 2010).

8. According to an ABC News / *Washington Post* poll conducted in 2011, we have hit a record low (26) in the percentage of Americans who are optimistic about our government system and how it works. This is the lowest confidence marker since 1974. See http://www.langerresearch.com/uploads/112112%202011%20Politics.pdf.

9. Lorraine C. Minnitte, *How to Think about Voter Participation*, report prepared for the New York City Charter Revision Commission, July 2010, p. 35.

The production of a new book always involves many collaborators. For edited volumes of this sort, it begins with the fine work contributed by the chapter authors themselves, in this case an extraordinary group of scholars and writers who interrupted busy schedules to make the project a priority. They have acknowledged their own debts by citing those who granted interviews and shared information that allowed us to assemble the historical record.

I also want to thank the Michael and Margaret Picotte Foundation, the Robert and Teresa Lindsay Family Foundation, Roy M. Goodman, Hamilton Rabinovitz & Associates, Robert M. Kaufman, Mary Lindsay, Stephen McDonald, Carter F. Bales, Sid Davidoff, Herb Elish, Donald H. Elliot, the Francis E. and Frederick S. Nathan Philanthropic Fund, Robert Heller, Joan Leiman, C.S. Heard, and Thomas D. Thacher. All gave generously, while without hesitation respecting the independence of our inquiries and conclusions.

Suzanne Flinchbaugh and Michele Callaghan of Johns Hopkins University Press were key partners in seeing the project through from its inception to its conclusion. Prudence Katze of the Hunter College Graduate Program in Urban Planning provided excellent backup as my research assistant and occasional artistic advisor.

I am grateful to Hunter College President Jennifer Raab for her early and continuous support of the project throughout and to Jonathan Fanton, Fay Rosenfeld, and all my friends at the Roosevelt House Public Policy Institute for planning a conference around the book's publication.

Finally, I want to thank Jay Kriegel, who gave my authors and me access to people, places, and things, and without whose help this project would not have been possible.

Summer in the City

Martin Luther King Jr. talks with President Lyndon B. Johnson in the White House Oval Office. December 3, 1963; photographer Yoichi Okamoto. From the Lyndon Baines Johnson Library and Museum White House Photo Office Collection. (W28-12)

CHAPTER ONE

Times a-Changin'

A Mayor for the Great Society

JOSEPH P. VITERITTI

On March 7, 1965, a twenty-five-year-old black man by the name of John Lewis led six hundred protesters across the Edmund Pettus Bridge in Selma, Alabama, to demand the right to vote.[1] When they disobeyed police orders to disburse, the marchers were beaten with whips and clubs. Lewis had his skull cracked. The violence that erupted on "Bloody Sunday" was not unusual. It had become an ordinary part of telecasts on the evening news. The civil rights movement was already ten years old. Just the summer before, three freedom riders were murdered in Mississippi. The year before that Martin Luther King wrote his "Letter from Birmingham Jail," appealing to the conscience of the nation and defending acts of civil disobedience as a means to advance the cause of justice.[2] It was a time when protest was the only form of activism available to people who were denied the right to vote, the same people who could be barred from a lunch counter or a park bench in the South because of their skin color, the same people who fled to New York and other cities in the North.

Lewis is now a member of the United States Congress, where he serves as a delegate from Georgia. His face among those who are seated in the House of Representatives is a measure of how far the country has come in the past fifty years, but the deep scars it bears are a cruel reminder of how long that journey has been. John Lindsay declared his candidacy for mayor on May 13, 1965, while the country was still on the first leg of that journey.

Racial animosity was not an entirely Southern affliction. On August 11, 1965, a young black man by the name of Marquette Frey was stopped on a Los Angeles street by a white policeman on suspicion of drunk driving. An argument ensued. Crowds gathered as police reinforcements were called to the scene to make an arrest and impound the car. Bottles began to fly, and soon the incident escalated into a full-scale riot. An estimated thirty-five thousand residents of the mostly black community of Watts partook in arson, looting, and other acts of violence. More than

2,400 national guardsmen were activated to impose martial law. The combined force of military and police personnel called to quell the disturbance exceeded seventeen thousand. Lasting for five consecutive days, the melee ended with thirty-five deaths, a thousand injuries, and four thousand arrests. There was $200 million in property damage. In one three-block area alone, forty-one buildings were destroyed. Most of those who died were black; most of the commercial property destroyed belonged to white-owned businesses.[3]

In a matter of days Watts became a national symbol of urban frustration and despair. The neighborhood had been plagued by poverty, unemployment, discrimination, and terrible schools. Two-thirds of all adults lacked a high school diploma; one in eight was illiterate. Watts was also a picture of simmering rage. It sent a message to the country that the struggle for racial equality was entering a new phase. Many African Americans had become impatient with the peaceful demonstrations espoused by civil rights leaders like Martin Luther King and John Lewis. They had seen orderly demonstrations met with brutality and jail time. They had seen civil rights laws flouted. Nine months prior to the Watts riots, an overwhelming majority of voters in California passed a referendum that nullified the Rumford Fair Housing Act, which had been passed in 1963 to outlaw discrimination in home sales and rentals.

The anger spread. Riots broke out in thirty-eight urban areas in 1966, including Chicago, Cleveland, Philadelphia, Milwaukee, Atlanta, and Minneapolis.[4] Cities were ablaze. The appearance of armed military personnel filing through the streets stoked white fears that the country was under siege. It was the worst domestic violence since the New York City Draft Riots of 1863. The National Advisory Commission on Civil Disorders appointed by President Lyndon B. Johnson in 1967 (referred to as the Kerner Commission after its chair, Governor Otto Kerner of Illinois, for which John Lindsay served as vice chair) recorded 187 urban disturbances in that year alone, eight of which it categorized as major. That same year a Senate committee investigating urban unrest counted eighty-three fatalities resulting from the outbursts. Most of the deaths occurred in Detroit and Newark, where the level of violence was reminiscent of Watts.[5] The key observation of the Kerner Commission, written by Lindsay staff in its terse introduction, was profound. The words rung out across the land warning, "Our nation is moving toward two societies, one black, one white—separate and unequal."[6]

The separation was happening in both body and spirit.[7] Observing the great migration that had taken place since World War II, the commission found that between 1950 and 1965, the black population in the United States had grown by 6.5 million. More than 98 percent of that growth occurred in metropolitan areas, 86 percent in central cities. During that same period, the white population had increased by 35.6 million. Approximately 78 percent of that growth was found in the suburbs. In the five years leading up to 1965, more than six hundred thousand black people moved from the South to the North and the West, with 98 percent ending up in metropolitan areas. At the same time, the white population in central cities declined by 1.3 million, while 78 percent of white population growth occurred in the suburbs. In 1966, 11 percent of whites and 40.6 percent of blacks lived below the poverty level. In 1967, the unemployment rate for blacks was double that of whites.[8]

Washington Acts

It was in the late spring of 1965, just weeks before rioting broke out in Watts, that Daniel Patrick Moynihan, then an assistant secretary of labor in the Johnson administration, wrote his controversial report on the disintegration of the black family.[9] Documenting high incidences of illegitimacy (as it was called then), child abandonment, and crime, some African American scholars condemned the report for its depiction of harsh stereotypes. Even well-meaning Americans wondered whether the portrait of rampant pathology was a cause for pity or fear, the latter of which was further fed by urban violence and disruption. White House aides had hoped that the report would help the nation understand the causes of poverty; Moynihan intended it as a call to national action.[10] In the end, it further muddied the country's turbulent political waters.[11]

Thanks to the skillful leadership of President Johnson, 1965 also would go down as the most productive year in American legislative history.[12] A year earlier, at Johnson's behest, Democratic and Republican leaders managed to overcome a fourteen-hour filibuster in the Senate to pass the most sweeping Civil Rights Act since the Civil War. With Southern Democrats leading the opposition, a larger proportion of Republicans voted for the bill than did Democrats. Johnson confided to aides that his actions could cost him reelection and dislodge the Democratic Party from control of the South for generations to come, but he persevered.[13] For the first time ever, it became illegal to practice racial discrimination in hotels, motels, theaters, or public facilities or to set unequal qualifications for voting. Although the United States Supreme Court had prohibited segregation in schools in 1954, racial separation was still widely practiced in the South. The new law empowered the United States attorney general to file suit to enforce school desegregation and expanded the powers of the Civil Rights Commission. It also prohibited discrimination on the basis of race, color, religion, gender, or national origin in government agencies that received federal funding. The Twenty-fourth Amendment was adopted earlier that year barring poll taxes in federal elections.

Johnson understood that the enactment of laws defining legal rights was insufficient to achieve true equality at a time when injustice and poverty had penetrated so many aspects of American life. Henceforth, in 1965 an avalanche of Great Society legislation was enacted to bring full citizenship and a decent life to all people. By the time the Eighty-ninth Congress had adjourned in 1966, two hundred measures had been proposed, and 181 (90.5 percent) were passed, which was an unprecedented and yet unmatched legislative record.[14] Lyndon Johnson had declared war on poverty in 1964. The bundle of programs adopted over the next two years was expansive. It covered food stamps, Medicare, Medicaid, elementary and secondary education, bilingual education, higher education, Head Start, the Teacher Corps, housing, immigration reform, law enforcement, the health professions, high speed transit, clean air, clean water, manpower training, child safety, urban mass transit, auto safety, farms, Appalachia, the wilderness, community health, vocational rehabilitation, rent supplements, a minimum wage increase, arts and the humanities, narcotics rehabilitation, bail reform, drug control, and affirmative action—and that was not even the full extent of the legislative torrent.

In order to emphasize his commitment to cities and the increasingly depressed population that was living in them, President Johnson created a Department of Housing and Urban Development (HUD) in 1965. He chose Robert Weaver as secretary, who was the first African American to hold a federal cabinet position. The following year he appointed Thurgood Marshall to the United States Supreme Court.[15] Johnson saw the Elementary and Secondary Education Act of 1965 as an antipoverty program. He had hoped that making one billion federal dollars available to poor children would help close the learning gap and that the threat of losing it would discourage segregationists from defying the law. Later additional legislative measures were enacted as part of the Great Society initiative that dealt with age discrimination, increased Social Security benefits, public broadcasting, college work-study, summer youth programs, product safety, fair housing, school breakfasts, aid to handicapped children, consumer protection, and vocational education. The era of big government had fully emerged. Washington had decided to right what was wrong with the country. There had been nothing like it since Franklin Roosevelt's New Deal, nothing since.

In some ways the strategy behind Johnson's War on Poverty was rather simple. If people are poor, the logical way to fix it is to give them jobs and resources. The approach was unambiguously redistributive. As White House aide Joseph Califano explained, "We are now asking the many to give to the few—the 15 percent of our society who comprise the 'have nots' in the wealthiest nation in the world."[16] With the creation of the Office of Economic Opportunity, government outlays to the poor increased from $13 billion in 1963 to $20 billion in 1966.[17] Between 1964 and

1967 federal spending on education went from $4 billion to $12 billion; in health it jumped from $5 billion to $16 billion. The inception of a welfare rights movement (National Welfare Rights Organization), organized by New York–based activists to get assistance for people who qualified, swelled the welfare rolls nationally and the commensurate costs. Aid to Dependent Children would increase fourfold. By 1967, Washington was appropriating $4,000 per year for each poor family in the country, quadruple of what was spent in 1961. There were tangible results. The number of Americans described as poor fell from 38 million in 1961 to 25.9 million in 1965.[18]

Johnson won support in the business community for his ambitious spending plan with the enactment of a massive tax cut of $11 billion in 1964, which he promised would fuel the economy. It worked, at least for a while. The gross domestic product increased from $569.7 billion in the first quarter in 1964 to $631.2 billion in the last quarter of 1965; disposable personal income jumped from $423 billion to $486.1 billion.[19] The invigorated economy added 8.4 million jobs between 1960 and 1966.[20]

If a real social revolution were to take place, however, political power would need to pass to those who by manner of law, custom, or deprivation were consigned to the sidelines of the democratic process. This had to start at the ballot box. The march on Selma in 1965 provided Johnson and Congress with the impetus to pass a comprehensive Voting Rights Act that voided literacy tests and authorized the attorney general to supervise elections. The law would have an extraordinary impact on Southern politics over time, which its opponents anticipated. The eventual election in Old Dixie of men like John Lewis, who before 1964 could not drink from a water fountain reserved for whites, proved the point.

The revolution also needed to move beyond the South. While black people were replacing white people in metropolitan areas, city politics was still controlled by old white ethnic machine organizations. African Americans needed to overcome the psychology of helplessness and take control of their own destiny. Black power advocates like Stokely Carmichael—a Black Panther who eventually replaced John Lewis as head of the Student Nonviolent Coordinating Committee in 1966—were already gaining influence among minority activists.[21] They demanded access to institutions and control over government resources. Washington policy makers complied.

The Community Action Program (CAP) operated by the Office of Equal Opportunity (OEO) required "maximum feasible participation of the poor" in the administration of the antipoverty programs. Federal funds were allocated directly to more than a thousand local corporations throughout the country, whose boards were chosen by community residents.[22] The results were chaotic. In many neighborhoods, control was taken by the most combative organizers, further inflaming race relations. As was the case with prior generations in urban politics, there was petty corruption. Local leaders did not always represent the best interests of the community. Nevertheless, this was a turning point. People who had regularly been excluded from having a say in government relished the opportunity to participate. And those politicians who wanted to keep the same poor and minority people in their place for a little bit longer reacted fiercely.

CAP managed to shake, though not at all shatter, the power structure of American cities. Ordinarily federal monies appropriated from Washington would be disbursed through elected officials at City Hall. With CAP, local chief executives were bypassed in favor of a new inexperienced black leadership. In 1965, the United States Conference of Mayors, led by Mayor Richard Daley of Chicago, drafted a resolution accusing OEO of fostering "class struggle" and demanded that local programs be put under their control. President Johnson, persuaded by his fellow Democrats that things were getting out of hand, ordered OEO Director Sargent Shriver to avoid political warfare and work through the usual governmental channels. In 1967, the mayors, just to be sure, took their case to Congress and persuaded it to amend CAP. A new provision removed the "maximum feasible participation" language from the statute and allowed municipalities to set up their own agencies to administer the program.

With Robert Weaver in place at the newly created HUD, the administration had hoped to bring together business, labor, and community leaders in a coordinated effort to save decaying cities. The idea for such a program was planted in the president's mind during a White House meeting with Walter Reuther, the powerful head of the United Auto Workers, which had deep roots in the declining city of Detroit. The goal of the resulting Demonstration Cities Act of 1966 was to coordinate programs in housing, education, health, employment, and recreation at the local level so that they would be effective. Also referred to as the Model Cities Program, the new HUD initiative was a break from the urban renewal programs of the past that relocated poor people out of their homes and neighborhoods. Model Cities would encourage people to maintain roots in their communities and make them better places to live through cooperative planning. In its final form, the program reached six large (500,000 people or more), ten medium-sized (250,000 to 500,000), and fifty small (fewer than 250,000) cities.[23] The law called for "widespread citizen participation." Already stung by criticism directed at the CAP from big city mayors, the administration put control of the program in the hands of local governments.

The toned-down rhetoric evident in the Model Cities initiative would be part of a larger retreat from the Great Society agenda, as domestic spending became a casualty of the Vietnam War, which drained both dollars and credibility from the

Johnson White House. In order to pay the bill for the war, the president proposed a 10 percent surcharge on corporate and business incomes for the 1968 fiscal year. The country was becoming fed up with a senseless war in a far-off land and a war on poverty that seemed to incite racial strife. On March 31, just two weeks before Martin Luther King was killed, Johnson announced that he would not seek another term. Robert Kennedy was assassinated in June while campaigning for his party's nomination, opening the door for Richard Nixon to assume the office in a campaign built around the theme of "law and order." An economic recession was on the horizon.

New York Reacts

Robert F. Wagner Jr. of New York was one of the local chief executives behind the resolution passed by the United States Conference of Mayors in 1965 urging President Johnson to back off from the strong participatory credo of CAP. By this time in the last year of his third term, Wagner had gained a reputation as a reformer of sorts. Scion of the prominent New Deal senator who had sponsored legislation carrying his name that gave organizing and collective bargaining rights to workers in certain industries, Wagner had assumed easy credibility in reform circles. Wagner also had learned at his father's knee that a man does not get elected in New York without the backing of party bosses. The father had close ties to the machine throughout his career. The son had been elected in 1953 with support from the Democratic machine at Tammany Hall, but the savvy politician eventually understood that the power of the legendary political clubs was waning. After Senator Hebert Lehman declared war on boss Carmine De Sapio and reformers began to exert influence in the party organizations, Wagner made a dramatic break in 1961 with the man who once helped him win office.[24] Until then De Sapio and Wagner had enjoyed a close alliance that enhanced the power of both men.

The break with De Sapio also helped Wagner cement his association with black leaders in Harlem, whose relationship with the party boss grew tense after Representative Adam Clayton Powell endorsed Republican presidential candidate Dwight Eisenhower over Democrat Adlai Stevenson. As pastor of the Abyssinian Baptist Church, with ten thousand loyal worshipers, Powell was the most powerful black politician in New York and the nation. Nowhere in the country had there been such a high concentration of dedicated black votes. Wagner also enjoyed a close friendship with J. Raymond Jones, Harlem's crafty political strategist who was known among his cronies as "The Fox."[25] Jones helped organize black voters throughout the city on the mayor's behalf; Wagner, in return, relied on Jones to dispense whatever political patronage there was for African Americans. Like most liberal politicians of his day, Wagner supported civil rights and gave lip service to school integration. As mayor, he built schools, provided assistance to the poor, expanded the police and fire departments, built health centers, opened three new city hospitals, and was responsible for a massive public housing program for the middle class.[26]

If Wagner had a single driving passion though, it was organized labor. He wanted to do for New York City what his father had done for the country. As a candidate for office in 1953, he promised to pass a "Little Wagner Act" that would grant collective bargaining rights to city workers. A few months after being sworn in, he issued an executive order guaranteeing the right of municipal workers to organize into unions. In 1958, as he was beginning his second term, Wagner created a city Department of Labor that was authorized to certify which organizations could represent workers in collective bargaining. Placing this function in an executive agency guaranteed that the mayor would have enormous discretion in determining which unions really mattered at the negotiating table. It enabled Wagner to empower both labor organizations and their leaders. Official recognition granted unions exclusive representation, a dues check-off, and collective bargaining privileges. The new municipal department not only negotiated wages, benefits, and working conditions; it also could hear grievances regarding allegations of unfair labor practices.

By the time Wagner broke with the party bosses in 1961, he was already in the process of building a new political base, which would prove more useful than the withering machines that once brought loyal voters to the polls. In order to alleviate Wagner's fear that he might lose the Democratic Party nomination to run for a third term, the mayor's close friend Harry Van Arsdale, who was head of the Central Trades and Labor Council, founded the Brotherhood Party. The Council brought together the leadership of many large unions, including the Teamsters, the Building Trades Council, the Transport Workers Union (TWU), the Building Services Employees, the Hotel Trades Council, the Utility Workers Union, the Brotherhood of Sleeping Car Porters, and the Retail, Wholesale, and Department Store Union.[27] Backing by the new party guaranteed the votes of many Irish and Italian workers, who habitually pulled the Democratic lever. While its leaders would loudly rail against the influence of the bosses, the Brotherhood Party was not about reform. Its main objective was to enhance the power of organized labor. Like the aging political clubs of New York, most municipal agencies were bastions of ethnic influence. As unions became more a factor in electoral politics, and eventually racial politics, they could frequently be counted on to reflect these ethnic identifications. John Lindsay would later learn this the hard way, especially when he clashed with unions representing policemen and schoolteachers.

Like the rest of the country, New York had been experiencing seismic demographic changes. Federally built highways and G.I. Bill loans that became available after World War II helped to drive the middle class from the city to the suburbs. Blacks fleeing discrimination and unemployment in the South came to New York seeking a better life, as many immigrants from Southern Europe had done generations before them. Between 1950 and 1970, the non-Hispanic black population grew from 9 percent (728,000) to 19 percent (1,526,000) of the total.[28] New York was also a convenient port of entry for Puerto Ricans and other Hispanics, whose ranks especially began to grow in the 1960s. In 1950, only 3 percent (246,000) of New Yorkers were Hispanic; by 1970, 16 percent (1,279,000) were.[29] Between 1959 and 1968 the proportion of the public school population that was black grew from 20.2 percent to 32.2 percent; that of Hispanics went from 15 percent to 21.5 percent.[30] Despite their hopes for a better life, blacks and Hispanics suffered from higher poverty and unemployment rates than did other New Yorkers. In 1969, the poverty rate for non-Hispanic whites was 4 percent, while that of non-Hispanic blacks was 11.1 percent, and for Hispanics it was 18.2 percent.[31] The unemployment rate among blacks exceeded that of whites by 44 percent, the rate among Puerto Ricans was more than double that of whites.[32]

Like other cities, New York was also the scene of growing racial unrest. The Kerner Commission, in its review of urban riots across the country, had found that most such incidents had been ignited by an altercation between a white police officer and a black civilian. New York was no exception. On July 16, 1964, two weeks after the Civil Rights Act was signed into law, a scuffle broke out on the Upper East Side between three black teenagers and a white building janitor. Thomas Gilligan, a white off-duty police lieutenant, happened to be passing by. He tried to break up the fight and drew his gun. In a matter of minutes, fifteen-year-old James Powell lay dead on the sidewalk with a bullet wound in his body. The spark of rage was ignited. Poet Langston Hughes captured the collective fury of the community when he wrote about the historic passage of black people "from the slave train to the lynch rope to the bullets of Yorkville."[33] The Congress of Racial Equality organized a march on the police station house. Gangs formed on 125th Street and moved north hauling Molotov cocktails. Five nights of mob violence in Harlem carried over into Bedford-Stuyvesant in Brooklyn. The destruction was eventually suppressed by the brutal use of police force.[34]

The Harlem riots contributed to the crisis atmosphere that had already begun to envelop New York. As early as 1959, *The Nation* magazine published a special edition on "the Shame of New York," highlighting the crime, filth, and corruption that was becoming an all too familiar part of city life.[35] The Harlem shooting and its aftermath brought the issue of police brutality center stage. Minority activists demanded the resignation of Police Commissioner Michael Murphy and called for

a civilian review board to oversee the department and investigate charges of misconduct. Mayor Wagner demurred. He expressed full confidence in the police review
board that had functioned since 1952 without civilian representation and offered to
change some of the procedures by which it operated. It was not Wagner's style to
move quickly on controversial matters, but the city was already racing into a new
era. Wagner was uncomfortable with confrontational politics, but angry clashes were
becoming the order of the day. Suffering from the loss of his wife in 1964, Wagner
seemed overwhelmed.

In 1964 and 1965 New York became the site of the World's Fair, which was held
in Flushing Meadows Park from the spring to the fall in each of the two years. It
was Robert Moses' last big act. The master builder had promised Mayor Wagner
and private investors that the fair would burnish New York's image as a world city
and generate much needed revenues. While the spectacle attracted 51 million visitors
who spent an estimated $750 million, it fell far short of Moses' predictions (70 mil-
lion attendees and $5 to $8 billion in spending). In fact the fair lost money and cost
the city treasury $50 million in addition to the $200 million absorbed by investors.[36]
Although Walt Disney Studios did its best to create a high-tech futuristic fantasy-
land, the fairgrounds were also the scene of disorderly racial demonstrations and
political protests that allowed a hostile press to portray New York as a "dying city
full of wrath and tears."[37] Marauding crowds ripped through the pavilion buildings
on its closing day, determined to carry off souvenirs—all under the watchful eye of
national television cameras.

In January of 1965 the *New York Herald Tribune* began a series than ran over four
months called, "New York City in Crisis." The series, eventually compiled into a
book, presented a portrait of a city in transition. Between 1950 and 1965, eight hundred thousand middle-class whites left the city and were replaced by newly arrived
blacks and Puerto Ricans who were more dependent on city services. Of the thirteen
thousand applications being submitted to the Department of Welfare each month,
72 percent were from black and Puerto Rican residents who could not find work in
an economy that once provided jobs for unskilled and undereducated immigrants.
In the five-year period between 1960 and 1965, more than two hundred manufacturing firms relocated from New York City to other parts of the state, while dozens
of others were finding new homes in Connecticut, New Jersey, and other parts of
the country. All told, the city hemorrhaged eighty thousand manufacturing jobs.[38]

With a wider readership and more constant coverage than *The Nation*, the *Herald Tribune* series offered readers a daily dose of stories about a once great city that
was falling victim to unsafe streets, an ailing hospital system, a government crippled
by bureaucracy, and an environment polluted by dirty air and water. The series was

National guardsmen face heckling protestors on Newark's Springfield Ave. as violence continued into a third day. Eleven died, and hundreds were injured during the 1967 riots. July 15, 1967; photographer Mel Finkelstein. © Daily News, L.P. (New York). Used with permission.

politically motivated, designed to discourage Mayor Wagner from seeking another term so that he could be replaced by a leader who was more forward thinking. The first article quoted a young Congressman from Manhattan named John Lindsay criticizing the inept leadership of Mayor Wagner, which, he warned, could transform New York into a second-class city.[39] The series was edited by Barry Gottehrer, who would later become a top aide to Lindsay in City Hall. John Hay Whitney, the owner of the newspaper, would become a major financial force behind Lindsay's campaign to get there.

Transitions

There were no poll taxes or literacy tests in New York City in 1965. These methods of deterrence were not needed to keep people down. Research shows that race, class, and education are reliable predictors of voting turnout and other forms of political involvement.[40] Since the African Americans and Puerto Ricans who came to New York were poor and undereducated, they did not vote in large numbers, nor were they seriously engaged in politics. While 76.5 percent of the eligible whites were registered to vote, only 15.5 percent of the blacks and 8 percent of the Puerto Ricans were.[41] Their minority status in the population was exacerbated by their underrepresentation in the political process. The frustration they expressed through protests and disorder presented them as a threat to the white political establishment, not to mention mainstream black politicians who had figured out ways to work with the white bosses.

Calls for civilian oversight of the police department grew, but so did resistance to real reform. A bill put forward in the City Council in 1965 to create an independent review board, later known as the Civilian Complaint Review Board (CCRB), was roundly defeated at the hands of the powerful Patrolmen's Benevolent Association. In June, as the mayoral election campaign was moving into high gear, five thousand policemen picketed City Hall urging Mayor Wagner and the local legislature to retain the existing police controlled board. Since candidate John Lindsay had announced support for the change during his first campaign speech a month earlier, the protest was as much against him as it was civilian review. The dispute would define Lindsay's relationship with the police union for years to come. A month after taking office, Lindsay delivered on his campaign pledge and announced plans to appoint a new board, which would be composed of four civilians and three policemen.[42] While the new mayor conceded that the police commissioner must have "exclusive charge" of internal operations and discipline in his department, he held that it was the mayor's ultimate responsibility as a duly elected city official to assure that the "Police Department is not a law unto itself."[43]

After unsuccessfully attempting to invalidate the board through state legislation and judicial action, the powerful police union decided to propose a popular referendum to amend the City Charter and require all members of any police review body to be full-time employees of the police department. It assembled a formidable war chest (for those days) of $500,000 from its own treasury to run television ads condemning the board as politically intrusive. It raised an additional $1 million from private donations.[44] It also garnered substantial support from the state Conservative Party, which was becoming a more influential force in local politics. William F. Buckley's run for mayor in 1965 on the Conservative Party line had been designed to provide an alternative for Republicans who could not warm to Lindsay's left-of-center politics. The police issue gave Conservatives a cause to rally.

Several aspects to the review board controversy would serve as harbingers of things to come.[45] For liberals, demands for external scrutiny of charges against the police were seen as a civil rights issue; conservatives lined up behind the police whom they believed needed popular support in the battle against rising street crime. Trumping all else was the explosive issue of race. A survey completed in Harlem by psychologist Kenneth Clark indicated that a black person was five times more likely to be a victim of police brutality than a white person was.[46] At that point in time, the police force was still more than 90 percent white.[47] More than 40 percent of those in uniform were Irish, and they controlled the upper ranks. The department was also corrupt and in need of closer supervision. In Lindsay's second term, an investigatory commission chaired by Whitman Knapp documented widespread systemic corruption that had been imbedded into the department's institutional culture throughout most of its existence.[48]

Lindsay further irritated the rank and file of the Police Department when, upon taking office in 1966, he replaced Commissioner Vincent Broderick with Howard Leary, an outsider of German ancestry who had been the Police Commissioner of Philadelphia. Broderick, a Wagner appointee with a good reputation, had clashed with Lindsay early on over the review board issue, saying publicly that the board would "hinder the administration of the Police Department" and provide an incentive for some officers "not to take action where they should take action."[49] Leary embraced the review board. He then jolted the Irish establishment in the department once again when he replaced Chief Inspector John Shanley with Sanford Garelik and Assistant Chief Inspector William McQuade with Lloyd Sealy.[50] Garelik was a Jewish lawyer from the force; Sealy, a deputy chief, was the first black man ever to be promoted to that rank. Lindsay was clearly using the appointment process to challenge the old ethnic strongholds that formed the career civil service system. He already had done the same in the fire department, the agency with the lowest representation of minorities in the workforce, when he chose a black firefighter by the name of Robert Lowery to serve as commissioner.

The Civilian Complaint Review Board went down to spectacular defeat at the polls in 1966 by a margin of 63 percent to 36 percent. This was not Lindsay's first brush with the newly emboldened forces of organized labor, nor was it to be his last beating at their hands. His first day in office was greeted by a transit strike that halted the city subways and buses for two weeks. During his first term, the city endured a nine-day sanitation men's strike that filled the streets with mountains of stinking garbage. Growing labor militancy was also evident in the private sector, where workers called strikes in the airline, construction, newspaper, and electrical utility industries; cabdrivers, deliverymen, oil truck drivers, and gravediggers did the same. In his second term, Lindsay was faced with work slowdowns and walkouts in the police and fire departments. Because of labor disputes at the state level, bridge tenders left the drawbridges open for two days, while their union brothers in treatment plants let tons of raw sewage run into the city waterways.[51]

But no episode had such a lasting impact on the new mayor or the city than his confrontation with the United Federation of Teachers (UFT). There were actually three teacher strikes in the fall of 1968, the last of which closed the schools for five weeks. Earlier that May, 350 teachers in Brooklyn staged a walkout after twelve white teachers and six white administrators were summarily "transferred" by the school board in the experimental Ocean Hill–Brownsville district.[52] During the prior summer, racial disturbances had broken out in East Harlem after a Puerto Rican teenager was critically wounded in an altercation with the police.[53] While the flare-up was not of the same magnitude of the earlier Watts riots or those that would take place in Detroit or Newark that same July, they contributed to the racial tension that had begun to ensnarl the city.

UFT president Albert Shanker had been one of the few labor leaders in the city to support Lindsay's campaign for a Civilian Complaint Review Board in the Police Department. He had a strong commitment to social justice and had been active in supporting human rights issues both at home and abroad. Shanker was also a dedicated union man and a driving force behind the organizing of teachers in New York.[54] He had led a major teachers' strike and several job actions during the Wagner years to protest low wages, meager benefits, and poor working conditions.

As policemen, firemen, sanitation men, bridge workers, and treatment plant operators were predominantly Irish and Italian Catholics, the teachers' union was controlled by the Jews, who had previously been more receptive to Lindsay's liberal politics. They were an important part of the reform coalition that put Lindsay in office. The confrontation in Ocean Hill–Brownsville between black school board members and Jewish teachers, nonetheless, epitomized the conflagration of forces that were exploding in New York during the volatile 1960s.[55] African Americans who had been segregated into failing public schools were growing more militant and demanding control over services that had overlooked their needs. These new demands put both jobs and power at stake. Charges of racism and anti-Semitism inflamed ethnic tensions and spilled over into the larger city population, which was already primed for confrontation. A newly emboldened labor organization followed its natural inclination to protect the status quo, which had acquired hard-earned legitimacy in its own right.

New York had been the first city in the country to implement a civil service merit system of recruitment based on competitive examinations. Dating back to 1883, the civil service was designed to replace the ward-based patronage system that had exchanged jobs for service to the corrupt party clubhouses. In 1954, Mayor Wagner sought state legislation that abolished the sixty-eight-year-old Municipal Civil Service Commission and established a three-member commission whose chair would serve a director of a newly created City Department of Personnel. The declared purpose of the new commission was to serve as the "guardian of the merit system."[56] It placed oversight of recruitment, hiring, placement, and promotion under the direction of an administrator appointed by the mayor.

By 1965, however, the civil service system was coming under increased criticism for setting up unfair barriers to minorities who were underrepresented in the work force. The Personnel Department was given responsibility for coordinating training and employment that became available through the federal antipoverty program. While Wagner welcomed the federal dollars as an opportunity to create more jobs for minority candidates, he continued to defend the exam-based merit system.

Lindsay took on the civil service system. He understood that, while symbolic appointments at the commissioner level were useful for communicating new priorities, the only way to deal with high levels of unemployment was to open up jobs to those who did not have them. He was critical of the exam structure. During his second year in office, he sent the three members of the Civil Service Commission to the state constitutional convention in Albany to plead for an amendment to provisions governing the merit system, which they called "discriminatory against those who can perform the jobs to be done, but who cannot do equally well on competitive tests."[57] Lindsay deliberately circumvented the exam structure to increase minority employment during his first two years in office, raising the number of city positions classified as "exempt" (not requiring a civil service test) from 1,500 to 12,000.[58] Between 1963 and 1971 the percentage of black employees in the city workforce grew from 23 percent to 28 percent; that of Puerto Ricans went from 3 percent to 6 percent.[59]

The transition from Robert Wagner's mayoralty to John Lindsay's represented a historic turning point from the moderate liberalism of a city dominated by white working-class traditions to the angrier politics of a city growing more diverse and disconnected from the old institutions. In the former, political parties provided access to politics, the civil service furnished jobs and mobility, and the private sector offered the possibility of accumulating wealth. In 1965 these paths were closed to newcomers who were not welcome by party operatives, could not pass qualifying exams, or suffered from downright racial discrimination. These new arrivals were the New Yorkers with whom John Lindsay aligned himself most. And he approached the task of helping them and the city he loved with an idealism that some would say bordered on naïveté.

Lindsay saw the politics of moderation as a remnant of the past that was ill suited for the changing times. He wanted to be an activist mayor and made a studied effort to separate himself from the ways of his predecessor. In a speech that he made to a group of foreign dignitaries soon after his election, Lindsay outlined three possible styles of leadership that a local chief executive might chose to follow.[60] One type would ignore the conflicts around him, "follow a deliberate policy of avoidance," and hope that the problems would go away. Another type would assume the "passive role" as mediator and pretend that the problems of the city "cannot be resolved, only mediated." Each of these approaches could allow a politician to have a long career in office. But it was the third course of action, associated with Fiorello LaGuardia, to which Lindsay aspired. He would "plunge into the current that sweeps over the city" and "channel it towards progressive and positive goals."

A New Vision

John Lindsay had developed a strong record on civil rights during his seven years in the House of Representatives. He did not just champion the causes of racial minorities; he was also sensitive to the challenges of all those who had been excluded from full participation in American life. As mayor he would be ahead of the rest of the country in advocating for the rights of women and gays. In 1970 he signed a local ordinance outlawing discrimination against women in public accommodations, after McSorley's, the landmark tavern in the East Village that catered to a male only clientele, resisted a federal court order to serve women. He also issued an executive order requiring city contractors to take affirmative action to eliminate sex discrimination on the job.

Gender issues took on a whole new meaning in late June of 1969 when the gay patrons of the Stonewall Inn on Christopher Street put up resistance during a menacing early morning raid by the police, resulting in a series of demonstrations in Greenwich Village and other parts of the city. In 1971, Lindsay supported a bill in the City Council to eliminate discrimination against homosexuals. After the bill was defeated in early 1972, Lindsay signed an executive order prohibiting employment discrimination against gays in the public sector. It was the first government provision enacted anywhere in the country for the protection of gay rights.

In addition to fighting for those who suffered from discrimination, Lindsay was also ahead of his time on a variety of other issues that are now within the mainstream of public policy. He established an Environmental Protection Administration (EPA) in 1968, before any agency of its kind existed either at the state or federal level, to coordinate sanitation services with efforts to control air and water pollution. During his first summer in office, Lindsay shut down Central Park to street traffic on weekends to encourage people to walk, bike, run, skate, and stroll through it more freely. Lindsay also mounted a campaign in Washington and Albany to support mass transit and discourage automobile traffic. It is hard to believe what it was once like in New York City during the hot summer months, when the sweaty bodies of commuters were crushed together in oven-like tunnels underground; it was Lindsay who finally established a policy to ensure that every new subway car and bus purchased by the city would be air-conditioned.

The changes all fit with Lindsay's grand vision for the city: cities in general and New York City in particular. He would not let his idealistic vision of urban life be deterred by the budding crises around him. During the same hot summer that racial disturbances were breaking out in East Harlem, Newark, and Detroit, the Metropolitan Opera Company was performing *La Bohème* in Central Park for the first time. Street fairs that New Yorkers now take for granted were put on all over the five boroughs. At a time when people and corporations were giving up on cities, Lindsay communicated optimism. He organized the nation's mayors to advocate on their behalf in Congress and through the popular media. As Lindsay himself explained to a London audience, "Cities are the centers of civilization—the peopled places where culture and commerce flourish—where free men together fashion a future for themselves and their children. They must have a purpose higher than survival."[61]

But for many New Yorkers, it was exactly survival that was at stake. Lindsay knew that for sure, and accordingly he responded vigorously to Lyndon Johnson's antipoverty program. To some later critics, Lindsay's sympathetic attitude toward poor people and their empowerment was interpreted as a pragmatic response by a politician in need of allies. Lindsay after all was a Republican mayor in a Democratic town, and he was too progressive for most voters in his own party. His mayoral campaign, which he won with 43 percent of the popular vote, was a volunteer operation run out of 122 neighborhood storefronts. His movie star looks made him one of the first elected officials to run a successful television campaign; and in the hands of media genius David Garth, it became a lesson on the future of American politics. Nonetheless, he started out in a weak position when he was sworn into office on January 1, 1966.

Lindsay had worked very hard to win the support of African American and Puerto Rican voters. Yet, no elected official could rely entirely on minority voters as a base of support in 1965 while white ethnic coalitions continued to dominate the political process. To do so was impolitic, almost suicidal. Beyond their status as a numerical minority, black and Hispanic people did not vote in great numbers. Moreover, many black political leaders who had worked successfully with the white establishment through the Wagner years were unhappy with how Lindsay used the poverty programs to cultivate new leadership in their communities. As former Lindsay aide Sid Davidoff bluntly explained, "We reached out to black leadership that wasn't being heard. We reached out to people who were not part of the black power structure. The black leadership establishment was pissed off at us for not always working with them."[62]

There was more than politics behind the outreach in minority communities. Even before the Community Action Program was conceived in Washington, Richard Cloward and Lloyd Olin, two New York–based social scientists, had developed an "opportunity theory" for dealing with alienated young people in minority neighborhoods, which held that constructive involvement in their communities could give youths a sense of control over their own futures and offer them an alternative to delinquent behavior.[63] This was the thinking behind the Mobilization for Youth Program that was launched on the Lower East Side with support from the Ford Foundation and other philanthropies. The same theory was applied to adults who were alienated from the political process when the Office of Equal Opportunity in Washington created CAP.

Lindsay had supported President Johnson's War on Poverty as a congressman. During his first summer in office, Lindsay began to work directly with community organizers after a violent confrontation had broken out between black and white gangs in the East New York section of Brooklyn and more than a thousand police personnel were summoned to the scene.[64] This time the police exercised restraint and conducted themselves in a professional manner. Lindsay learned quickly that summer, after meeting with a bunch of local tough guys in the back of a neighborhood bar, how his personal intervention could prevent the street fight from escalating into a full-scale riot. He began to appreciate the need to keep lines of communication open in troubled communities by showing his own face regularly and assigning members of his administration to keep tabs on key pressure points.

From that point onward, Lindsay and his staff took walking tours of city neighborhoods several times a week—a different location each night. His aides made contacts in dicey neighborhoods. They identified local leaders, many of whom were out of reach for the police and agency officials. Federal antipoverty money allowed them to put local leaders on the payroll. Some of the streetwise operators put to work for the city had shady backgrounds. The sense of legitimacy City Hall granted them was a source of consternation in mainstream circles; but it was the very same characters that functioned on the margins of society who understood the dynamics of the rotting communities that the mayor was trying to penetrate. They were an early warning system and an emergency response team all in one.

Before his second summer in office, Lindsay had put together a Summer Task Force operation that assigned high-level administrators to serve as community liaisons with city agencies. Lindsay wanted to establish a network of neighborhood city halls, but the City Council, suspecting that the mayor was setting up a clubhouse operation to rival their own party-based storefronts, refused to approve the funding. Lindsay persisted with his own Urban Action Task Force plan that reached out into twenty-two of the most troubled communities throughout the five boroughs.[65] Such involvement allowed the administration to build social capital in communities so that, in times of crises like the evening that Martin Luther King was assassinated, he could walk the streets of Harlem calmly and keep it from exploding as other cities burned.

Cooperative, community based government would become a hallmark of the administration. In a speech he gave at a conference for professional city planners, Lindsay proclaimed, "Politics and the art of planning—your craft, must go along together—or else other forces will surely decide whether our great, decaying, but beautiful cities will live or die." He further emphasized, "planning is now too important to be left only to public officials and professional planners. It demands in addition the effective participation of another kind of expert—the citizen on whose life planning decisions have the most profound effect."[66]

Lindsay endorsed the concept of advocacy planning put forward by activists like Paul Davidoff, who urged his professional colleagues to abandon the notion that planners are objective actors in policy making and instead assume a role that advances the cause of social justice.[67] Lindsay was in basic agreement with the Model Cities approach outlined earlier in the chapter to development that replaced urban renewal programs with cooperative planning. He criticized the former approach in which only 15 percent of the resources were spent on areas that needed the most help and focused his energy on three communities: Harlem, Central Brooklyn, and the South Bronx.[68] As the Model Cities Program evolved, conflict erupted between African American and Puerto Rican representatives. Lindsay subsequently grew more cautious about ceding too much control of Local Policy Committees to neighborhood people and relied on his own administrators to coordinate programs.[69]

In 1969 Lindsay reluctantly signed a local law that established sixty-two Community Boards with advisory power regarding planning, budgeting, and service delivery in their respective districts. The Community Boards were adapted from a plan that Robert Wagner developed for Manhattan in 1953 when he was borough president. Under both plans, only the borough presidents were empowered to make appointments to the boards. The following year Lindsay put forward his own proposal that would have merged the Community Boards with the Urban Action Task Forces, in which the power of appointment would be shared by the mayor, the borough presidents, and City Council members.[70] Lindsay's model suggested that board members should eventually be directly elected by their respective communities, but it included no specific date for the change to be enacted. The plan was never adopted by the City Council. In 1972 Lindsay created his own Office of Neighborhood Government (ONG), administered by a cabinet official, that placed district managers in eighteen locations throughout the city to coordinate services.[71] ONG became a model for the community districts that were written into the City Charter in 1975 following the recommendations of a panel chaired by State Senator Roy Goodman, who had previously served as finance commissioner under Lindsay.

Like most local chief executives, Lindsay resented the fact that cities lack the autonomy for real self-governance. According to American law, cities are creatures of the states, and the powers cities enjoy are entirely dependent on state discretion.[72] This not only means that states need to approve city taxes, borrowing, and governance, but states can also make policies that obligate cities. For example in 1971, as the city was facing budget deficits, the state legislature imposed a $22 million increase for police, fire, and teacher pensions, which were outside the scope of local collective bargaining. Work rules set by state legislation were also beyond the purview of City Hall. Reliance on regressive property taxes constrained the capacity of the city to meet the expenses that resulted from deals made in Albany by suburban legislators and union leaders. Like nearly every mayor who preceded and followed him, Lindsay demanded greater home rule. But state-city relations were only part of the problem. In Lindsay's mind, these limitations were a piece of a larger narrative in which cities became depositories of the nation's problems but lacked the means to resolve them.[73]

The federal government, with all its generosity during the years of the Great Society, was partly responsible for this discouraging outcome. As Lindsay explained it, the poverty that was growing in urban centers was a migratory problem. Seventy percent of the mothers receiving family relief in the city had been born elsewhere. Poor people sought opportunities in cities, because their needs were not being met in other parts of the country. Since the sources of poverty were national in scope, Lindsay believed, the federal government should furnish the resources for dealing with it. Instead, the federal government required the states and localities to provide matching funds to meet the costs. In New York, state law required the city to pick up 35 percent of the welfare burden. The revenue provided by federal and state lawmakers created expenses in the city budget.[74] It had the effect of converting assets into liabilities, imposing one problem to solve another.

A Perfect Storm

John Lindsay served as mayor of New York during one of the most volatile periods in the history of the city and the country. The challenges he faced were particularly daunting because he sought to make the city a better place for people who were most in need, many of whom were newcomers that lacked a political base of their own. He was a WASP in a city dominated by ethnic politics. He was a Republican in a Democratic town. He brought many African Americans and Hispanics into the political process, but in so doing he antagonized more established minority politicians who felt compromised by the inroads he made into their communities. He soon learned that newly empowered unions who had supported liberal policies in the past were capable of great resistance when it came to issues of racial justice. The arcane ways of the bureaucracies they protected were irreconcilable with methods of modern management.

While Lindsay welcomed federal money that poured into cities as a result of the Great Society programs, these same programs forced the city to spend money it did not have. As more poor people came to New York, middle-class taxpayers and businesses started to leave. Manufacturing jobs that once employed unskilled laborers disappeared. The city was overcome by fear. White residents felt threatened by the new black militancy and the rising crime rates that they associated with the growing minority population. Black and Puerto Rican people lost faith in government and its capacity to treat them fairly.

Lindsay walked into a perfect storm that swept over the country in 1965, when the eye of the storm was hanging over New York City. This was the reality, but it is not an excuse. History still needs to judge him, and scholars need to determine what we can learn from that history to plan for the future. Was Lindsay a true leader that others should emulate? Or, was he a naïve idealist? Was he ill prepared for the monumental challenges that faced him? Or was he a courageous politician who acted according to the dictates of his conscience? Did his commitment to the needs of poor minorities blind him from the concerns of the white middle class who already had begun to depart for the suburbs? Did he ask the right questions? Did his response to them make matters better or make matters worse? To what extent was he responsible for the fiscal crisis that nearly made the city go bankrupt? These issues are better addressed after we have had an opportunity to take a closer look at the record in the following chapters. We will return to them in the conclusion.

NOTES

In addition to those cited below, I would like to thank the following who granted interviews: Carter Bales, Vincent Cannato, Gordon Davis, Ronnie Eldridge, Dick Ravitch, Herb Sturz, and Robert Sweet.

1. See John Lewis and Michael D'Orso, *Walking with the Wind: A Memoir of a Movement* (New York: Simon & Schuster, 1998), pp. 335–362.

2. See Jonathan Reider, *Gospel of Freedom: Martin Luther King Jr.'s Letter from Birmingham Jail and the Struggle That Changed the Nation* (New York: Bloomsbury Press, 2013).

3. Gerald Horne, *Fire This Time: The Watts Uprising and the 1960's* (University of Virginia Press, 1995) pp. 3–5, 53–115. In 1960, blacks in L.A. had an official unemployment rate of 12.5 percent, and 44.5 percent were below the poverty level. Horne, *Fire This Time*, p. 248.

4. Robert Dallek, *Lyndon B. Johnson: Portrait of a President* (Oxford University Press, 2004), p. 239.

5. Report of the National Advisory Commission on Civil Disorders (New York: Bantam Books, 1968), pp. 5–6.

6. Ibid., p. 1.

7. See Isabel Wilkerson, *The Warmth of Other Suns: The Epic Story of America's Great Migration* (New York: Random House, 2010).

8. Report of the National Advisory Commission, pp. 12–14, 242–246.

9. Daniel P. Moynihan, *The Negro Family: The Case for National Action*, Office of Policy Planning and Research, United States Department of Labor (March 1965).

10. Joseph Califano, interview with author, November 28, 2012.

11. See generally, James T. Patterson, *Freedom Is Not Enough: The Moynihan Report and America's Struggle over Black Family Life from LBJ to Obama* (New York: Free Press, 2010).

12. There is a voluminous literature on the Johnson legislative record. For an early journalistic account, see Robert Evans and Robert Novak, *Lyndon Johnson: The Exercise of Power* (New York: New American Library, 1966), pp. 406–434. For insider accounts, see Joseph A. Califano, *The Triumph and Tragedy of Lyndon Johnson: The White House Years* (College Station: Texas A&M University Press, 2000), pp. 106–164; Eric F. Goldman, *The Tragedy of Lyndon Johnson* (New York: Knopf, 1968), pp. 305–399. For fuller biographies, see Robert Caro, *The Passage of Power: The Years of Lyndon Johnson* (Knopf, 2012), pp. 558–570; Robert Dallek, *Flawed Giant: Lyndon Johnson and His Times* (New York: Oxford University Press, 1998), pp. 185–237; Randall B. Woods, *LBJ: Architect of Ambition* (Cambridge: Harvard University Press, 2006), pp. 440–482, 557–592, 649–692.

13. Califano interview.

14. Califano, *Triumph and Tragedy*, p. 150.

15. After serving as an attorney for the NAACP who argued the landmark *Brown v. Board of Education* case in 1954, Marshall sat on the United States Court of Appeals for the Second Circuit and was subsequently appointed solicitor general by President Johnson before taking a seat on the Supreme Court.

16. Woods, *LBJ*, p. 710.

17. Dallek, *Lyndon B. Johnson*, p. 243.

18. Woods, *LBJ*, p. 710.

19. Ibid., p. 446.

20. Dallek, *Lyndon B. Johnson*, p. 243.

21. Stokely Carmichael and Charles V. Hamilton, *Black Power: The Politics of Liberation* (New York: Vintage Books, 1967).

22. See generally, Sar Levitan, *The Great Society's Poor Law: A New Approach to Poverty* (Baltimore: Johns Hopkins Press, 1969); John Donavan, *The Politics of Poverty* (New York: Pegasus, 1967); Daniel P. Moynihan, *Maximum Feasible Misunderstanding* (New York: Free Press, 1969); Richard Cloward and Frances Fox Piven, *Regulating the Poor* (New York: Vintage, 1971).

23. Califano, *Triumph and Tragedy*, p. 131.

24. See generally, Chris McNickle, *To Be Mayor of New York: Ethnic Politics in the City*

(Columbia University Press, 1993), pp. 91–179. See also James Q. Wilson, *The Amateur Democrat: Club Politics in Three Cities* (Chicago: University of Chicago Press), pp. 32–65.

25. Charles V. Hamilton, "Needed, More Foxes: The Black Experience," in *Urban Politics, New York Style*, edited by Jewel Bellush and Dick Netzer (Armonk, NY: M. E. Sharpe, 1990), pp. 359–384.

26. McNickle, *To Be Mayor*, pp. 116–117.

27. Wilson, *Amateur Democrat*, pp. 276–277.

28. Joseph J. Salvo and Arun Peter Lobo, "Population," in *Encyclopedia of New York City*, 2nd ed., edited by Kenneth T. Jackson (New Haven: Yale University Press, 2010), p. 1020.

29. Ibid.

30. "Annual Census of School Population, Trends in Distribution of Pupils," Board of Education of the City of New York, Bureau of Educational Program Research and Statistics, 1968.

31. Mark K. Levitan and Susan S. Wieler, "Poverty in New York City, 1969–99: The Influence of Demographic Change, Income Growth, and Income Inequality," *FRBNY Economic Policy Review* (July 2008).

32. "Employment Status of Persons in NY City UES Area," U.S. Department of Labor, Bureau of Labor Statistics, 1969.

33. Langston Hughes, "Death in Yorkville," in *The Collected Works of Langston Hughes: The Poems, 1951–1967*, vol. 3, edited by Dolan Hubbard (University of Missouri Press, 2003).

34. R. W. Apple, "Police Defend the Use of Gunfire in Controlling Riots in Harlem," *New York Times*, July 21, 1964, p. 1.

35. Fred Cook and Gene Gleason, "The Shame of New York," *The Nation*, October 31, 1959.

36. Miriam Greenberg, *Branding New York: How a City in Crisis Was Sold to the World* (New York: Routledge, 2008), p. 48.

37. Ibid., p. 49.

38. Barry Gottehrer, ed., *New York City in Crisis: A Study in Depth of Urban Sickness* (New York: David McKay, 1965), pp. 10, 30, 95, 196.

39. *New York Herald Tribune*, January 26, 1965.

40. Kay Lehman Schlozman, Sidney Verba, and Henry E. Brady, *The Unheavenly Chorus: Unequal Political Voice and the Broken Promise of American Democracy* (Princeton University Press, 2012); Norman H. Nie, Jane Junn, and Kenneth Stehlik-Barry, *Education and Democratic Citizenship in America* (University of Chicago Press, 1996); Sidney Verba, Kay Lehman Schlozman, and Henry E. Brady, *Voice and Equality: Civic Voluntarism in American Politics* (Harvard University Press, 1995).

41. Report by Deputy Mayor Timothy Costello, City of New York, 1968.

42. John V. Lindsay, "Statement on the Appointment of a New Police Commissioner," February, 21, 1966. Lindsay actually appointed the new board by executive order in May of that year.

43. Ibid.

44. Algernon Black, *The People and the Police* (New York: McGraw Hill, 1968), p. 209.

45. Joseph P. Viteritti, *Police, Politics and Pluralism in New York City* (Beverley Hills, CA: Sage Publications, 1973).

46. Kenneth Clark, *Dark Ghetto: Dilemmas of Social Power* (New York: Harper & Row, 1967), p. 36.

47. Arthur Niederhoffer, *Behind the Shield: The Police in Urban Society* (New York: Doubleday, 1967), p. 134.

48. Michael F. Armstrong, *They Wished They Were Honest: The Knapp Commission and New York City Police Corruption* (New York: Columbia University Press, 2012).

49. Eric Pace, "Broderick Is Firm on Review Board," *New York Times,* January 29, 1966.

50. Eric Pace, "Two More Have Quit High Police Posts," *New York Times,* March 2, 1966, p. 1.

51. Joshua B. Freeman, "Lindsay and Labor," in *America's Mayor: John Lindsay and the Reinvention of New York*, edited by Sam Roberts (New York: Columbia University Press, 2010), pp. 118–131. See generally, Joshua B. Freeman, *Working-Class New York: Life and Labor since World War II* (New York: The New Press, 2000), on the rise of labor in New York.

52. There were originally thirteen teachers according to Richard Kahlenberg, one of whom was white and was mistakenly included on the transfer list, who was subsequently reinstated. See Kahlenberg, *Tough Liberal: Albert Shanker and the Battles over Schools, Unions, Race, and Democracy* (New York: Columbia University Press, 2007), p. 93.

53. Homar Bigart, "12 Hurt in Violence Here," *New York Times,* July 25, 1967, p. 1.

54. See generally, Kahlenberg, *Tough Liberal.*

55. See Diane Ravitch, *The Great School Wars: A History of the Public Schools as a Battlefield of Social Change* (New York: Basic Books, 1974), pp. 251–404; Clarence Taylor, *Knocking at Our Own Door: Milton Galamison and the Struggle to Integrate New York City Schools* (New York: Columbia University Press, 1997), pp. 176–207.

56. City of New York, Municipal Civil Service System, and the Department of Personnel, *Annual Report,* 1954, p. 5.

57. City of New York, Civil Service Commission and Department of Personnel, *Annual Report,* 1967, p. 13.

58. Martin Shefter, *Political Crisis / Fiscal Crisis: The Collapse and Revival of New York City* (New York: Basic Books, 1985), p. 90.

59. These data are drawn from citywide employment surveys conducted by the City Commission on Human Rights. See Joseph P. Viteritti, *Bureaucracy and Social Justice: The Allocation of Jobs and Services to Minority Groups* (Port Washington, NY: Kennikat Press, 1979), pp. 94–107.

60. John V. Lindsay, "Remarks before the Society of Foreign Counsels," March 10, 1966.

61. John V. Lindsay, "Address before the Institute of Directors," London, November 5, 1970.

62. Author interview with Sid Davidoff, February, 15, 2012.

63. Richard A. Cloward and Lloyd E. Ohlin, *Delinquency and Opportunity: A Theory of Delinquent Gangs* (New York: Free Press, 1960).

64. For a vivid account, see Barry Gottehrer, *The Mayor's Man: One Man's Struggle to Save Our Cities* (New York: Barry Gottehrer, 2007), pp. 3–30.

65. Robert F. Pecorella, *Community Power in a Postreform City: Politics in New York City* (Armonk, NY: M. E. Sharpe, 1994), pp. 104–105.

66. John V. Lindsay, "Remarks before the American Society of Planning," April 7, 1970.

67. John V. Lindsay, "Remarks before the Student Body of Columbia University," December 12, 1968. See also Paul Davidoff, "Advocacy and Pluralism in Planning," *Journal of the American Institute of Planners* 31 (Sept. 1965).

68. John V. Lindsay, "Broadcast Message to New Yorkers on the Urban Renewal Program," September 19, 1966.

69. *Report on Model Cities,* Study Prepared by the State Charter Revision Commission for New York City, November 1973.

70. John V. Lindsay, "Plan for Neighborhood Government for New York City," June 1970.

71. Pecorella, *Community Power,* pp. 104–110.

72. Gerald Frug, "The City as a Legal Concept," *Harvard Law Review,* vol. 91 (Apr. 1980): 1057–1154.

73. John V. Lindsay, "Testimony before the Wagner Commission on Home Rule," April 28, 1971.

74. John V. Lindsay, "Remarks at New York University Law School," April 15, 1971.

Congressman John V. Lindsay speaking at a Board of Estimate meeting at City Hall regarding the controversial Lower Manhattan Expressway. April 15, 1963; photographer Fred Palumbo. Library of Congress, Prints & Photographs Division, NYWT&S Collection, LC-USz62-132500.

CHAPTER TWO

On Principle

A Progressive Republican

GEOFFREY KABASERVICE

John Lindsay, in the view of his critics, embodied the failures of liberalism. But in fact Lindsay was not a liberal—he was a progressive. This is not a mere semantic distinction. Lindsay emerged from the distinctive milieu of post–World War II progressive Republicanism. The ideas, influences, and aspirations he brought to politics were different from those of Democratic politicians. Since progressive Republicans essentially have become extinct, it is difficult for contemporary observers to see Lindsay as anything other than a liberal. But an analysis of the entirety of Lindsay's career—from his beginnings as a Republican activist through his congressional service as well as his tenure as New York mayor—can illuminate the contours of his progressivism and provide a better understanding of his vision and successes, as well as the limitations of that vision and the ways in which he failed to live up to it. It can also help explain the transformation of politics since the 1960s and why Lindsay's experience still offers relevant lessons.

The historian Robert Darnton, taking a cue from anthropology, observed that the "best points of entry in an attempt to penetrate an alien culture can be those where it seems to be most opaque." When we cannot understand a historical phenomenon, "we know we are on to something."[1] In the present era of polarized politics, when "progressive Republican" seems to be a contradiction in terms, it is unsurprising that historians have been puzzled by Lindsay's Republican affiliation and in effect have treated him as a liberal Democrat in all but name. But Republican progressivism was not merely an imitation of Democratic liberalism. It had its own history, ideals, and political philosophy. In order to comprehend Lindsay, it is necessary to understand how he situated himself in the Republican progressive tradition.

Lindsay's Republican Origins

Lindsay's Republicanism was to some extent a consequence of his background. He was born in New York City in 1921 to a prosperous White Anglo-Saxon Protestant (WASP) family. Moderate Republicanism of the Theodore Roosevelt variety was the usual political expression of upper middle-class New York families like the Lindsays.[2] The New York Republican position in turn reflected the gentlemanly code of the Eastern Protestant elite, which held among other things that great advantages carried great responsibilities including the obligation of public service in the national interest.[3] These cultural-political influences were reinforced at the private schools Lindsay attended (Buckley and St. Paul's) as well as during his undergraduate years at Yale.[4]

Lindsay identified himself as a Republican from a young age. In the summer of 1940, John and his twin brother, David, worked as pages at the Republican national convention in Philadelphia. They became enthusiasts for the dark horse candidate Wendell L. Willkie, a moderate and internationalist Wall Street lawyer, and were thrilled when he secured the party's presidential nomination. Later that summer, they met New York mayor Fiorello LaGuardia, an independent-minded, good-government Republican who was another of Lindsay's political heroes.[5]

Lindsay was an academic and social success at Yale, but his undergraduate career was foreshortened when the Japanese bombed Pearl Harbor midway through his sophomore year. He accelerated his studies and graduated a year early in 1943. He entered the U.S. Navy and served as a destroyer gunnery officer in the Mediterranean and Pacific theaters. "The war had a lot to do with my eventual decision to go into public service," he later recalled. "I lost a barrel of friends. One of my roommates was killed, and one of my closest friends was among the initial casualties at Guadalcanal. Twenty percent of my class at St. Paul's was wiped out. I felt something had to be done to make sure it wouldn't happen again."[6] He enrolled at Yale Law School after the war and then began his law career at the New York firm of Webster, Sheffield, Fleischmann, Hitchcock & Christie. There Lindsay came under the influence of his first moderate Republican mentor, Bethuel M. Webster, one of the firm's founding partners. "No one was a better or greater influence on me than Bethuel," Lindsay attested. "He believed in an independent bar, and in the protection of individual liberty and rights."[7] Webster encouraged him in the Eastern WASP elite's longstanding conviction that public service was the highest calling. "By the time I finished Yale," Lindsay once commented, "I had all the 'advantages,' and what the hell was all that money for if I didn't do more with my education than just make a good living?"[8]

Lindsay had campaigned for fiscally conservative yet socially tolerant Republicans while still in law school, and as a young lawyer he gave street-corner speeches on behalf of Republican candidates in the 1950 elections. He joined the New York Young Republican Club, the oldest YR club in the country and at that time still an all-male organization, and became vice-president in 1951. An early advocate of Dwight Eisenhower's presidential candidacy, Lindsay was one of the eleven founders of Youth for Eisenhower and traveled to Paris to urge the general to run for the Republican nomination. After Eisenhower's victory in the 1952 election, Lindsay became president of the New York YRs. The Young Republican organization was more important in the Empire State than in most other states, because Governor Thomas Dewey had used it to build his national political network. Dewey even had a secret action group, called the Mallards, made up largely of his YR supporters.[9] The network was instrumental in Dewey's gubernatorial and presidential campaigns as well as in 1952 and 1956, when he put it at the disposal of Eisenhower's presidential campaigns.

As leader of the New York Young Republican Club, Lindsay became involved in a factional dispute that would impact his later political career. Lindsay was part of a clique led by his close friend Charles Metzner, a law secretary to Judge William Hecht of the New York Supreme Court. Opposing Metzner's clique in city and state YR contests was a clique masterminded by F. Clifton White, a Cornell University political science instructor who was to become a prominent conservative strategist. The divisions between the Metzner and White cliques were not initially ideological, as both groups worked for Thomas Dewey's 1950 New York gubernatorial campaign and Eisenhower's 1952 presidential campaign. The statement of principles formulated at the New York state YRs' 1950 convention reflected moderate Republican fiscal conservatism blended with a pragmatic acceptance of the New Deal. The platform, written principally by White, conceded that "when any individual American, through no fault of his own, lacks adequate food, shelter, clothing, or medical care, it is the responsibility of society, through both private and governmental sources, to provide these basic requirements of life as a matter of simple justice." Republicans still agreed, however, that the "well-being of the nation as a whole is enhanced by the degree to which every individual relies upon his own abilities, his own thrift, his own sacrifices, and his own initiative."[10]

Despite their overall political and ideological agreement, there were serious personal antipathies between the factions, and particularly between the Metzner group and White's ally William A. Rusher, who at that time was a lawyer in New York. As one historian of the New York YR clubs observed, Metzner's group had a "sworn personal vendetta" against Rusher and prevented him from succeeding White as the president of the association in 1952.[11] Rusher's conversion to ideological conservatism in the mid-1950s preceded the similar rightward trajectory of the White clique (also known as the Syndicate). Eventually White and Rusher would use their network to displace Dewey's network and seize the Republican presidential nomination for Barry Goldwater in 1964. Rusher would be a poisonous ideological enemy of Lindsay for the remainder of his political career and, as longtime publisher of the conservative *National Review* magazine (which he joined two years after its 1955 founding), would do considerable damage to Lindsay's prospects and reputation.[12]

The dominant political figure in New York Republican circles during the 1940s and 1950s was Thomas Dewey, the three-term governor and twice-unsuccessful GOP presidential candidate in 1944 and 1948. Dewey was a fiscal conservative but believed that Republicans should not attempt to repeal the New Deal; rather, they should advance competing social welfare programs that emphasized individual freedom and economic incentives instead of the Democrats' tendency toward centralization and collectivism. Dewey also believed that Republicans had to appeal to voters in heavily urban and Democratic areas, with a particular effort to reach middle-class professionals who would respond to a program of social reform and internationalist foreign policy. Pennsylvania's moderate Republican Senator Hugh Scott believed that "the rise of the moderates in the party was due as much to Dewey in New York as to any other factor. . . . Most of the new moderates in the party took their cues from Dewey."[13] Dewey's failed presidential runs meant that he was not a name to conjure with after 1948, but he remained an extremely important influence on Lindsay and his cohort of New York Republicans.

Lindsay's friend Charles Metzner had been a member of the Youth for Dewey organization and had worked with the Dewey leadership on tactics for the 1948 Republican national convention. He formed a close association with Herbert Brownell, who had been campaign manager for both Dewey and Eisenhower and whose moderate Republican outlook was similar to both of those candidates. When Brownell became attorney general after Eisenhower's victory, Metzner followed him to Washington as his executive assistant. When Metzner left his position in 1954, Brownell named Lindsay as his replacement. Lindsay served in the Eisenhower administration for about three years, during which time he worked on various issues including civil liberties, immigration, and the 1957 Civil Rights Act. He became a protégé of Brownell, who advised him to return to his law practice in New York and run for the Seventeenth District congressional seat held by Republican Representative Frederic R. Coudert Jr.

Coudert's old-fashioned conservatism had once struck a chord with the wealthy

Republicans of the so-called Silk Stocking District, which encompassed Manhattan's East Side from Greenwich Village in the south to Harlem in the north. But that ideology was increasingly unappealing to the growing numbers of minorities and educated professionals who were moving in; the district was moving left politically, and Coudert was not moving with it.[14] In 1958, Lindsay announced that he would challenge Coudert for the Republican nomination, and Coudert soon let it be known that he would not seek reelection. Lindsay overcame the more conservative challenger put forward by the district's Republican regulars, then defeated the Democratic candidate in the general election by a 54-to-46 percent margin despite the district's heavy Democratic registration edge. In subsequent elections, he rolled up ever-widening percentages of the vote: 60 percent in 1960, 68 percent in 1962, and 71.5 percent in 1964.[15] From his earliest appearances in Congress, his fellow Republicans saw Lindsay as a "young, adventurous crusader" who would be the party's "bright star of the future."[16]

Lindsay and the History and Heritage of Republican Progressivism

Lindsay quickly became identified as a leader of the Republican Party's progressive faction, which had experienced a significant revival in the late 1950s after a long period of dormancy. Even so, Republican progressives did not consider themselves newcomers but heirs to the party's deepest traditions, who could trace their heritage directly to Abraham Lincoln and the first generation of Republicans. They believed that they were faithful to the Lincoln values of civil rights and civil liberties, social reform, and government efforts to promote economic growth and national development. Progressives countered the small-government arguments of conservatives by pointing out that the Republican Party had laid the groundwork for modern society through active-government achievements such as abolishing slavery, opening public lands in the West to homesteaders, chartering the first transcontinental railroad, and establishing a national banking system and land-grant colleges.

Progressives also emphasized their spiritual kinship to Theodore Roosevelt and the progressive movement of the late nineteenth and early twentieth centuries, which had reformed civil service, passed the first conservation legislation, and created the skeletal frame of a social welfare safety net. Progressives had lost force within the GOP after Roosevelt's bolt from the party in 1912 to form the Progressive Party, popularly known as the Bull Moose Party. Progressivism retained a foothold in the Republican Party, however, in the form of a bloc of mainly Western Congressmen, known derisively as the "Sons of the Wild Jackass." Senators such as Robert

LaFollette of Wisconsin and George Norris of Nebraska were early champions of many of the social welfare reforms later incorporated into the New Deal under Franklin Roosevelt.

There were few prominent Eastern progressives in office during the interwar years, with the notable exception of LaGuardia in New York City. But progressives made common cause with Republican moderates, who were descended from the wing of the progressive movement that had not bolted the party in 1912. Like the progressives, moderates also favored political reform but were more conservative on economic and social issues. Moderates succeeded in gaining the GOP presidential nomination for Willkie in 1940, Dewey in 1944 and 1948, and Eisenhower in 1952 and 1956. The Eisenhower years witnessed the reemergence of progressives, including senators such as Jacob Javits and Kenneth Keating of New York, Mark Hatfield of Oregon, and Thomas Kuchel of California, and a considerable number of governors whose acknowledged leader was Nelson Rockefeller of New York (first elected in 1958). Rockefeller would come to be a significant rival of Lindsay's, both personally and on account of his office and the perennial tensions between New York City and state. Even so, his example and success were important influences on Lindsay.

Lindsay was acutely conscious of his party's progressive legacy. Richard Aurelio, who eventually served as Lindsay's deputy mayor, remembered that when he first encountered Lindsay at gatherings of New York Republicans in the early 1960s, "he would talk often about the party following in the tradition of Lincoln, Theodore Roosevelt. . . . He often mentioned George Norris of Nebraska, LaFollette of Wisconsin, LaGuardia, of course, but also Wendell Willkie, and publishers like William Allen White [*Emporia Gazette*] and Eugene Meyer [*Washington Post*] as well as Ogden Reid [*New York Herald Tribune*]."[17] The *Herald Tribune*, in particular, epitomized the moderate-to-progressive Republican position that Lindsay espoused, which was dedicated to strengthening civil rights and liberties, wary of unions, firmly though not zealously anticommunist, dismissive of the growing conservative movement, and sharply critical of New York's Democratic leadership for its willingness to preside over worsening urban decay.

The Democratic Party had little appeal to Lindsay, in part because its dependence on the "solid South" and the long-serving Southern Democratic committee chairmen in Congress meant that the party as a whole resisted passage of civil rights legislation, despite the liberal rhetoric of most northern Democrats.[18] Lindsay was pleased to point out that the GOP was the "party which has spearheaded every major civil rights measure in the last century."[19] Lindsay also opposed the corruption and inefficiency that he associated with urban Democratic machines in cities like New York. He had looked up to LaGuardia in his youth because "he was a good guy fighting the bad guys, and the bad guys were the Tammany Hall bosses."[20] The good-government position, in Lindsay's view, implied that Republicans in power should not only be honest but should also use government to do good. Indeed, Republicans should be better able to run effective government programs, because they were not beholden to either Southern reactionaries or urban bosses.

As a New Yorker as well as a progressive, Lindsay wanted Republicans to compete with Democrats for the allegiance of groups that had not been well represented in the party over the previous decades, including urbanites, young people, minorities, intellectuals, and blue-collar workers. He also called for Republicans to develop constructive and affirmative solutions to social and economic problems that could not adequately be addressed through private means. A. James Reichley, who both participated directly in GOP political efforts and analyzed them as a political scientist, pointed out that Republican progressives like Lindsay shared the Democrats' belief in active government but differed on several significant points. On economic issues, the "progressive Republicans instinctively sought ways to work with business," while Democrats continued to regard business with deep suspicion and occasionally outright antipathy.[21]

The Republicans' business orientation permeated their consideration of other issues such as civil rights, where Lindsay and his allies criticized racial discrimination for its economic costs as well as its affront to American principles.[22] Progressives attempted to devolve administrative government to the state and local levels, where liberal Democrats pushed for centralized federal control. Progressives also tended to remain "true to the puritan heritage of the Republican Party" by relating their proposals to moral absolutes, "whereas the liberal Democrats more often emphasized various kinds of personal and group 'liberation.'" Reichley concluded that, while the progressives cast themselves as reformers, they "remained essentially conservative in that they viewed reform as a means for preserving the underlying soundness of the existing system."[23]

Lindsay's Progressive Republican Faction and His Opponents

The revival of progressive Republicanism coincided with the emergence of a new conservative movement. Adherents of the New Right were militant economic, social, and cultural right-wingers, antigovernment in rhetoric if not always in practice, who for the most part came from what would later be called the Sunbelt regions of the South and West. The movement benefited from the powerful sense of cause offered by populist politicians such as Senators Joseph McCarthy of Wisconsin and Barry Goldwater of Arizona, the ideological contributions of intellectuals like William F. Buckley Jr. and Russell Kirk, the forum provided by magazines such as *Na-*

tional Review (where Lindsay's antagonist Rusher was publisher), and the creation of networks and organizations at the grassroots to raise funds and rally foot soldiers for battles against both Republican moderates and Democratic liberals.[24]

Conservatives saw progressive Republicans not as misguided comrades but as "crypto-Democrats," in Rusher's words, who needed to be purged from the party. Rusher scoffed that, if Lindsay had been a Democrat, he would have been seen as just one more liberal loyalist, while "as a Republican, his record gives him the rarity value of a giant panda."[25] Rusher helped to establish the Conservative Party of New York to run candidates against progressive Republicans like Lindsay and Rockefeller, with the aim of forcing them to switch parties or exit public life.[26] In the conservative view, progressives like Lindsay were more dangerous than liberal Democrats, because they fuzzed and distorted the ideological clarity of the Republican Party. Only when Democrats and Republicans were polarized into liberal and conservative parties would the GOP gain the support of the allegedly conservative majority of American voters. As Buckley more eloquently expressed it, conservatives needed to "build an opposing party which is other than a purely organizational alternative." He predicted that the struggle within the Republican Party in the coming years would be between "those who feel that history requires an assent to socialism, and those others who believe that we can take history by the scruff of the neck and force it to acknowledge the eternal validity of the idea that created this republic and made it prosperous and free."[27]

Conservatives and progressives alike considered Lindsay, with his good looks and political gifts, as presidential material. For conservatives, therefore, it was imperative to destroy Lindsay as a potential national figure in the party. In 1961, the *Herald Tribune* reported that a Buckley challenge to Lindsay in a Republican congressional primary was a "prospect that has been discussed in conservative circles for some time."[28] When Lindsay announced that he would run for mayor of New York City, Buckley believed it was his duty to run against him on the Conservative line in order to draw off enough votes to ensure the election of the Democrat.[29] For Buckley, the decisive evidence that Lindsay needed to be stopped came when Representative John Ashbrook of Ohio, a conservative member of the White-Rusher Syndicate, reported that his constituents were excited by the Lindsay candidacy.[30] Buckley wrote to a friend that "John Lindsay will do as much harm to the Republican Party, if he is elected and becomes powerful, as anyone who has threatened the Party's role as defender of the tablets in recent history. If the Republican Party is transformed in his image, I shall give you the Republican Party, and go elsewhere."[31]

But the conservative assertion that Lindsay's outlook was indistinguishable from that of a liberal Democrat was incorrect, and neither was he as out of step with his party as they claimed. Lindsay voted for almost all measures advocated by the Eisenhower administration; for this reason, Rusher griped in 1960 that an index measuring Republican Party loyalty was "primarily a test, not of a man's conservatism, but of his allegiance to the Law as laid down by Prophet Dwight. No wonder Messrs. Javits and Lindsay score high, compared to southern Democrats!"[32] Lindsay supported the Republican stance against diplomatic recognition of Communist China and what the GOP construed as excessive Democratic spending bills. In keeping with Eisenhower's mistrust of the "military-industrial complex," Lindsay proposed legislation to encourage competitive procurement of materials and supplies by the armed forces. He was also one of the loudest voices calling for the executive branch to implement the recommendations for more efficient and economical government proposed by a commission headed by former Republican president Herbert Hoover.[33]

Even in the area of civil rights, Lindsay was willing to follow the lead of Ohio Representative William McCulloch, the chief Republican negotiator on the Civil Rights Act of 1964, who was principally responsible for removing proposed provisions that struck him as unconstitutional or overreaching. These included federal controls on banks and mortgage companies, racial quotas for employers, and busing to eliminate racial imbalance in education.[34] Lindsay endorsed these limitations and emphasized his opposition to busing and what became known as affirmative action.[35] In the various orderings of members of Congress from left to right, compiled by political scientists and ideological outfits, Lindsay was to the right of other New York Republicans such as Javits and House members Seymour Halpern and Ogden Reid and well to the right of most New York Democrats.[36] He maintained that the "Republican Party in the past has represented the great center core of America, and this has been ultimately the reason why America has turned to it . . . for leadership."[37]

True, Lindsay did occasionally play the maverick, as when he cast the sole dissenting vote against a bill allowing the postmaster general to impound books and periodicals thought by one official in the U.S. Post Office to be obscene, a provision that he argued was an unconstitutional assault by government on the personal right of free speech.[38] Lindsay's dedication to civil rights meant that he was one of twenty-two Republican dissenters who defied their party leadership by voting to enlarge the Rules Committee in 1961, thereby overturning the controlling conservative majority that had bottled up civil rights initiatives and other domestic legislation.[39] Lindsay also butted heads with stand-patters in his party when he tried to advance positive alternatives to Democratic legislation. For example, his legislative assistant Anthony Morella recalled that Lindsay proposed an excellent substitute for a Democratic housing bill in the early 1960s, which would have achieved many of the same aims but would have been more economical. Javits was able to get strong Republican support for the measure in the Senate, but the Republican minority on the House Banking and Currency Committee killed it because "in fact [they] did not want a really attractive Republican housing bill to get to the floor." They wanted the GOP "to be against housing in any form, and that was that."[40] Further, like many progressives, including Rockefeller, Javits, and Keating, Lindsay refused to endorse Republican presidential nominee Barry Goldwater in 1964, in protest against the conservative senator's vote against the Civil Rights Act and efforts to court Southern segregationists' support.[41]

But some fifty of the 140 Republicans in the entering Eighty-ninth Congress (Lindsay's last) could be classed as moderates and progressives. While still only a minority within a minority, their numbers were growing. They were passionately committed to retaking the GOP from the conservative forces that had led the party to electoral disaster in 1964, and they wielded considerable heft inside the Republican caucus.[42] Lindsay provided inspiration and advice to other progressive Republicans who wanted to run for Congress.[43] The GOP moderates' increasing political influence was augmented by the House Wednesday Group, a social and intellectual congressional organization that Lindsay had helped create in the wake of the Rules Committee battle.[44] And in many ways, the conservatives were more out of step with the Republican mainstream than the progressives. Eighty percent of House Republicans voted for the 1964 Civil Rights Act, for example, while the final version of the 1965 Voting Rights Act passed with 111 Republicans voting in favor and twenty against. Senate Republicans supported the 1964 and 1965 bills by margins of 27–6 and 30–1, respectively, and a greater proportion of Republicans than Democrats in both houses voted for both measures.[45]

In certain respects, Lindsay was one of the most prominent Republican critics of Democrats, particularly in the areas of civil liberties and civil rights. Lindsay believed that Robert F. Kennedy, in particular, was a partisan menace to traditional American freedoms, and they clashed repeatedly. Lindsay attacked the attorney general's pressure for legislation allowing the FBI to place wiretaps without court orders, criminalize the "obstruction" of government investigators, and broaden the Sedition Act of 1918 to prohibit Americans from speaking or uttering disloyal, profane, scurrilous, or abusive utterances anywhere in the world.[46] Lindsay charged that the "basic grabs by the Kennedys for power . . . are offensive to conservatives and liberals alike."[47]

Lindsay also blistered the Democrats for their broken promises on civil rights, which he attributed to the Kennedy administration's deal making with the segregationist Southern committee chairmen. The Democrats' inaction was made worse by the cynical instances of "legislative gamesmanship" through which the administration and congressional leadership tried to make it look as though they were taking action.[48] When Robert Kennedy testified before the House on the administration's 1963 civil rights bill and Lindsay accused him of undercutting the public-accommodations section, Kennedy snapped back that "neither the President nor I have to defend our good faith to you or to anyone else." Lindsay baited Kennedy into admitting that he had not read the Republican version of the bill, which in several respects was stronger than the administration's, and further that he was too busy to waste his time reading Republican legislation.[49]

At the same time, while Lindsay maintained deeply held principles, particularly on matters relating to constitutional rights and freedoms, he was not a rigid ideologue. He was willing to work with and befriend other members of Congress regardless of political party or ideology. Robert Blum, who was Lindsay's legislative assistant in his first year in Congress, remembered that Lindsay was immensely popular with his House colleagues, not only because of his sociability but also "because he didn't care about where anyone hung their hat politically. He was an intensely pragmatic guy. He cared about solving problems. His guiding question was: How do you get it done?"[50] Lindsay opposed Southern Democrats on civil rights and immigration reform, for example, but worked comfortably with many of them on issues such as medical care for the aged, middle-income housing, and liberalization of Social Security benefits and coverage.

In one of his early congressional speeches, Lindsay defined himself as a "practical idealist," opposed to both starry-eyed utopians and cynical realists. He recognized that humans were capable of avarice and aggression but also aspired to "moral and spiritual fulfillment." The non-perfectionist politician, in his view, had to hold to a "set of moral goals and values which we must attempt to realize in our political life while recognizing that our attempts are often likely to fail." The "practical idealist" in public life would accept the "necessity of compromise, concession, adjustment, and strategic retreat in the pursuit of a morally worthy objective," though in rare and extreme conditions he might be compelled to use the "methods and policies of power politics."[51]

Lindsay and the New York City 1965 Mayoral Election

When he announced his decision to run for New York mayor in May 1965, Lindsay didn't play down his party affiliation, but neither did he highlight it. This was a pragmatic calculation in a city where Democrats outnumbered Republicans by a more than three-to-one ratio, and where Goldwater's anti–civil rights conservatism had caused the GOP to be pummeled in the 1964 elections. Lindsay cast himself as a progressive more than a Republican, which was a posture distinctively in the Republican tradition of progressivism. Partly this approach was dictated by political realities, but Lindsay's approach to governance had a lot in common with that of earlier Republican progressives like Hiram Johnson, Earl Warren, Robert LaFollette, and (to some extent) Fiorello LaGuardia.

Progressives were hostile to political parties, believing (like the Founding Fathers) that factionalism worked against the public good. Their watchword was bipartisanship—or nonpartisanship. They stood for clean government, an active and educated citizenry, and opposition to machine bosses. They believed that the nonpartisan political culture of progressivism would require successful officeholders to base policies on factual analysis and justify them with concrete results. Progressives also blended the seemingly antithetical impulses of elitism and populism. On the one hand, progressives upheld the importance of disinterested, technocratic experts who could make difficult trade-offs and implement necessary but politically unpopular long-term changes. On the other, progressives also espoused a faith in the wisdom of the people and their ability to govern themselves responsibly.[52] Lindsay was an ideal progressive candidate, because he straddled both the elitist and populist camps: he came across as an incorruptible upper-class paragon with a popular touch.

The nonpartisan, progressive approach also carried obvious liabilities. Democrats made much of the difficulties that a Republican mayor of New York might expect to encounter in seeking funds from the Democratic administration of President Lyndon Johnson. "I know he's pretty," Rep. Adam Clayton Powell smirked during Lindsay's mayoral campaign. "I know he's glamorous. I know he's glib. But that ain't gon' bring him that Federal money here."[53] Curiously, conservatives like William Rusher agreed that only Democrats had the ability to govern big cities: "not because they are capable administrators (let alone honest ones), but because they know where the power levers are (the labor unions, the mobs, the pressure groups), and thus have a better chance of forestalling trouble than any Republican—able or otherwise."[54] Upper-class WASP progressives also had a history of alienating the working-class white members of ethnic groups who were often the targets of their good-government reforms.[55] This was the context to the observation of one leader of the (largely Catholic and white ethnic) Conservative Party of New York that its opponents were the "good, the well-born, and the able."[56]

Even so, Lindsay enjoyed considerable resources, particularly of a Republican variety, in seeking the mayoralty. His rationale for running, as mentioned in the previous chapter, came from the "City in Crisis" series in the moderate Republican *New York Herald Tribune*.[57] The *Herald Tribune* actively solicited Lindsay's entrance into the mayoral race, editorializing on the city's need for the "excitement and ferment of a new administration, tied neither to the mistakes of the past nor to a self-perpetuating organization too long in power," as well as the "kind of political challenge only a revitalized Republican party, behind a clearly outstanding candidate, can provide."[58]

Most of Lindsay's campaign donors were wealthy Republicans, including John Hay Whitney and Walter Thayer of the *Herald Tribune*, William Paley of CBS, and the pillars of Wall Street and the New York bar. Support also came from Washington-based organizations like Charles P. Taft's Republicans for Progress, out-of-state Republicans like Leonard Firestone, and some of Lindsay's fellow Yale University trustees.[59] The campaign's largest donor was Nelson Rockefeller, and indeed Lindsay's willingness to run was contingent on receiving Rockefeller's half-million dollar contribution.[60] Lindsay asked national Republicans to stay out of his campaign but relied heavily on Dewey, Brownell, and Javits (his campaign chairman) to rally the party faithful in New York.[61]

Conservatives professed outrage at Lindsay's refusal to stand forthrightly as a Republican.[62] Indeed, Lindsay lobbied for and received the nomination of the Liberal Party, a third-party New York organization that cross-endorsed major-party candidates who were sympathetic to its anticommunist liberal philosophy. In the tradition of Fiorello LaGuardia, Lindsay ran as a Republican-Liberal fusion candidate, with Liberal Party member Timothy Costello as his running mate for City Council president. Lindsay also blurred his party identity by running alongside Milton Mollen, a Democrat who had been part of the Wagner administration but was willing to criticize his party.

William Rusher claimed that Lindsay's fusionist campaign, as well as his successful effort to get endorsements from left-leaning organizations such as Americans for Democratic Action and the *New York Post,* meant that he "has for all practical purposes abandoned the Republican Party: its candidates, its machinery, and (not least) its principles."[63] But most New York Republicans did not see Lindsay's campaign as party apostasy. In the recollection of Richard Aurelio, who was an assistant to Javits and coordinated his participation in the Lindsay campaign, the New York Republican establishment saw Lindsay's candidacy as a "chance to emerge as a significant force." The party hierarchy welcomed the campaign as a demonstration of the "party's willingness to join a progressive fusion movement of Republicans, liberals, disgruntled Democrats, and independents. The decision was consistent with Lindsay's hope to influence the party nationally along progressive lines, spurred on by the perceived lessons of the disastrous Goldwater defeat, and his feeling that once reelected, he could put into practice progressive ideas that could influence the party nationally."[64] Conservative Party challenger William F. Buckley Jr. confessed his dismay to Barry Goldwater about "Lindsay's successful co-option of the Republican Party organization in New York."[65]

Republicans knew that Lindsay offered a rare opportunity for the GOP to win in New York City politics and that even a meritocratic, nonpartisan administration nonetheless would be much more open to Republicans than the preceding Democratic regimes. Indeed, a history of the New York Young Republican Club recorded that "Club members, too numerous to list, flocked to the Lindsay headquarters and headed almost every area of activity at headquarters or in the field" and that, of the twenty-five members of the club's board of governors, twenty-three joined the Lindsay administration.[66] In the verdict of columnist Walter Lippmann, "John Lindsay is a Republican in the main line of Republicanism as it comes down from Lincoln and Theodore Roosevelt. The notion that he is a 'Leftist' or a 'pinko' is utter nonsense. . . . The Republican credentials of John Lindsay would have been validated in any Republican convention except the one the Goldwater faction raided last year."[67]

Lindsay had attracted and recruited a core group of young and enthusiastic followers from the time of his 1958 GOP primary campaign. In subsequent years, his allies had taken over most of the Manhattan Republican leadership, culminating in the 1962 election of Lindsay ally Vincent F. Albano Jr. as chairman of the New York County Republican Committee. It was this central core of Republican supporters that formed the nucleus of Lindsay's 1965 mayoral race.[68] Lindsay's gifted campaign manager Robert Price ran what was in essence an old-school retail campaign, building on the model he had established in running all of Lindsay's congressional campaigns as well as Nelson Rockefeller's 1964 GOP presidential primary victory in Oregon. Price created 122 storefront campaign headquarters throughout the city, staffed by Lindsay's core of young enthusiasts and other volunteers. The result, according to *New York Times* reporter Warren Weaver Jr., was "to create a whole new political apparatus and super-impose it" over the Republican Party organization in the outer boroughs.[69]

Lindsay won the November 1965 mayoral election with a 43.3 percent plurality, trailed by Beame with 39.5 percent and Buckley with 12.9 percent. Lindsay carried Manhattan, Queens, and Staten Island. A Louis Harris poll found that three-quarters of Republican voters had chosen Lindsay, while he cut into traditional Democratic constituencies by taking 40 percent of the Jewish vote, 40 percent of the black vote, and 25 percent of the Puerto Rican vote. While he did best among WASP voters, with 61 percent support, he did well among white ethnic voters as well, winning half of the German vote and 40 percent of the Irish and Italian vote.[70]

Progressivism in Practice: Lindsay's Mayoral Initiatives

Most of Lindsay's campaign white papers were compiled by progressive Republican activists from organizations such as the Ripon Society, Republican Advance, and Republicans for Progress.[71] The ideas that he brought to the mayoralty after his victory were different from those of liberal Democrats, Tammany Democrats, and conservative Republicans. They revolved around distinctively progressive Republican concepts such as modernization, decentralization, individualism, and racial neutralism. And they resulted in initiatives that few Democrats of any description would have put forward in the same form.

The programs that best illustrate the distinctively progressive nature of Lindsay's mayoralty include the Little City Halls, the Civilian Complaint Review Board, the school decentralization effort, the campaign against unaccountable and racially exclusive unions, and the move to end the tradition of ethnic and racial fiefdoms in city government. The specific details and overall assessments of these policies appear in subsequent chapters of this book as well as in numerous other sources. But an analysis of the often-forgotten Republican coloration of these initiatives can help to illuminate Lindsay's motivations and the extent to which his efforts failed or succeeded according to his own reckoning as well as the assessment of outside observers.

The campaign white paper that probably offered the most telling insight into what became Lindsay's political outlook as mayor was the one with the cumbersome title of "Organization of New York City's Government to Achieve Effective Planning and Administration and Responsiveness to Local Need." In it, Lindsay laid out the principle of solving New York's administrative chaos by securing the "fullest participation in the determination of governmental policy by the citizens who are affected by that policy, while at the same time achieving the economies of large operation and the consistent coordinated use of city-wide resources."[72]

One of the commonalities between moderate and conservative Republicans was that they all worried about the dangers of big, centralized government. Unlike Democrats, who since the New Deal had placed their faith in the power of federal government, Republicans touted the virtues of state and local government and cited Abraham Lincoln's dictum that "government should do for the people only that which they cannot do for themselves." By the mid-1960s, the increasingly obvious difficulties of the Soviet Union pointed to the inherent failings of a centralized, command economy. Moderate Republicans did not agree with the extreme libertarian view that government was unnecessary but were more likely than Democrats to criticize the federal government and its bureaucracies as remote, impersonal, unaccountable, and out-of-touch, and therefore ineffective. Massachusetts attorney general Elliott Richardson, a prominent moderate Republican and close friend of Lindsay's, spoke for many in the GOP when he declared that in an era when Americans felt depersonalized and insignificant, it was imperative that government operate "as close to the people as possible."[73]

One consequence of the growth and centralization of big institutions of all kinds over the previous decades, according to Lindsay, was that city residents were becoming increasingly mistrustful of the institutions of established authority, which often seemed to be "closed to the individual who wants to better his position, to alter his place in society or to change his way of life."[74] The Republican tradition therefore required that institutions of government had to be decentralized, opened, and democratized in ways that would lessen citizen mistrust of government power. Lindsay's arguments were in the mainstream of then-current Republican discourse and anticipated the "New Federalism" rhetoric of Richard Nixon and Ronald Reagan.[75]

In the late nineteenth and early twentieth centuries, Tammany Hall and the Democratic clubhouses had to some extent provided the sort of decentralized, neighborhood-based government assistance that Lindsay extolled and in a way that avoided the impersonality and dependency-inducing effects of contemporary social welfare.[76] But after the New Deal, according to Lindsay, the clubhouses had lost their original functions and decayed into a political spoils system. Key jobs were "staffed with district people from the clubhouses, people without the qualifications for the jobs they hold. These are machine politicians, not professional public servants. They spend two or three days a week on the job, the rest of the time in the clubhouses."[77] The problem of the clubhouses was the problem of Democratic city bureaucracy writ large: the system was closed (particularly to minorities), inaccessible, and incompetent. By the tail end of the Wagner administration, once effective government machinery had become outmoded, uncoordinated, unresponsive, unable to cope with growing urban problems, and often corrupt and counterproductive.[78] As Lindsay's assistant Jay Kriegel put it, "The status quo was not only unjust, it was also archaic and unsustainable."[79]

As mayor, Lindsay called for a "revolution in the administrative processes of New York City," a modernization program that would complement the decentralization program.[80] He emphasized that, in keeping with the progressive tradition, "I have filled appointive positions by seeking out the finest available men and women without obeisance to party affiliations and I have insisted that those who serve give up whatever political offices they may hold."[81]

Modernization, too, would be in the Republican tradition, and particularly in Thomas Dewey's tradition of bringing order and efficiency to New York State government. Robert Sweet, a longtime YR ally of Lindsay's who served as deputy mayor from 1967 to 1969, felt that Lindsay's program of modernization "was an effort to do for the city what Dewey had done for the state."[82] Modernization also had an inescapably partisan dimension, since in pursuing his program Lindsay inevitably would run up against the city's Democratic forces, which had vested interests in the status quo.

Lindsay's mayoral effort to set up Little City Halls combined his emphases on decentralization and modernization in a Republican vein. His campaign white paper on organization had called for "centralized planning supplemented by up-to-date information from every community in the City" and a partnership between citizens and government at the local level that would help to shape citywide programs.

Moderate Republicans who wanted to regain the loyalties of African American voters that had been lost with Goldwater's 1964 campaign were devising similar initiatives elsewhere. In 1965, aspiring GOP senatorial candidate Charles Percy launched the New Illinois Committee (NIC), a Republican effort to deliver private sector assistance to Chicago's minority ghettos. The NIC functioned as a sort of ombudsman and intermediary between South Side residents and the city government, connecting local businesses and job seekers with Republican employers, assisting citizens with complaints about ineffective city services, and offering literacy classes and legal aid.[83] Michigan's Republican chair Elly Peterson opened a Republican Action Center, patterned after the NIC, at the party headquarters in an inner-city district of Detroit; later, as co-chair of the Republican National Committee, she launched action centers under RNC auspices in cities across the country.[84] Peterson had high hopes for the program's potential to lure minorities away from the Democrats and acknowledged that it "resembles the function once performed by old-style political organizations."[85]

Democrats unsurprisingly viewed Lindsay's Little City Halls plan as a covert attempt to set up a Republican political network and recruit candidates. Indeed, deputy mayor Robert Price, another old comrade of Lindsay from YR days, hoped to use a neighborhood-based network of Civic Improvement Agencies to build a political organization around the mayor.[86] Lindsay raised private funds to open six neighborhood centers in mainly poor minority areas. While Lindsay never succeeded in setting up a citywide network of these local offices, the ideas and planning that went into the Little City Halls spilled over into the creation of the Office of Neighborhood Government (ONG) in 1970. Although the ONG was abolished under Lindsay's Democratic successor, the New York City Charter revisions of 1975 revived the Little City Hall plan for district managers and district cabinets and empowered them to plan and review land use in the community. The charter revisions thereby provided the capstone to reform efforts started under Lindsay and were influential for other mayors such as Kevin White in Boston.[87] In a sense, the reforms marked the culmination of the progressive program of decentralization, modernization, and professionalization of city government.

Few observers would describe Lindsay's effort to establish a Civilian Complaint Review Board for the police department as a success (see chapter 3). But the CCRB sprang from the same progressive Republican impulses of modernization and decentralization that had motivated Lindsay to create the Little City Halls. The racial aspect of the debate over the civilian review board has obscured the extent to which it originally was conceived as an instrument of progressive reform.

Lindsay made the creation of an independent civilian review board central to his 1965 mayoral run. It was the focus of his first major campaign speech and came two days after a City Council subcommittee had declared that such an independent review board was unnecessary.[88] Lindsay agreed that the police department had to be meritocratic, nonpolitical, and professional. But he emphasized that there had been a breakdown in relationships and communication between the police and a substantial part of the city's law-abiding citizens—particularly its poor and minority citizens. The question of how widespread police brutality actually was in minority communities was something of a moot point for Lindsay, even though police misconduct toward minorities and its potential for provoking riots usually framed the debate around the establishment of a civilian review board. The real point was that minority communities *had* lost confidence in the police, and the existing internal review procedures for police misconduct could not restore that confidence.[89]

In a campaign speech the following month, Lindsay made clear that the CCRB was only part of a program of progressive reform and modernization of the police that would liberate the department from "archaic concepts of law enforcement and municipal administration." The solution to rising crime rates was not the addition of more officers, since seven thousand men had been added to the force over the previous dozen years and yet crime rates were exploding in every category. Looking to the example of the Chicago Police Department, Lindsay believed that a modern police force needed access to computers, fax machines, advanced training, and the use of "systems applications in manpower distribution and data analysis." The police also needed the cooperation of the community in solving crime, which meant that the community had to have confidence in the police—hence the need for the CCRB.[90]

Although he didn't use the term, Lindsay was picking up on the gathering movement of law enforcement across the country toward the concept of community policing. The traditional model of policing—itself the product of a late nineteenth-century reform movement—called for a highly centralized, nonpolitical, well-trained, and well-disciplined force, emphasizing competence, leadership, and manpower. But the traditional model failed to contain either the skyrocketing rates of crime during the 1960s or the wide-scale riots that erupted in predominantly poor and minority urban areas. As noted in the report of the 1968 National Advisory Commission on Civil Disorders (better known as the Kerner Commission), of which Lindsay was a leading member, many of the most serious disturbances of that era took place in "cities whose police are among the best led, best organized, best trained and most professional in the country."[91]

The increasingly evident failure of the traditional policing model led to what one study called a "reexamination of law enforcement philosophy and practice unprecedented in American history."[92] A consensus slowly formed around the central insight of what later became known as community policing. Studies such as the 1967 report of the President's Commission on Law Enforcement and Administration of Justice emphasized that citizens played a critical role in crime prevention. Antagonism between police and ghetto inhabitants fostered community tolerance for lawlessness as well as citizen reluctance to cooperate with police in reporting crimes, providing information, or testifying as witnesses.[93] An improvement in police-community relations, therefore, was a precondition of successful crime control. This, in turn, implied a move away from the traditional standard of impersonal and efficient service toward personal interaction and face-to-face contact and understanding between neighborhood-based police and local residents, and a move toward restraint in dealing with certain forms of disorder rather than the traditional use of force and intimidation. Like other agencies of city government, then, the police department needed to be modernized, decentralized, and opened up.

Lindsay believed that, in the words of the Kerner Commission report that he helped to formulate, "Civil disorders are fundamental governmental problems, not simply police matters." As the chief elected official, the mayor should not leave the responsibility to the police but should exercise authority and control in times of disorder, much as the state governors and attorneys general had responsibility over state law enforcement activities.[94] Although the New York City Police Department resisted both the policies and practices of Lindsay's approach at almost every level, the strategy of containment over confrontation was critical in allowing New York to escape the kind of large-scale rioting that afflicted other cities during the 1960s, which most historians count as one of Lindsay's most significant achievements.[95]

The CCRB, for Lindsay, was only one component of his broader effort to change the attitudes of the community (to make them more trusting of the police and more willing to cooperate with law enforcement) and of the police (to make them more responsive and accountable to the community). It was driven by the same progressive impulses that led him to revamp the precinct community councils, which attempted to "make precinct personnel aware of the local community's point of view" through town hall meetings, informal local gatherings, and youth field trips to police head-quarters.[96]

The police fought the CCRB as well as other aspects of community policing, in a dynamic that recalled past tensions between progressive WASP elites and white ethnic groups. It didn't help that Lindsay made his case in moralistic terms, as progressives were prone to do, rather than argue for the broader reform of which the CCRB was a part. The CCRB's repeal undoubtedly was a political defeat for Lindsay and helped strengthen the perception that he sided with minorities against the white middle class.[97] But the CCRB arguably had been a symbol of the Lind-say administration's concern for minority neighborhoods more than a substantive institution in its own right. Its repeal set back but did not derail the movement to-ward community policing. Lindsay's program of police department modernization also went forward. The later achievements associated with the "Compstat" crime analysis process built on Lindsay's progressive approach that emphasized communi-cations and reporting technology, systems analysis, decentralized problem solving, empowered commanders at the precinct level, and accountability enforced through centralized information gathering.[98]

The battle over school decentralization in the Brooklyn neighborhood of Ocean Hill–Brownsville was another public relations debacle for the Lindsay administra-tion. It too, however, proceeded from the same progressive ideals that had driven Lindsay throughout his career. School decentralization was not initially one of his goals; while running for mayor, Lindsay said that he would favor decentralization that would improve school quality and give teachers and schools freedom to experi-ment, but that he would oppose a decentralization process that would merely add an extra layer of bureaucracy.[99] The worsening performance of minority education—by the mid-1960s, New York's minorities were reading two years below grade level, and dropout rates in ghetto schools averaged 70 percent—and the rising sense of crisis in race relations pushed the cause of school decentralization to the fore.[100]

For Lindsay, decentralization was both a practical necessity and a promising approach to improving education. The school system had swollen to an unmanage-able size, with over 1.1 million students, 70,000 teachers, and 43,000 administrators governed by a rigid and remote bureaucracy then housed at 110 Livingston Street in Brooklyn. The need to delegate some powers to local authorities had been proposed as early as 1954, and the advantages of decentralization had been demonstrated by Mitchell Sviridoff, the head of Lindsay's newly created Human Resources Administration. In his previous role as director of the antipoverty program in New Haven, Connecticut, Sviridoff had improved school performance by breaking up the centralized system into more manageable clusters and enlisting the cooperation of universities, businesses, teachers' unions, administrators, parents, and community leaders to help run the schools.

Lindsay believed that the bureaucracy had become too big and the principal teachers' union (the United Federation of Teachers) too rigid to function effectively. The bureaucracy-union complex was marginalizing parents and children and contributing to city residents' sense of powerlessness.[101] Lindsay viewed decentralization not only as a way to improve the functioning of the schools but also as a way of "distributing decision-making authority throughout the neighborhoods," as he put it. Decentralization was tangible evidence that "we are trying to . . . give government back to the people. We are trying to convert a machine that has for too long been externally operated into an organism that functions to satisfy its own internal needs."[102]

The school decentralization effort turned into a disaster for all the reasons described by Clarence Taylor in chapter 3. Even so, the Ocean Hill–Brownsville debacle did not invalidate the principle of decentralization or obviate the need for reform. The effort to make the school system more responsive and effective has been pursued by subsequent New York mayors and is still a matter of current debate.

Evaluating Lindsay in the Context of Progressive Republicanism

Many historians tend to forget that Lindsay remained one of the nation's most popular Republicans through the end of 1968. A March 1968 article by Nick Thimmesch pointed out that "it's hard to find a Republican on the Hill who doesn't like John Lindsay," and that even in traditionally more conservative upstate New York, "Lindsay is celebrated as that good-looking Republican mayor who maintains law and order in the nation's biggest city." In his speeches, the mayor continued to please his fellow party members by talking about fiscal integrity and hewing to the "Republican line on the need to decentralize city government and the school system, improve local neighborhood participation, make social welfare programs more productive and efficient, and involve the private sector—business and civic groups—in anti-poverty and urban renewal work."[103]

Lindsay commanded sufficient stature within the Republican Party in mid-1968 that he was considered a serious possibility for the vice presidential nomination at the party convention in Miami. Lindsay enjoyed reasonably good relations with the Nixon administration during its first months in office, judging that Nixon was "performing as a centrist, as I thought he would."[104] The Nixon administration gave tangible support to Lindsay in the form of the rapid public transfer of the Brooklyn Navy Yard, the announcement of the Gateway National Park, and generous funding of the Summer Youth Corps.[105]

But from mid-1969 onward, Lindsay angered the national Republican Party with his increasing attacks on the Nixon administration, particularly its policies in Vietnam and the turn toward populist conservatism. By the midpoint of Nixon's first term, Thimmesch would report that "regular Republicans everywhere [are] disgusted with [Lindsay]."[106] In addition, fallout from the Ocean Hill–Brownsville crisis and accompanying school strikes, the city's inability to clear Queens streets after the massive snowstorm of February 1969, and Lindsay's battle against municipal unions and racial backlash had made the mayor by his own private admission a polarizing figure to the city's white ethnic voters.[107] To some extent this was his fault for failing to seek common ground with the city's more culturally traditionalist voters, which he might conceivably have done through means such as playing up his World War II military service as a counterbalance to his ever more outspoken pronouncements against the Vietnam War.[108] To some extent it was also because Lindsay moved away from the progressive emphases of the early years of his mayoralty. In the first months of his mayoralty, for example, he had emphasized that "no particular ethnic group owns any particular job" and had faced down hostile groups accustomed to the ethnic and racial spoils system that had prevailed under the Democrats.[109] But the pressing needs and growing tensions of New York's minority communities produced the widespread impression that Lindsay was giving disproportionate attention and resources to them, an impression he did little to dispel. A reporter accompanying the mayor on one of his walks through a predominantly white ethnic neighborhood in Brooklyn recorded that one resident asked Lindsay "why all the taxes came out of white pockets only to be spent in the black neighborhoods. 'We have three hundred years of neglect to pay for,' Lindsay said, and half the sidewalk audience was shuffling in impatience."[110]

Lindsay's departures from the progressive Republican message he had campaigned on were arguably a consequence of the departure of Robert Price, his principal political advisor, at the end of 1966.[111] Robert Sweet, another of Lindsay's Republican deputies, believed that the mayor's loss to Conservative candidate John Marchi in the 1969 Republican primary was avoidable "if only John had paid a little more attention to the party structure and its needs."[112] Other observers saw the hand of Lindsay's rival Nelson Rockefeller in Marchi's decision to challenge the mayor in the Republican primary rather than on the Conservative Party line in the fall elections. The Ripon Society charged that Rockefeller was offering covert support to Marchi in the hope of minimizing Conservative Party opposition to his 1970 gubernatorial reelection bid.[113] Richard Aurelio pointed out that Marchi was a state senator who was "a major figure in Albany, close to Rockefeller and the GOP leadership. There certainly was no doubt that Rockefeller had the power to persuade Marchi not to contest Lindsay. Instead, he allowed his Lieutenant Governor [Malcolm Wilson] and many of his allies to help Marchi both financially and with other resources."[114]

Lindsay's defeat in the 1969 primary strengthened the conservative forces in the Republican Party and Nixon administration who sought to remove progressives from the party. Barry Goldwater crowed to Buckley that Lindsay's defeat "could well be the turning point that all of us have been looking forward to—a division in the Republican Party whereby we might shuffle off the Javits, the Goodells, the Rockefellers and the Lindsays . . . and begin to build strength on the conservative side."[115] Nixon's conservative advisor Pat Buchanan accurately assessed that the defeat meant that "Lindsay's advisors and the mayor himself are now *unleashed* to go where their predilections would lead them—and that is to the left."[116]

In the lead-up to the 1969 mayoral election, Lindsay made peace with the city's labor leaders, as a number of unions received generous deals. For the most part, he ran a New Politics campaign that tilted to the left of both Marchi and the Democratic nominee Mario Procaccino, whose campaign combined ineptitude, outer-borough resentment, and a traditional machine-politics approach. Running on the Liberal-Independent line, Lindsay won with 42 percent of the vote, beating out Procaccino with 33.8 percent and Marchi with 22.1 percent. Lindsay took Manhattan with a resounding two-thirds of the vote and eked out a victory in Queens. While many of his longtime Republican supporters stuck with him, the outlines of his new and more liberal coalition were evident in the fact that he received 85 percent of the black vote, 65 percent of the Puerto Rican vote, and 45 percent of the Jewish vote.[117]

Although Lindsay had won an impressive personal victory, his national standing in the Republican Party was damaged, and the Republican presidential candidacy he and his aides had long contemplated seemed considerably less likely. Lindsay's first open move toward switching parties came with his endorsement of Nelson Rockefeller's Democratic opponent in the 1970 New York gubernatorial election, perhaps as payback for Rockefeller's presumed support of Marchi. "I can only assume that he wants to 'go for it' in 1972," Lindsay's longtime backer Walter Thayer lamented, "and he thinks this is his only chance."[118]

Lindsay defected to the Democrats in August 1971, emphasizing his opposition to Nixon's war policy and "Southern strategy" on race while accusing the Republican Party of having "stifled dissent and driven progressives from its ranks" and becoming the sort of "closed institution" that he had fought throughout his career.[119] He resisted the pleas of moderate Republican activists in the Ripon Society, who warned that his switch would contribute to the growing conservative dominance within the GOP, and of his heaviest Republican contributors such as Whitney, Thayer, and David Rockefeller.[120] Lindsay's assistant Jay Kriegel recalled that even amid the worst troubles of the late 1960s and early 1970s, the mayor's Republican backers "were steadfast in their political loyalty to him. When they saw what was going on in the rest of the country, they admired and respected and appreciated what Lindsay was doing. The switch to the Democrats was wrenching, because he was breaking with his whole background."[121]

Lindsay proved a poor fit for the Democratic Party precisely because the progressive ideals that motivated him were alien to Democratic liberalism. His positions on urban issues, civil rights, and the Vietnam War seemed to position him on the left wing of the Democrats, but he had always spoken the language of moderate Republican communitarianism and New Federalism rather than that of big-government, interest-group liberalism, or racial/ethnic/gender/sexual identity politics. At a time when many left-wing Democrats were hostile to capitalism, Lindsay had courted and cultivated big business in an attempt to keep existing business in New York and attract new ones. Gustave L. Levy, the senior partner of Goldman Sachs, had chaired Lindsay's finance committee in his mayoral reelection campaign, and Lindsay's 1972 presidential run was bankrolled by industrialist J. Irwin Miller.[122] To be sure, the Wall Street bankers and corporate leaders who supported Lindsay mostly subscribed to traditional ideals of prudence and trustworthiness that were later displaced by an ethos of "greed is good," but progressives like Lindsay were still too close to corporate America for many Democrats' comfort.[123]

In the end, Democrats mistrusted Lindsay for his ideas and principles, his antagonistic relations with unions, and his friendly relations with business as well as for his opportunism in running for president less than a year after switching parties. Lindsay performed poorly in the 1972 Democratic presidential primaries, coming in a poor fifth in Florida with a meager 7 percent of the vote.[124] The remainder of his mayoral term witnessed improvements in the city's finances, safety, physical appearance, and administrative performance. But Lindsay's reputation suffered after the city slid into financial crisis in 1975 under his Democratic successor, Abraham Beame, though Lindsay maintained that his fiscal policies had not contributed to the city's near-bankruptcy. The collapse of Lindsay's political stock was confirmed by his weak third-place finish in the 1980 Democratic senatorial primary in New York.

Many commentators on Lindsay have taken him as the embodiment of 1960s urban liberalism, a symbol of the dual crisis of the cities and the political left.[125] But equating Lindsay's progressive Republicanism with the Democratic liberalism of the period is a mistake and leads commentators to misunderstand his goals and programs. By the same token, Lindsay's efforts to create new institutional structures and patterns have not been properly assessed. There is no doubt that, in casting himself as a reformer, Lindsay underestimated the resistance he would encounter in his attempts to modernize the city and its administration, while he overestimated his ability to achieve change without the backing of established interest groups and longstanding party organizations. But any New York mayor would have had to attempt to reform the city's outdated institutions and governance or face terrible consequences. Lindsay's distinctively progressive program of modernization, decentralization, and democratization helped New York to avoid some of the disasters that befell other cities in that era. In many little-recognized respects, his efforts have had lasting and productive impact. People who seek to understand today's New York City may well find that the foundation for its success was laid by Lindsay's progressive reforms.

NOTES

1. Robert Darnton, *The Great Cat Massacre and Other Episodes in French Cultural History* (New York: Vintage, 1984), pp. 5, 78.

2. As various accounts have pointed out, the Lindsays were not old-stock blue bloods and were not rich by the elevated standards of New York's elite. John Lindsay's grandfather, John James Lindsay, was a Scottish immigrant who came to New York after the failure of his brick kiln on the Isle of Wight, and his father, George Lindsay, began his career as a clerk. However, George Lindsay became a leading figure on Wall Street and a member of the Social Register, and Florence Vliet Lindsay, John's mother, was a Wellesley College alumna (at a time when fewer than one percent of American women were college graduates) and a descendant of Dutch settlers in colonial New Jersey. It seems fair to say that someone who grew up, as John Lindsay did, in a family with four servants and a chauffeur and a sixteen-room summer home on Long Island's North Shore, enjoyed significant advantages, however "middle class" is defined.

3. The classic analysis of the political culture of the nineteenth- and twentieth-century WASP elite is E. Digby Baltzell, *The Protestant Establishment: Aristocracy & Caste in America* (New Haven: Yale University Press, 1964).

4. See Geoffrey Kabaservice, *The Guardians: Kingman Brewster, His Circle, and the Rise of the Liberal Establishment* (New York: Henry Holt, 2004), which describes the influence of background and education on future establishment leaders like Lindsay during the 1930s and 1940s.

5. Nicholas Thimmesch, *The Condition of Republicanism* (New York: Norton, 1968), pp. 199–200.

6. Nat Hentoff, *A Political Life* (New York: Alfred A. Knopf, 1969), p. 55.

7. Thimmesch, *Condition of Republicanism,* pp. 202–203.

8. Hentoff, *Political Life,* p. 53.

9. Richard Norton Smith, *Thomas E. Dewey and His Times* (New York: Simon & Schuster, 1982), p. 218.

10. Tanya M. Melich, "Youth Politics: A Study of Cliques within the Association of New York State Young Republican Clubs, 1932 to 1959" (unpublished master's thesis in political science, Columbia University, 1961), p. 177.

11. Ibid., pp. 189–191.

12. For an assessment of Rusher's career, see David M. Frisk, *If Not Us, Who? William Rusher,* National Review, *and the Conservative Movement* (Wilmington, DE: ISI Books, 2012).

13. Nicol C. Rae, *The Decline and Fall of the Liberal Republicans from 1952 to the Present* (New York: Oxford University Press, 1989), p. 33.

14. Robert S. Bird, "Lindsay Wins in 17th Over Democrat Akers," *New York Herald Tribune,* November 5, 1958.

15. Thimmesch, *Condition of Republicanism,* pp. 205–206.

16. Stuyvesant Wainwright in *Congressional Record* 106, March 12, 1959, pp. 4089–4090.

17. Richard Aurelio to Jay Kriegel and Steven L. Isenberg, March 15, 2010.

18. Geoffrey Gould, "Southerners Stall GOP's Rights Talk," *Washington Post,* June 5, 1963.

19. *Congressional Record* 109, January 31, 1963, p. 1561. Lindsay's deputy mayor Richard Aurelio interviewed Lindsay in the early 1960s while he was assisting Jacob Javits with his book *Order of Battle* (see note 21 below). He remembered that Lindsay "stressed even more passionately than Javits his feeling that the Republican Party must logically be the party of civil rights and civil liberties in the Lincoln tradition and must acknowledge its moral obligation to redress the country's years of neglect of minorities. This latter point was a dominant and provocative theme during all the years I knew him." Richard Aurelio to Geoffrey Kabaservice, August 8, 2012.

20. Jo-Ann Price, "Door Left Open on Race for Mayor, Lindsay Says," *New York Herald Tribune,* February 17, 1965, p. 19.

21. Arthur Schlesinger Jr.'s *The Vital Center,* for example, consistently caricatures capitalists (and their Republican tools) as top-hatted villains and destroyers of society. According to Schlesinger, "business rule tends to bring public affairs to a state of crisis and to drive the rest of the community into despair bordering on revolution." Compare this with Jacob Javits' comparable Republican manifesto, *Order of Battle:* " 'Business,' properly understood, is so central to every aspect of our civilization that Republicans should proudly announce that they are indeed 'the party of business' and intend to make business operate in the public interest, and should boldly follow through on the implications of this identity." Arthur Schlesinger Jr., *The Vital Center: The Politics of Freedom* (orig. pub. 1949; rev. ed. New York: Da Capo, 1988), p. 25; Jacob K. Javits, *Order of Battle: A Republican's Call to Reason* (New York: Atheneum, 1964), p. 131.

22. The Republicans on the House Judiciary Committee charged that racial discrimination was denying the nation the "full benefit of the skills, intelligence, cultural endeavor, and general excellence which the Negro will contribute if afforded the rights of first-class citizenship. The failure of our society to extend job opportunities to the Negro is an economic waste. The purchasing power of the country is not being fully developed. This, in turn, acts as a brake upon potential increases in gross national product." Additional views to accompany HR 7152, submitted by William McCulloch, John V. Lindsay, William T. Cahill, Garner E.

Shriver, Clark MacGregor, Charles McC. Mathias, and James E. Bromwell, December 2, 1963. Robert Taft Jr. Papers (Library of Congress) 38:2.

23. A. James Reichley, *Conservatives in an Age of Change: The Nixon and Ford Administrations* (Washington, DC: Brookings Institution, 1981), p. 33.

24. For further analysis of Republican factionalism in the early 1960s, see Geoffrey Kabaservice, *Rule and Ruin: The Downfall of Moderation and the Destruction of the Republican Party, from Eisenhower to the Tea Party* (New York: Oxford University Press, 2012), especially chapter 1.

25. William A. Rusher memo, n.d. [Sept.? 1965]. William A. Rusher Papers (Library of Congress), reel 32.

26. George J. Marlin, *Fighting the Good Fight: A History of the New York Conservative Party* (South Bend, IN: St. Augustine's Press, 2002).

27. William F. Buckley Jr. to John M. Olin, April 1, 1965. William F. Buckley Jr. Papers (Yale University) 1:36: "Olin, John M. (1965)."

28. Keith R. Johnson, "Conservatives Eye Lindsay Seat in '62, Hail Nash Showing," *New York Herald Tribune,* September 9, 1961.

29. William Rusher later wrote to James Buckley that the desired outcome was "the election of Beame rather than Lindsay—since, after all, the Conservative Party's long-range strategic objective is to influence the Republican Party to nominate more conservative candidates by taking away conservative voters when they fail to do so." William A. Rusher to James Buckley, January 25, 1966. Rusher Papers, reel 33.

30. Peter Maas and Nick Thimmesch, "The Fight for City Hall: Anatomy of a Victory," *New York (New York Herald Tribune),* January 2, 1966, p. 9.

31. William F. Buckley Jr. to Robert Strausz-Hupe, July 16, 1965. Buckley Papers 1:37: "Strake–Strausz-Hupe (1965)."

32. William A. Rusher to William F. Buckley Jr., March 23, 1960. Buckley Papers 1:10: "Milbank, Jeremiah J. (1960)."

33. "The Activities of Representative John V. Lindsay in the 86th and 87th Congresses," August 18, 1962. John Vliet Lindsay Papers (Yale University) 9:21:9.

34. "The Evolution of the Civil Rights Bill from the Kennedy Administration Proposal to the Bill Ordered Reported by the House Judiciary Committee," January 29, 1964. William M. McCulloch Papers (University of Northern Ohio) 43: "Civil Rights of House and Senate."

35. *Congressional Record* 110, April 22, 1964, p. 8833; Lindsay campaign white paper on education, October 20, 1965. Lindsay Papers 6:91:79.

36. See for example Stricker Research Associates survey of 87th Congress, March(?) 1962. Charles McC. Mathias Papers (Johns Hopkins University), 1:2:2.

37. John V. Lindsay on *Meet the Press,* November 8, 1964. Source courtesy of Robert Price.

38. Lindsay seems to have cultivated his maverick reputation while also worrying that "I'm sufficiently independent to have come close to the edge of being ineffective." "Maverick Republican: John Vliet Lindsay," *New York Times,* August 4, 1964; James Lynn, "N.Y.'s Second-Best-Known Republican," *New York Herald Tribune,* November 1, 1964, p. 34.

39. "Lindsay Defends House Rules Vote," *New York Times,* February 26, 1961; National Committee for an Effective Congress, "Legislative Report," March 4, 1961.

40. George E. Agree notes on conversation with Anthony Morella, October(?) 1961. George L. Hinman Papers (Rockefeller Archives) 4:J2-1–34:204.

41. "Lindsay Bolts Barry to Run on Own Record," *New York Daily News,* August 4, 1964.

42. Numbers derived from the 1964 endorsements of the Committee to Support Moderate Republicans and the Ripon Society, plus *National Review*'s listing of House Republicans who permitted Democratic victories on "crucial Administration measures of an anti-conservative nature." See Committee to Support Moderate Republicans press release, October? 1964. Ripon Society Papers (Cornell University) 1:58. Ripon Society press release, October 28, 1964. Ripon Society Papers 3:185; "The Democratic Margin of Victory," *National Review* (Nov. 3, 1964): 960–964.

43. Author interview with Paul N. McCloskey, December 7, 2005.

44. Stanley Meisler, "15 Seeking 'New' G.O.P.," *Washington Star*, April 24, 1964.

45. *CQ Almanac 1964*, p. 96; *CQ Almanac 1965*, pp. 976, 984, 1042, 1063.

46. John V. Lindsay, "A Special Duty for Republicans," *Harper's*, September 1963.

47. Thimmesch, *Condition of Republicanism*, p. 208.

48. *Congressional Record* 108, August 27, 1962, pp. 17659–17660.

49. Thimmesch, *Condition of Republicanism*, pp. 207–208.

50. Author interview with Robert Blum, June 28, 2012.

51. John V. Lindsay address to the National Religious Publicity Council national convention, April 17, 1961. Lindsay Papers 9:21:7.

52. A good analysis of the progressive mind-set, of the West Coast variety, is George E. Mowry, *The California Progressives* (Berkeley, CA: University of California Press, 1951). The inescapable reference for any discussion of Eastern progressivism is still Richard Hofstadter, *The Age of Reform* (New York: Vantage, 1955).

53. James F. Clarity, "Wagner Speaks Out for Beame; So Does Powell," *New York Herald Tribune*, October 19, 1965, pp. 1, 10.

54. William A. Rusher to Charles B. Goldberg, July 15, 1969. Rusher Papers 34:8.

55. See for example Shelton Stromquist, "The Crucible of Class: Cleveland Politics and the Origins of Municipal Reform in the Progressive Era," in *Who Were the Progressives?* edited by Glenda Elizabeth Gilmore (Boston: Bedford/St. Martin's, 2002).

56. Paul L. Adams, address to the New York County Conservative Party dinner, February 22, 1972. Rusher Papers 56:5.

57. The editorial inaugurating the series declared that "the nation's greatest city cries out for a greatness of civic vision, translated into reality by get-it-done performance." "The City in Crisis," *New York Herald Tribune*, January 26, 1964, p. 22. The series was later published as a book: Barry Gottehrer, ed., *New York City in Crisis: A Study in Depth of Urban Sickness* (New York: David McKay, 1965).

58. "New York's Three Wise Men," *New York Herald Tribune*, February 24, 1965, p. 24.

59. Charles Taft to Leonard Firestone, November 29, 1965. Charles P. Taft Papers (Library of Congress) 216: "Republicans for Progress (Sept.–Nov. 1965)."

60. Author's interview with Jay Kriegel, March 14, 2012.

61. Marquis Childs, "Division and Dollars in N.Y. Campaign," *Des Moines Tribune*, October 14, 1965; Paul Hope, "Washington Close-Up," *Washington Star*, November 12, 1965.

62. Lindsay's critics anonymously mailed copies of Paul Weissman's June 20, 1965, *New York Herald Tribune* article, "Lindsay, Liberals Agree on Cabinet for Mayor," in which Lindsay was quoted as saying, "Personally, I'll get as far away from the Republican party as possible." Hinman Papers 4:J2–1–13:71.

63. William A. Rusher to William Rentschler, November 11, 1965. Rusher Papers, reel 32.

64. Richard Aurelio to Geoffrey Kabaservice, August 8, 2012.

65. William F. Buckley Jr. to Barry Goldwater, July 23, 1965. Buckley Papers 1:35: "Goldwater, Barry (1965)."

66. Morton Lawrence, "History of the New York Young Republican Club," http://nyyrc.com/history/.

67. Walter Lippmann, "The New York Election and the Nation," *New York Herald Tribune,* November 4, 1965, p. 22.

68. Author's interview with Robert Price, March 8, 2013.

69. Warren Weaver Jr., "This Tuesday's Winner and Loser," *New York Times Magazine,* October 31, 1965, p. 149.

70. Louis Harris, "New Yorkers Analyze Lindsay," *Washington Post,* November 8, 1965.

71. Stephen Horn address to the "Academic Involvement in the Republican Party" conference sponsored by Arts and Sciences Committee of the California Republican State Central Committee, December 4, 1965. Kenneth Keating Papers (University of Rochester) 7–37:20.

72. Lindsay campaign white paper on organization, October 22, 1965. Lindsay Papers 6:91:75.

73. Elliott L. Richardson, "Beyond the Marlboro Man," *Ripon Forum,* May 1967, p. 1.

74. John Lindsay address to the Liberal Party of New York State dinner, October 11, 1967. Lindsay Papers 16:349:251.

75. Of course, arguments for more democratic forms of governance and "participatory democracy" were also bubbling up from left-wing organizations like Students for a Democratic Society at that time. To some extent, such left-leaning ideas also were reflected in the Democratic reform movements of the 1950s and 1960s, which found expression in the provision for the "maximum feasible participation" of the poor in poverty programs that was written into the Economic Opportunity Act of 1964. One could also point to older Democratic experiments in decentralization such as the creation of the Community Boards in Manhattan in 1951 under then Borough President Robert Wagner. However, these developments don't seem to have much influenced Lindsay in the early-to-mid-1960s, or to have significantly altered the broad preference of Democrats for centralized federal power. A May 1967 *New York Times* article on Richard Goodwin, a liberal Democrat and former speechwriter for Kennedy and Johnson, noted that his warning against the dangers of centralized government carried "accents normally used by political conservatives." "Decentralized Government Called Decisive Issue," *New York Times,* May 21, 1967. See also Allen J. Matusow, *The Unraveling of America: A History of Liberalism in the 1960s* (New York: Harper Torchbooks, 1984), chapters 4 and 9.

76. Jack Beatty, *The Rascal King: The Life and Times of James Michael Curley, 1874–1958* (Reading, MA: Addison-Wesley, 1992), p. 77.

77. Lindsay campaign press release, October 6, 1965. Lindsay Papers 6:104:232.

78. Charles R. Morris noted that by the mid-1960s the city was in dire need of management reform: "System after system was clanking almost to a halt, wheezing with age and the pressures of new service demands. . . . The inability to perform cut right across the most routine business." Charles R. Morris, *The Cost of Good Intentions: New York City and the Liberal Experiment, 1960–1975* (New York: Norton, 1980), p. 49.

79. Author's interview with Jay Kriegel, March 14, 2012.

80. Lindsay campaign white paper on organization.

81. John V. Lindsay Lincoln Day speech, February 12, 1966. Lindsay Papers V-59:17.

82. Author interview with Robert Sweet, April 19, 2012.

83. David Murray, *Charles Percy of Illinois* (New York: Harper & Row, 1968), pp. 67–70.

84. Sara Fitzgerald, *Elly Peterson: "Mother" of the Moderates* (Ann Arbor, MI: University of Michigan Press, 2011), pp. 105–109, 139–145.

85. David S. Broder, "GOP Drive Is Aimed to Break Democrats' Grip on Ghettos," *Washington Post,* April 29, 1969, p. A17.

86. Vincent J. Cannato, *The Ungovernable City: John Lindsay and His Struggle to Save New York* (New York: Basic Books, 2001), p. 111; Kerry Gruson, "New York's Quiet Revolution: John Lindsay Builds a Machine to Dethrone City's Democrats," *Harvard Crimson,* April 29, 1967.

87. Seth Forman, "Community Boards," *Gotham Gazette,* September 20, 2000.

88. "Majority Report of a Special Subcommittee to Study the Feasibility of Creating an Independent Civilian Complaint Review Board to Investigate, Hear and Make Recommendations Concerning Allegations of Police Brutality," City Affairs Committee, New York City Council, May 18, 1965. Lindsay Papers 16:366:493.

89. John V. Lindsay address to the New York County Lawyers Association, May 20, 1965. Lindsay Papers 10:26:25.

90. John V. Lindsay address to Idlewild Lions Club, June 17, 1965. Lindsay Papers 10:26:25.

91. *Report of the National Advisory Commission on Civil Disorders* (New York: Bantam Books, 1968), p. 301.

92. Vera Institute of Justice, *Programs in Criminal Justice Reform: Ten Year Report, 1961–1971* (New York: Vera Institute of Justice, 1971), p. 43.

93. "Text of Summary of 18-Month Study Made by a Special Presidential Commission," *New York Times,* February 19, 1967, p. 68.

94. *Report of the National Advisory Commission,* p. 333.

95. Morris, *Cost of Good Intentions,* pp. 76–78.

96. *Spring 3100,* December 1966, p. 11.

97. On the positive side, however, Lindsay's campaign for the CCRB, into which he had pressured a clearly reluctant Robert F. Kennedy, strengthened his appeal among reform Democrats, independents, and civil libertarians as well as minorities, which helped him greatly in his 1969 reelection campaign.

98. Franklin E. Zimring, *The City That Became Safe: New York's Lessons for Urban Crime and Its Control* (New York: Oxford University Press, 2012), pp. 120–121.

99. Lindsay campaign white paper on education, October 20, 1965. Lindsay Papers 6:91:79.

100. Mario Fantini, Marilyn Gittell, and Richard Magat, *Community Control and the Urban School* (New York: Praeger, 1970), p. 103.

101. Victor Ratner to Walter N. Thayer, November 25, 1968. Walter N. Thayer Papers (Hoover Presidential Library) 3:4:7.

102. John V. Lindsay address at Occidental College, November 17, 1967. Lindsay Papers 16:349:251.

103. Nick Thimmesch, "Lindsay's Political Timetable," *New York,* March 27, 1968, p. 26.

104. Nick Thimmesch, "Nixon and the New York Republicans," *New York,* April 7, 1969, p. 39.

105. "Editorial," *Ripon Forum,* June 1969, p. 3.

106. Nick Thimmesch, "Lindsay Boxes Himself into a Corner," [Washington, PA] *Observer-Reporter,* November 20, 1970.

107. Josiah Lee Auspitz to John V. Lindsay, June 2, 1970. Steven Livengood Papers (Cornell University) 2: "Auspitz—Chron file."

108. However, the conservative charge that Lindsay boarded the bandwagon of antiwar opposition when it became a popular cause is completely wrong. Lindsay had been one of the earliest critics of the Johnson administration's conduct of the war and was among the few outspoken congressional opponents of the intervention. See *Congressional Record* 110 (Jan. 31, 1964): 1555–1556.

109. Jerome Zukosky, "Mayor Warns against Ethnic Job Pressure," *New York Herald Tribune,* February 3, 1966, p. 1.

110. Larry L. King, "Lindsay of New York," *Harper's,* August 1968, p. 41.

111. Author's interview with Anthony Morella, July 9, 2012.

112. Author's interview with Robert Sweet, April 19, 2012.

113. "Editorial," *Ripon Forum,* June 1969, p. 3.

114. Richard Aurelio to Geoffrey Kabaservice, August 8, 2012. Aurelio also emphasized that, while he advised Lindsay to conserve resources during the Republican primary, the better to prepare for the possibility of an independent run in the fall, Lindsay's GOP backers "unanimously rejected that idea, and pledged to fund a stepped-up campaign to try to win the Republican primary, indicating their determination to hold on to Lindsay as a future national hope to lead a progressive Republican movement. With this additional financial help, we boldly increased our media activity, our canvassing and retail campaigning. Nonetheless, we lost by 6,000 votes with a total turnout of about 200,000."

115. Barry Goldwater to William F. Buckley Jr., June 21, 1969. Buckley Papers 1:61: "Goldwater, Barry (1969)."

116. Patrick J. Buchanan to Richard M. Nixon, June 20, 1969. Nixon Presidential Materials (National Archives II) POF—President's handwriting, box 2: "1969."

117. Cannato, *Ungovernable City,* pp. 437–438.

118. Walter N. Thayer to Richard Shields, October 26, 1970. Thayer Papers 1:4.

119. David S. Broder, "Lindsay Shifts to Democrats, Pledges '72 Role," *Washington Post,* August 12, 1971, p. A4.

120. Martin Tolchin, "City G.O.P. Group Bids Lindsay Stay," *New York Times,* August 11, 1971, p. 1.

121. Author interview with Jay Kriegel, March 15, 2012.

122. In the 1969 campaign, Levy wrote: "During the last four years, John Lindsay has become the nation's chief spokesman for all urban areas—not exclusively New York City. At this time when the cities are America's most expedient concern, we can ill-afford to sacrifice John Lindsay." Gustave L. Levy to Charles P. Taft, August 29, 1969. Charles P. Taft Papers 219: "Republicans for Progress (Sept. 1968–Sept. 1969)." Fred Siegel, an indefatigable critic of Lindsay, has pointed to the 1969 campaign as an example of a "top-bottom" leftist coalition pitting the rich and poor against the middle class. Siegel errs by equating the middle class with the "remnants of the old Democratic machine," omitting the fact that Lindsay received labor union backing and claiming that Lindsay won only in Manhattan. Still, it was only up to 1969 that there were many journalists asserting that Lindsay's administration "represented a new and very middle-class style of leadership." Fred Siegel, "The Liberal Top-Bottom Coalition," *City Journal,* winter 2012, available at http://www.city-journal.org/2012/22_1_snd -top-bottom-coalition.html; Paul H. Weaver, "The Phantom Deflator," *New York,* March 27, 1968, p. 38.

123. See William D. Cohan, *Money and Power: How Goldman Sachs Came to Rule the World* (New York: Anchor, 2011); Karen Zouwen Ho, *Liquidated: An Ethnography of Wall*

Street (Durham, NC: Duke University Press, 2009); Steve Fraser, *Wall Street: A Cultural History* (New York: Faber & Faber, 2005).

124. Aurelio maintained that, although Lindsay knew his chances in the Democratic presidential race were slim, he felt that a "presidential run would give him a pulpit to talk about the problems of urban America, the disastrous Vietnam War, women's rights, and a host of other issues that had obsessed him." After he pulled out, "he was satisfied that he had made the effort, even though he failed to achieve his major objective—to put the plight of the cities on the forefront of national attention." Richard Aurelio to Geoffrey Kabaservice, August 8, 2012.

125. Cannato, *Ungovernable City,* p. ix.

A smiling Mayor Lindsay shares the delight of uptown kids after he opened a spray cap on a fire hydrant at 122nd Street, between Seventh and Eighth avenues. It was the first of three hundred spray caps installed. July 15, 1966; photographer Frank Russo. © Daily News, L.P. (New York). Used with permission.

CHAPTER THREE

Race, Rights, Empowerment

CLARENCE TAYLOR

This chapter examines Mayor John Lindsay's efforts to make the city more racially inclusive by giving those who were powerless the opportunity to address their concerns. I argue that the most racially charged episodes—the fight over a civilian complaint review board for the police, the attempt to create community control of schools, and the scatter-site housing controversy in Forest Hills—laid the groundwork for important structures by giving people an opportunity to make government agencies work for them. Another important part of Lindsay's legacy was the appointment of a group of young black leaders to local agencies who would help shape a better future for the city by taking action against racial discrimination and injustice. And finally Lindsay's creation of the Urban Action Task Force was an early step in a larger effort to build lines of communication between City Hall and troubled communities so that the government could be more responsive to people in need.

Civilian Complaint Review Board

The creation of a civilian complaint review board was John Lindsay's first major attempt to address racial tension in the city. Lindsay knew too many people felt they were not being treated fairly by the police. In May of 1965, in his first major speech as a candidate for mayor, Lindsay declared, "So long as we have large numbers of our population who believe that society cares nothing for them, we cannot hope to be successful." This sentiment of feeling uncared for led to resentment. And, he continued, "Resentment breeds resentment; misunderstandings become serious incidents, tempers flare and people are injured."[1]

At the heart of the problem was the fact that people did not have any recourse to express their grievances. Lindsay understood that the existing complaint review board was not trusted by black and Latino communities, because it was controlled by the police, with three white deputy police commissioners serving on it and no outsiders. The board was simply part of the police department; therefore it could not be seen as an impartial party. Lindsay proposed adding four civilians to the existing board, who would be selected by the mayor from a list of names "submitted by a committee made up of men and women of unquestionable stature." Because large numbers of people did not trust the police, Lindsay insisted, "It is time for an independent review board to be joined with professional police knowledge."[2] He had hoped that better relations between the police and the communities they served would eventually improve the overall effectiveness of the department. Lindsay's demand for a more just review of citizen complaints also put him on the side of the civil rights community, which had called for better oversight of police misconduct and abuse.

To no one's surprise, the police opposed Lindsay's plan. As explained previously in chapter 1, the leadership of the department believed that the proposed board would undermine their ability to properly protect the city. They accused Lindsay of caving in to the demands of blacks and Latinos. John Cassese, president of the Patrolmen's Benevolent Association (PBA), even used racially inflammatory rhetoric to appeal for public support, claiming that he was "sick and tired of giving into minority groups with whims and their gripes and shouting." He contended that the misconduct issue was a fabrication, made up by blacks and Latinos.[3] Cassese's rhetoric was effective in appealing to the majority population of New Yorkers who were fearful of the rising crime rate. In November of 1966, New Yorkers voted almost two to one in favor of the referendum that outlawed the review board Lindsay had appointed. While black and Latino areas of the city voted overwhelmingly against the referendum, white areas chose by a three to one margin to favor it.[4]

The battle over a review board was a bold illustration of a racial divide that had existed in the city long before John Lindsay announced his candidacy for mayor. Since the Great Migration in the early part of the twentieth century led to a dramatic increase in the black population in New York, racial inequality in housing, public services, employment, and health services had been a matter of concern for many New Yorkers. Civil rights and other groups had led campaigns to address racial discrimination by private businesses, the police, schools, and other public and private entities, leading to a strain in race relations. Lindsay was well aware that his campaign to create a police review board might further contribute to existing racial tensions. He publicly admitted being "terribly concerned" a month before the referendum was held, but he would not back down. He told the press that he was "totally committed because it is an issue that lies at the very root of American democracy."[5] At the heart of the story was the struggle for citizens to gain a voice in city policing, the same people who had been victims of police brutality.

Although the civilian review board was defeated in 1966, the city would eventually create a board where civilians served with non-uniformed police officers. In 1993, Mayor David Dinkins and the City Council created an all civilian complaint review board.

The larger picture for Lindsay was to assure that those who felt alienated from city government were given an opportunity to be heard. That was the way to guarantee that the government properly served the community. As Lindsay noted in his inaugural address on January 1, 1966, "My administration will be a visible government. No longer will New Yorkers be obliged to seek out the distant, unfamiliar offices of their city; from this day on, their city will go to them."[6]

Community Control of Schools

The push for community control of schools, similar to the fight for a civilian complaint review board, did not originate at City Hall. It began with a campaign by citizens trying to improve their children's education. After the U.S. Supreme Court handed down its landmark *Brown v. Board of Education* decision in 1954, national civil rights organizations and grassroots groups accused the New York City Board of Education of separating children on the basis of race. The allegation was confirmed in 1955 when the Public Education Association released a study commissioned by the Board of Education indicating that children attending schools in black and Latino neighborhoods were relegated to segregated and overcrowded classes with the least experienced teachers. Advocates for the children living in the affected areas demanded that school officials take action to correct the discriminatory practices but to no avail.[7]

The group that led the struggle to integrate New York City's public schools after a decade of inaction by the state and local governments was the Parents Workshop for Equality in New York City Schools. Led by the Reverend Milton Galamison of Siloam Presbyterian Church in Brooklyn, the Parents Workshop was a grassroots organization made up of women and men whose children attended the public schools. Unable to persuade the board to accede to its demands, the Parents Workshop, joined by the NAACP, the Congress of Racial Equality, the Urban League, and the Harlem Parents Committee, created the Citywide Committee for Integrated Schools. The committee staged a citywide school boycott on February 3, 1964, hoping to pressure the Board of Education to develop a plan for integration. Once again the board refused to act.[8]

By 1965 it was clear to parents and community activists that the school integration movement had failed. At that point they began to call for community control. Community control proponents were part of a larger national movement advocating black empowerment, which sought to have local residents take charge of institutions in the black communities as a way to improve the circumstances of the people living there. Public schools that shaped the future of black children living in segregated neighborhoods were a key target of their efforts. Community control activists demanded the right to hire and fire teachers, to make decisions on curricula, to control budgets, and to negotiate contracts.

The Ford Foundation, which was philosophically sympathetic to the ideas of local participation and control, took an immediate interest in the school controversy. Under the leadership of McGeorge Bundy, the New York–based foundation saw community control as a way to advance racial equality and agreed to support their effort financially.[9] Community control of schools was also attractive to John Lindsay, who, according to one close associate, had an unwavering faith that poor people, if provided the opportunity, could alleviate their conditions.[10]

As a member of Congress in 1964, Lindsay had supported the maximum feasible participation prescription that was central to President Lyndon B. Johnson's War on Poverty (see chapter 1). At the time the national poverty rate was close to 20 percent. But the War on Poverty was not simply an assortment of government entitlement programs. The architects of the program had a larger vision that embraced the culture of poverty thesis articulated first by social scientist Oscar Lewis and later adopted by Richard Cloward, Michael Harrington, Charles Ohlin, and others to explain its causes. Proponents of the theory argued that a cycle of poverty kept the poor trapped. The roots of their condition could be traced to tangible structural barriers to opportunity as well as a host of environmental handicaps found in minority communities. In urban centers, these barriers were manifest in the process of ghettoization and in poor diets, inadequate education, and a lack of health care that pushed the poor in a downward trend, locking them into the lowest strata of society.[11]

The solution was not just a number of new funding programs. Indeed, early antipoverty programs had been ineffective because they were inflexible and bureaucratic. State governments and local municipalities were unresponsive to the poor. To assure that the new efforts were effective, it was essential that the people who were their intended beneficiaries participate in their creation and monitoring to the maximum extent feasible. Such involvement of the poor would help address the social disintegration and apathy that crushed the spirit and drained the will to succeed.[12] Allowing people to participate in eradicating their own poverty would give the poor a sense of worth, enabling them to participate in the democratic process.[13] Could this theory of democracy work to improve the New York City public schools?

After interviewing community groups, the Board of Education recommended that three experimental districts be created, one in lower Manhattan, the second in Harlem, and the third in Ocean Hill–Brownsville in Brooklyn. The major problem with the experiment was that there had been no clear definition of community control. Those elected to run the schools in Ocean Hill–Brownsville did have a transparent definition of community control. They meant to have complete control over curriculum, budget, and school professional staff. But legally the board was only given an advisory role and not the authority to determine the status of personnel. Despite its advisory role, the school board voted in the spring of 1968 to remove thirteen teachers, five assistant principals, and one principal from the district. The school board's actions prompted the United Federation of Teachers to take action in the form of three strikes over a two-and-half-month period.

The strike was settled when Mayor Lindsay decided that the schools could not remain closed. The agreement called for the removal of three principals from the Ocean Hill–Brownsville district, for the appointment of the Associate State Commissioner Herbert E. Johnson as the trustee of the district, and for the creation of a special committee by the state to protect the rights of teachers and supervisors. The local school board was not included in negotiations.[14]

On April 30, 1969, the state legislature passed a decentralization bill. The bill contained a decentralization plan advocated by Albert Shanker and the UFT. The Board of Examiners remained in place so that teachers and principals were selected by examination. The central Board of Education appointed by the mayor was replaced with a seven-person board, with each borough president selecting a member and the mayor appointing the other two. Thirty-one new districts (later thirty-two) with the authority to select a superintendent and principals were created to oversee elementary and middle schools. High schools and special education classes remained under the control of the central headquarters then at 110 Livingston Street. The local boards could select textbooks from a centrally approved list. Each new district had to have at least twenty thousand students, assuring that the Ocean Hill–Brownsville district would be placed into a larger district. Board members were selected by election.

The criticism directed at Lindsay for his handling of Ocean Hill–Brownsville seems almost unanimous. The strike divided the city along racial lines and deepened the rift between blacks and Jews.[15] Many accused the mayor of coddling black militants. There is no doubt that the 1968 teachers' strike was a horrible episode in the city's history that led to further distrust and animosity between New York City teachers and African Americans and Latinos.

Despite the deep racial division resulting from the episode, there were significant accomplishments. Lindsay's support helped lead to a system where parents had the opportunity to have a greater say in their children's education on the elementary and junior high school levels. Although community control was not fully realized, a decentralized structure was created with some power delegated to the new local boards. The new structure gave citizens the power to help determine educational policies. Local boards—elected by members of the community—overseeing elementary and middle schools selected the superintendent, hired school aides, made

repairs to school buildings, operated social centers, ran recreational and extracur-
ricular programs, and served as advisors to the chancellor on construction proposals.
The local school boards' executive powers, administered through a local superintendent, included the authority to appoint, promote, and fire all of its employees and
define their duties and determine their pay within the general rules and guidelines
set by the central Board of Education for the entire school system.[16]

Critics have rightfully criticized the decentralized system of not being effective.
Many of the local boards proved to be corrupt. Turnout in school boards elections was low. Community control, however, gave parents a place where they could
express their concerns about their children's education. The new system provided
parents with the right to elect school board members.[17] Even parents who were
not citizens could vote in school board elections. In many neighborhoods, local
school boards were effective in providing educational services. Teachers and parents
worked together in these districts on curricula and other matters.[18] Even though
participation was low, schools were still responsive to citizens.

Scatter-Site Housing

For historian Jerald Podair, the scatter-site housing episode that erupted in Forest Hills in 1971 was another indication of the withering away of New York City
liberalism in the face of growing racial strife. According to Podair, the liberalism
of politicians such as the Democratic Congressman Edward Koch was "dissolving
in New York's racial maelstrom. Forest Hills taught Koch, and a good many of his
colleagues as well, a lesson about the power of community—white community—in
the city's racial politics."[19]

Podair is correct that the battle in Forest Hills was an indication that New York
liberalism was beginning to waver in the 1970s. But Forest Hills was also a clear
sign that, while some politicians were abandoning their earlier liberal positions,
Lindsay refused to move away from a stance that he thought was morally right.
His views on race and particularly the housing question were spelled out in the
Report of the National Commission on Civil Disorders, for which he served as vice
chair. The report observed that in urban areas "segregation and poverty have created
the racial ghetto," which was a "destructive environment totally unknown to most
Americans."[20] It contended that white racism, white flight, and ghettoization were
responsible for urban unrest. But it also insisted that the growing racial divide was
not inevitable and could be reversed.

One solution to the growing divide in America was to address the housing crisis.
The report's recommendation on housing called for building low-income housing
outside of slums. This practice is sometimes known as scatter-site housing, because

the properties are not all concentrated in one location but rather scattered throughout the community. It proclaimed, "We believe that federally aided low-income and moderate income housing programs must be reoriented so that the major thrust is in non ghetto areas." It continued, "Public housing programs should emphasize scattered site construction, rent supplements in non ghetto areas, and an intensive effort to recruit below market interest rate sponsors willing to build outside the ghettos."[21]

Lindsay embraced the notion that structural forces were responsible for racial inequality. If the victims of racism were provided opportunities, they would improve their lives. At the start of his first term, he decided to build low-income housing in the Corona neighborhood of Queens. After residents protested, a compromise was worked out between the residents, the Queens borough president, and the Lindsay administration that scatter-site housing would be developed on 8.5 acres of a vacant lot in nearby Forest Hills.[22] However, when the Housing Authority finally announced in December 1970 that it would start building low-income housing projects in the middle-class neighborhood there, residents became furious and organized to stop the project.[23]

The racial tension created by the Forest Hills housing controversy exacerbated the animosity across the city that was already growing out of the teachers' strike. White, mostly Jewish residents of the Forest Hills community expressed fears that the movement of low-income minorities into the area would reduce Forest Hills to a slum. Some even asserted that, if low-income blacks were allowed into the neighborhood, white women would be in danger of being raped. To make matters worse, residents charged Lindsay and his black Housing Authority Chairman Simeon Golar with anti-Semitism, claiming that the two were intent on destroying a Jewish neighborhood.[24]

Lindsay did not want the confrontation to drag on, so in the fall of 1971 he asked a young Queens lawyer, Mario Cuomo, to serve as a fact finder and to recommend a solution to the conflict. Instead of the 840 units originally planned, Cuomo proposed 432 units that would be situated in three twelve-story buildings. Forty percent of the units were set aside for the elderly, and thirty units would be allocated to families on welfare.[25]

By the late 1960s America was experiencing a political backlash. Many white voters blamed the Democratic Party for giving in to the demands of black militants, antiwar protesters, and other "special interest groups," while ignoring the concerns of working- and middle-class families. Whites in the South, West, and parts of the North were beginning to flock to the Republican Party fearing crime, urban unrest, and what they believed was a decline in moral values. While New York City remained strongly Democratic, whites in the boroughs outside of Manhattan could no longer be counted on to vote the party line, especially for candidates who continued

A political conflict in the Ocean Hill–Brownsville neighborhood in Brooklyn sets the teachers' union and local community activists in opposition over control of the schools. 1969; photographer Richard Kalvar. Magnum Photos.

to carry a left-of-center agenda. Many in the outer boroughs blamed Lindsay for caring about the needs of blacks and Latinos while ignoring them. Despite this political shift, Lindsay did not walk away from his core principles. His willingness to champion scatter-site housing on behalf of poor working-class black families after a tumultuous confrontation in Ocean Hills–Brownsville testified to what one Lindsay close aide said was a "clarity of vision, commitment to principles" and a "personal courage" that allowed him to stand up for what he believed was right despite the difficulty.[26]

Why did Lindsay decide to pursue scatter-site housing soon after the school strike that racially divided New York? According to his close aide, Sid Davidoff, Lindsay stuck with scatter-site housing because he thought it was the right thing to do and that "was who he was."[27] The mayor saw scatter-site housing as a benefit to the poor. But he also saw advantages for the entire city. Scatter-site housing would help address the problem of crime by moving people concentrated in poor housing to places in stabilized neighborhoods. Having access to better public services and better local amenities would give them a greater stake in their communities. Because residents of scatter-site housing would live in close proximity to people in middle-class communities, there was greater possibility of more positive relationships developing between the two groups. The resulting racial and class integration would challenge the social isolation that led to ghettoization and urban decay.[28]

A New Black and Latino Leadership

Mayor Lindsay's appointment of many talented blacks and Latinos to high-level positions in city government remains one of the most significant legacies of his administration. Their opportunity to serve at a time when men and women of color were severely underrepresented in the upper echelons of government opened the door to influential careers that they would have in decades to come. The list of notables is endless: Walter Washington, who served as Chair of the Housing Authority under Lindsay went on to become mayor of Washington, D.C. Amalia Betanzos, the head of Youth Services, went on to serve in high positions for four subsequent mayors. Major Owens, who was head of Community Services, went on become a prominent member of the U.S. House of Representatives, where he held a seat for a quarter century. Lindsay's human rights commissioner, Eleanor Holmes Norton, has also had a long career in Congress, where she is still the delegate from the District of Columbia. Carl McCall, a deputy commissioner in Human Rights, was later elected state comptroller and now serves as chair of the board of trustees for the State University System. Former mayoral assistant Victor Marerro is a federal judge. Gordon Davis, another mayoral assistant, later served on the City Planning Commission and then became parks commissioner before embarking on a distinguished law career. As top mayoral advisors and members of his cabinet, these same individuals would devote a good part of their energies challenging discriminatory practices and other barriers to fair representation. The result of their activity was a more inclusive city that befitted all New Yorkers.

Mayor Lindsay's very first cabinet appointment—that of Robert O. Lowery as fire commissioner—was clearly an extraordinary event. It sent a strong message to the city that the new mayor was committed to racial inclusion. Lowry became head of the largest fire department in the nation with fifteen thousand employees and an annual budget of $300 million. The New York City Fire Department was also the whitest of all major city agencies. There were only six hundred black firefighters, making up just 4 percent of the staff. But Lowery's appointment was more than symbolism. During his eight-year tenure as the fire commissioner, Lowery undertook a variety of measures to increase the number of black and Latino firefighters, to improve the relationship between the fire department and the black and Latino communities, and to reduce the high number of fires taking place in minority communities, where 53 percent of the alarms occurred.[29] Lowery understood that the "fire problem" was a "major sign of a deteriorating community" and that it was closely related to a host of other social problems. Overcrowding and "rundown buildings which are built so close together that when a fire occurs, it can endanger a whole block" were important spatial considerations to take into account in black and Latino communities that suffered a higher fire mortality rate than other communities.[30]

To address this problem, Lowery created additional fire companies and relocated fire units to poor communities. To foster better relations, he created a community and news service and expanded the role of the Community Relations Bureau. He worked to increase the number of black firefighters by initiating a review of recruitment procedures and advocating that additional credits be given to residents of New York City who took the civil service entry exam.[31]

Another early Lindsay appointment was that of William H. Booth, who was appointed chair of the City's Human Rights Commission. Booth, an African American attorney, had been chair of the state conference of the NAACP. He had also been an outspoken critic of employment discrimination, having protested the lack of black and Puerto Rican construction workers at the Roachdale Village construction site in Jamaica, Queens, in 1963.[32] The mayor gave Booth a "very wide mandate," directing him to assure that "every citizen is given a fair shake and treated properly," and he instructed Booth to "make determined efforts to eliminate bias in labor unions."[33]

One of Booth's largest targets in his fight to end racial discrimination in employment was in the building trades. Booth demonstrated that blacks made up only 4 percent of those involved in the crafts compared with 23 percent employed in the city.[34] A commission report, based on data on eleven trade unions submitted to it by Peter Brennan, president of the New York Building Trades Council, revealed that employment of minorities by construction contractors made "insubstantial and spotty progress." There were only about seven thousand nonwhite journeymen and about five hundred nonwhite apprentices of the sixty-four thousand union members. The hardline approach taken by Booth led to some gains. In August 1966 he reported that black and Puerto Rican employment in firms doing business with the city increased by 23 percent.[35]

Booth's aggressive approach on racial parity was also a source of controversy, and his tenure as chair of the Human Rights Commission was short lived. In February 1967 Rabbi Julius G. Neumann resigned his post on the commission, complaining that Booth only investigated discrimination against blacks and ignored discrimination against Jews.[36] Subsequently, Gilbert Klaperman, president of the New York Board of Rabbis, asked Mayor Lindsay not to reappoint Booth as human rights commissioner because of his "singular insensitivity to anti-Semitic incidents." Klaperman was alarmed, because Booth had failed to investigate allegations that black teachers at I.S. 201 in Harlem made anti-Semitic remarks during a memorial service for Malcolm X. The Board of Rabbis was the largest representative rabbinic body in the nation, with eight hundred Orthodox, Reform, and Conservative rabbis.[37] Lindsay had taken a political beating during the teachers strike and did not want another controversy that threatened to increase the tension between blacks and Jews. He decided not to reappoint Booth for another term. Instead he appointed him as a judge to the Criminal Court. Lindsay's decision drew criticism from Donald Lee, chairman of the State NAACP, who charged that Booth had been removed due to a "white backlash."

Booth's troubles should not overshadow the significance of his time as chairman of the Human Rights Commission. Lindsay's selection of Booth to head the agency and the mayor's willingness to provide him with a mandate to eradicate racial discrimination meant that the nation's largest city had adopted the agenda of the civil rights community. Unlike previous administrations, Lindsay was willing to challenge forces that for decades practiced discrimination with impunity. Lindsay's announcement in April 1970 that he would issue an executive order requiring that one trainee from a minority group be hired for every four journeymen working on a construction site being built with city funds was a demonstration of Booth's impact. It was estimated that the executive order would involve four to five thousand trainees.

Despite the replacement of Booth, Lindsay did not walk away from an assertive agenda to end discrimination in both public agencies and private firms. Neither did the mayor turn away from the civil rights community when deciding on a chair for the Human Rights Commission. Indeed, Lindsay renewed his commitment when he selected Eleanor Holmes Norton as chair in 1970. Norton was active in the national civil rights movement. As a law student she participated in the Mississippi Freedom Campaign in 1964. After graduating Yale Law School, she became a civil rights lawyer and worked for the American Civil Liberties Union (ACLU) in New York City. As a lawyer for the ACLU, Norton drew the attention of John Lindsay, when she successfully defended the right of a white supremacist to use Shea Stadium for a rally. For Norton, the defense of a member of a white supremacist organization had nothing to do with race. It was a constitutional issue.

Norton's appointment as chair was historic, because she was the first woman to serve in that position. Norton's appointment was more than symbolic. As chair of the commission, she carved out an agenda that was more expansive than those of her predecessors. She not only addressed the problem of racial discrimination; she also focused on sex discrimination.[38] Norton drew attention to the condition of poor and working-class women. One of her goals was to get "women to understand that civil rights meant women's rights.[39] Norton convened conferences targeting the concerns of women. At one such conference held in April 1971, the commission focused on household work. Participants at the conference examined the problems of domestic workers and suggested both immediate and long-term recommendations to help improve the situation for household workers. She told conference participants that her reason for highlighting the plight of domestic workers was to make people recognize that such work was a "question for the women's rights movement." She noted, "The civil rights movement and the trade union movement must of course feel equal responsibility." However, it is the women's movement alone that "embraces both household workers and those who employ them."[40]

In July 1972 Title VII of the 1964 Civil Rights Act was amended to include state and municipal governments as employers. Thus, state and local governments fell under the jurisdiction of the Equal Employment Opportunities Commission and were obligated to submit annual reports to the commission on the racial and sexual makeup of their workforce. By this time, Norton already had convinced Mayor Lindsay to conduct a survey of the workforce. On October 1, 1971, Lindsay issued Executive Order Number 49, ordering the city's Human Rights Commission to conduct an annual survey noting the race, ethnicity, and sex of the city workforce. The commission was also required to reveal the number and percent of the workforce that classified as "handicapped."[41] Although the 1971 survey showed that the city had made gains in black and Puerto Rican employment in certain city agencies, their numbers were extremely low in others such as the uniformed services. Women were also virtually excluded from the uniformed services, while 93 percent of them were concentrated in health, housing, and education.[42]

As Commissioner of Human Rights, Eleanor Holmes Norton fought to make New York City a place where men and women of every race enjoyed the same opportunities in employment as other New Yorkers, and she began to establish information systems that allowed the city to monitor progress toward fair representation.

As previously mentioned, another active member of the civil rights community who served in the Lindsay administration was Major Robert Odell Owens. While serving as a community coordinator for the Brooklyn Public Library in the early 1960s, Owens had developed links with several community organizations. One of the groups was the Brownsville Community Council (BCC). It was one of twenty-six antipoverty groups created in response to Title II of the 1964 Economic Opportunity Act that required people eligible for antipoverty funds to help determine how the funds were used. Each council was expected to come up with a plan for economic development for its community.[43] In 1966 Owens became head of the BCC, one of the most effective in the city.[44] It was because of his success in Brownsville that Mayor Lindsay asked Owens to become commissioner of the Community Development Agency (CDA).[45]

When Owens took over as commissioner, close to two million New Yorkers lived in poverty. Seventy percent of the impoverished were black and Puerto Rican. To help in determining how federal antipoverty funds would be administered, Lindsay created the New York City Council Against Poverty. The group, along with the CDA, set policy for antipoverty programs. The CDA and the Council Against Poverty oversaw how the twenty-five community corporations operated the numerous programs under their purview, including health services, employment and economic development, consumer affairs, family planning, education, and legal services. Community corporations were vehicles for self-help government by local residents, because community people sat on the boards of the corporations that decided how the various programs would operate.[46]

While mayors in other cities throughout the country were opposed to maximum feasible participation, because it encouraged grassroots opposition to their policies, Owens notes that Lindsay was an ardent supporter of the idea. Speaking before the House of Representatives in 2001, Owens, then a congressman, asserted, "Assuming great political risks, Lindsay was one of the few leaders in the nation who seriously adopted Lyndon Johnson's 'maximum feasible participation of the poor' policy. His administration made a Herculean effort to institutionalize power sharing down to the local level. Instead of siphoning and resources from the federal programs like the Community Action Program and the Model Cities initiative, Lindsay added city support."[47]

Unfortunately, Lindsay's hope that community participation would lead to dramatic improvements in the life of impoverished minorities was never realized. Corruption and mismanagement existed in many of the antipoverty programs, undermining their effectiveness. But the administration's efforts provided respect and opportunity for poor people that was unprecedented and remains unmatched.

Urban Action Task Force

John Lindsay created the nation's first Urban Action Task Force that provided residents of neighborhoods who had no access to those in power an avenue to express their priorities and concerns. It was through the task force that poor blacks and Latinos were able to meet with city officials, convincing them to improve their communities. Lindsay pledged to create such a mechanism in his inaugural address in 1966 when he proposed to establish Little City Halls, promising "we can open direct lines of communication between the people and their government."[48] When Lindsay was drawn to the East New York section of Brooklyn the following summer, because of a violent turf war that had broken out between Italian and black youths, he gained an added insight. It was then, in an attempt to quell the disturbance, that Lindsay began his celebrated walking tours of troubled areas and realized that his personal presence could be calming. It was an unusual act for a white politician, and Lindsay took to the streets with just a few aides and no police entourage. It was then that Lindsay also learned that there were no channels of communication between City Hall and remote city neighborhoods. So Lindsay raised private funds to create an office in East New York and assigned a mayoral aide to oversee the delivery of services. The office, a precursor of the district cabinet system described more fully in chapter 5, coordinated interventions by the sanitation, parks, buildings, traffic, police, and fire departments to clean up blighted areas.

Simultaneously, City Hall developed a crisis communication system under special mayoral assistants Barry Gottehrer and Sid Davidoff, which evolved into the Urban Action Task Force. As head of the task force, Gottehrer assigned a team with street experience to build relationships with leaders in communities that the police and youth services agencies identified as trouble spots.[49] They included Central Harlem, East Harlem, the Lower East Side, Chinatown, Bedford-Stuyvesant, Bushwick, Brownsville, Williamsburg, East New York, and Coney Island.

Along with other key officials, especially Human Rights Commissioner William Booth, who understood the dynamics of these neighborhoods, Gottehrer turned to local people who might have street credibility and the ability to influence those most likely to be causing trouble. He reached out to people who were often referred to as rabble rousers and political extremists, street orators who could gather a crowd. Gottehrer built relationships with Sonny Carson in Brooklyn, and Charles Kenyatta of Harlem, with the Black Muslims and the mostly Latino political organization known as the Young Lords, and especially with a man who went by the name of Allah, the leader of a fringe youth organization called the Five Percenters.[50] Over time, as they became allies of the administration in keeping the peace, Gottehrer provided funds and support to help the Five Percenters to establish a series of street academies for outcast youth.

The efforts by Gottehrer offended many government officials and some in the established news media as well as traditional black leadership, who were sharply critical. But it gave Gottehrer and Lindsay sophisticated insights into the undercurrents of these minority communities and direct lines into those who could reflect the mood of the streets. The information was invaluable, not just to City Hall but to the police department as well. Gottehrer had built a unique intelligence network that allowed him to generate a detailed report on each potentially unstable community.

As Lindsay reported in his own memoir:

During the 1967 summer Barry Gottehrer, as the coordinator of the task force, received all reports of trouble—about a thousand of them. In two hundred cases that looked especially serious, Gottehrer got in touch directly with local task force leaders, who lived in the neighborhoods, who knew the people there, and who in fact acted as representatives from their neighborhoods to the city—instead of a representative of the city working in a neighborhood about which he knew little. On twenty-four occasions the task force leaders and Gottehrer took immediate action to head off an explosion.[51]

Through an executive order Mayor Lindsay assigned high-ranking city officials —including commissioners, deputy commissioners, assistants to the mayor, and police and sanitation—to chair the Urban Task Forces in the various troubled neighborhoods. These individuals, who reported directly to the mayor, met with civic leaders and local agency representatives. As Gottehrer explained, "Now, when a community group complained about a dirty street or a needed traffic light, the police could call their task force chairman and he would get action."[52] The task force operation helped the administration learn about the problems from residents who in the past had little means to express their concerns to city officials. The process led to greater trust between poor people and the administration.

Conclusion

The celebrated walk that John Lindsay took through Harlem on the warm April evening in 1968 that Martin Luther King was assassinated in Memphis was not fortuitous. It had not been his first walk through a troubled black neighborhood. Nor was his visit merely symbolic. When Mayor Richard Daley ordered his police department the next day to "shoot to kill" to end the rioting in Chicago, Lindsay responded, "We don't shoot kids in New York City."[53] On that fateful night when King was murdered, more than a hundred cities erupted in violence, and more than 66,000 federal and state troops were dispatched to end it. John Lindsay's presence in Harlem that night prevented a full-scale riot because he had been there before. He had already told people that he heard their pleas. He worked hard to curb police misconduct, improve services, empower the powerless, and establish lines of communication.[54] He was not only the mayor of New York; he was their mayor.

John Lindsay became a popular figure among black and Latino New Yorkers as a result of his efforts on their behalf. In his first run for mayor in 1965, Lindsay won 40 percent of the black vote and 25 percent of the Puerto Rican vote. In his second run for mayor in 1969, he received 80 percent of the vote in black districts and 60 percent in Puerto Rican districts.[55]

NOTES

1. *New York Times*, "Text of Lindsay's Address to New York Lawyers, May 21, 1965, p. 1.
2. Ibid., p. 12.

3. *New York Times*, "Policemen to Sue for Unit Banning Civilian Review Board," May 9, 1966, p. 1.

4. *Reading Eagle*, "New Yorkers Abolish Lindsay's Civilian Complaint Review Board," November 9, 1966, p. 34.

5. *New York Times*, "Lindsay Seeks Aid on Review Board," October 3, 1966.

6. *New York Times*, "Text of Lindsay's Inaugural Address at City Hall," January 2, 1966, p. 56.

7. Clarence Taylor, *Knocking at Our Own Door: Milton A. Galamison and the Struggle to Integrate New York City Schools* (New York: Columbia University Press, 1997), pp. 54–64.

8. Ibid., pp. 91–175.

9. Jerald Podair, *The Strike That Changed New York: Blacks, Whites, and the Ocean Hill-Brownsville Crisis* (New Haven: Yale University Press, 2002), p. 38.

10. Author interview with Major Owens, Brooklyn, New York, August 8, 2012.

11. Tara J. Melish, "Maximum Feasible Participation of the Poor: New Governance, New Accountability and a 21st Century War on the Sources of Poverty," *Yale Human Rights and Development Law Journal*, 13, no. 1 (2010): 13.

12. Ibid., p. 21; Richard W. Boone, "Reflections on Citizen Participation and the Economic Opportunity Act," Special Issue: Citizens Action in Model Cities and CAP Programs: Case Studies and Evaluation, *Public Administration Review*, 32 (Sept. 1972): 445.

13. Melish, "Maximum Feasible Participation of the Poor," p. 22.

14. Taylor, *Knocking at Our Own Door*, pp. 204–205.

15. Podair, *Strike That Changed New York*, pp. 132–133.

16. Kenneth R. McGrail, "New York City Decentralization: The Respective Powers of the City Board of Education and the Community School Boards," *Fordham Urban Law Journal*, 5, no. 2 (1976): 250–259.

17. Jim Leslie Gelbman, "Evolution of District 12: The Implementation of Public Policy in a Decentralized New York City District, 1969–1982" (Jan. 1, 1984), ETD Collection for Fordham University Paper AA18409257 http://fordham.bepressconm/dissertations/AAs8409257.

18. Anemona Hartocollis, "Consensus on City Schools: History; Growing Outrage Leads Back to Centralized Leadership," *New York Times*, June 7, 2002.

19. Podair, *Strike That Changed New York*, p. 188.

20. Ibid., pp. 1–5.

21. Ibid., p. 263.

22. Andrea M. K. Gill, "We Will Not Be Forced Out Again: The Scatter Site Housing Controversy in Forest Hills, Queens and the Reshaping of Public Policy" (master's thesis, Department of History, Simon Frazer University, April 2004).

23. Mario Cuomo, *Forest Hills Diary: The Crisis of Low-Income Housing* (New York: Random House, 1974), pp. 184; Podair, *Strike That Changed New York*, p. 187.

24. Author interview with Sid Davidoff, June 11, 2012.

25. Cuomo, *Forest Hills Diary*, pp. 139–143; Michael N. Danielson and Jameson W. Doig, *New York: The Politics of Urban Regional Development* (Berkeley, CA: The Institute of Governmental Studies, University of California Press, 1982).

26. Jay Kriegel remarks, at a panel discussion on "America's Mayor: John Lindsay and the Reinvention of New York," September 3, 2010.

27. Author interview with Sid Davidoff, June 11, 2012.

28. *The State of the Cities: Report of the Commission on the Cities in the '70's* (New York: Praeger Publishers, 1972), p. 98.

29. "Nation's Number One Fire Fighter: New York Commissioner Heads Largest, Busiest Department," *Ebony*, vol. 27, no. 12 (Oct. 1972): 116–118.

30. Ibid.

31. Ibid.

32. "William Booth, Judge and Civil Rights Leader Dies at 84," *New York Times*, December 27, 2006.

33. Terence Smith, "New Rights Chief Criticizes Unions," *New York Times*, February 3, 1966.

34. "City Rights Drive Raises Hiring of Minority Groups," *New York Times*, August 15, 1966.

35. Ibid.

36. Peter Millones, "Rabbi Quits Posts on Rights Agency," *New York Times*, February 5, 1967.

37. Joseph P. Fried, "Mayor Criticizes Inquiry by Booth," *New York Times*, December 18, 1968.

38. "Legends in the Law: A Conversation with Eleanor Holmes Norton, *Bar Report*, June–July 1997.

39. Ibid.

40. Edith P. Lynton, "Toward Better Jobs and Better Service in Household Work: A Report and Recommendations Based on a Conference on Household Work," New York Civil Rights Commission report, 1971.

41. "The Employment of Minorities, Women and the Handicapped in the City Government: A Report of a 1971 Survey," New York City Human Rights Commission report (n.d.).

42. Ibid.

43. "Community Development in New York City," Report from the Community Development Agency of the Human Resources Administration, City of New York (n.d.).

44. Ibid; author interview with Major Owens.

45. Author interview with Major Owens.

46. "Community Development in New York City."

47. Major Owens, "Death of Former Mayor John V. Lindsay," House of Representatives, February 6, 2001. basic.house.gov/member-profiles/profile.html

48. "Text of Lindsay's Inaugural Address at City Hall," *New York Times*, January 2, 1966, p. 56.

49. Ibid, pp. 40–41; author interview with Sid Davidoff, June 11, 2012.

50. See generally, Barry Gottehrer, *The Mayor's Man: One Man's Struggle to Save Our Cities.*

51. Author interview with Sid Davidoff; John Lindsay, *The City* (New York: Norton, 1970), pp. 99–102.

52. Gottehrer, *Mayor's Man*, pp. 42–43.

53. James Coates, "Riots Follow Killing of Martin Luther King," *Chicago Tribune*, April 5, 1968; Clay Risen, "The Night New York Avoided Riot," *The Morning News*, January 26, 2009.

54. Peter Levy, "The Dream Deferred: The Assassination of Martin Luther King Jr. and

the Holy Week of Uprisings," p. 5–6. www.temple.edu/tempress/chapters_1800/2148_ch1 .pdf; Clay Risen, *A Nation on Fire: America in the Wake of the King Assassination* (New York: Wiley, 2009), pp. 54–58, 63–66, 116–121, 145–155; Barrye La Troye Price, "The Use of Federal Troops in Quieting Unrest in Washington, D.C., April, 1968," (master's thesis, Texas A&M University, 1994), pp. 53–83.

55. Jack Newfield, "The Ups and Downs of John Lindsay," *Life*, 67, no. 20 (Nov. 4, 1969): 30B.

Mayor Robert F. Wagner Jr. (*left*) looks over the city budget with his director of the budget, Abraham D. Beame (*right*). 1960. The LaGuardia and Wagner Archives, LaGuardia Community College / The City University of New York. Used with permission.

CHAPTER FOUR

Of Budgets, Taxes, and the Rise of a New Plutocracy

CHARLES R. MORRIS

New York City's rise to the status of America's premier city dates from the opening of the Erie Canal in 1825. At a stroke, great chunks of interior trade were diverted from Boston and Philadelphia. As New York City's share of export business soared, it became the country's center both for trade finance and for wholesale and retail marketing and distribution. Any manufacturer who wanted to create a national presence opened a showroom in New York.

The focus on trade led to a thriving shipyard and dry-dock industry and later in the century to large-scale foundries, heavy machine shops, and marine engine manufacture. The city also had a wide range of iron and brass foundries and light machinery shops making small metal parts, toys, and later electrical motors. It became the national leader in clothing manufacture, upscale jewelry, and printing and publishing of all kinds. R. Hoe was founded in 1805 to make saws and hand printing presses. In the world's most literate nation, with a ravenous appetite for printed matter, Hoe came to specialize in the largest, fastest presses, which it supplied to most of the world's high-volume printers. The Hoe press at the New York *World* plant in the late 1880s turned out 48,000 eight-page editions an hour, all neatly cut and folded.[1]

Triple-crown leadership in finance, in wholesale and retail trade, and in important manufacturing sectors generated the wealth to support a world-city infrastructure, rivaling those of London and Paris—sewers, subways, reservoirs and aqueducts, splendid parks and museums, one of the nation's great school systems, fine beaches within easy reach, and later free colleges for top students and a comprehensive network of good-quality free municipal hospitals.

As the twentieth century opened, the United States was the world's greatest economic and financial power, with a GDP greater than that of Great Britain, France, and Germany combined. Two successive world wars only reinforced America's dominance. In the early stages of both, it supplied the financing and much of the equipment for its allies' armament, and, after a modest combat commitment in the first war and a much heavier one in the second, it supplied the financing and much of the goods for reconstruction of both sides. While the Great Depression was dreadful for everyone, New York City weathered it better than most, with the help of Robert Moses' massive federally subsidized public works, investments in new subway lines and bridges, and big private projects like the Empire State Building.

The post–World War II era was New York's golden age. No city could match its rich array of services. A serious housing deficit, stemming from the years of war and depression, was remedied by aggressive public-private building projects for working people, offering affordable rents for quite commodious spaces. Teachers associations and blue-collar unions had ready access to city financing for nonprofit rental cooperatives for their members. Neat brick row houses were built by the tens of thousands in the outlying areas of Brooklyn and Queens but still within convenient subway access to the center city. Neighborhoods were laid out along invisible ethnic-religious lines that had evolved as accidents of immigration timing. Crime rates were low, stability reigned, families enjoyed a standard of living once beyond their dreams.

And then it all came apart.

Urban Crisis

By the end of the 1950s, America's thriving cities quite suddenly found themselves victims of their own success. As the premier American city, New York's unraveling was especially painful and the most publicized. All older cities were hit by three tidal forces, all operating in the same direction and roughly at the same time. The first was the suburbanization of the population, the second the collapse of big-city manufacturing industries, and the third was the Great Migration of African Americans from the South, which was amplified in New York's case by a smaller migration from Puerto Rico and later from other Caribbean locations.

The Lure of the Suburbs

When the war ended, working-class families found themselves, for the first time ever, with money in their pockets. Heavy industry factories were on 24/7 shifts for almost the whole of the war, and workers piled up huge amounts of overtime pay, which wartime rationing forced them to save. Opportunity beckoned everywhere. GIs could go to college on the government's tab, opening up new worlds of advancement and ambition. Depression and war had delayed marriage and suppressed birth rates, and America indulged in a mass baby-making boom. The iconic American image of a home of one's own, with a white picket fence, rosebushes, and a yard for the kids, was no longer a fantasy.[2]

The cream of the working classes fled the cities in droves. The first wave of building in New York's outer boroughs was merely an early salient of a much bigger migration to Long Island, Westchester, New Jersey, and beyond. Throughout the 1960s and 1970s, city officials fought a losing battle on residence rules for city employees, especially police and firemen. Since they lived in the firehouses during their shifts and commuted only at the beginning and end of a tour of duty, firemen usually moved the farthest out from the city.

The Loss of Manufacturing

The population outflow coincided with the crumbling of New York City's old economic base. Manufacturing, along with wholesale trade, was the largest source of city employment in the 1950s. City manufacturing jobs peaked at 963,000 in 1959, or 6 percent of all manufacturing jobs in the country.[3] The garment industry was the biggest single employer and the first to be hit, as the sewing trades moved south to take advantage of a cheaper, less militant labor force. (A couple of decades later, the industry made another mass migration overseas.)

Cold economics drove the exodus. Wartime production records had demonstrated the power of rationalized manufacturing, with straight-line production processes in large one-story factories with big loading bays. Even the garment industry, traditionally a small-shop enterprise, modernized its production as new nationally branded clothes makers adopted high-volume manufacturing methods. The birth of the over-the-road trucking industry, with big rigs and diesel engines, decimated railroad traffic, undercutting big-city hub locations. As the narrow streets of older cities became congested with private cars, urban manufacturing made less and less sense.[4]

New York City's manufacturing establishments were more vulnerable than most. Individual operations tended to be very small; industry by industry, its manufacturers had more modest amounts of capital and only about half the employees as those in other big cities. The great part of its production was in nondurables, much of it consumed locally. There were tens of thousands of bakeries, for instance; and a third of all manufacturing operations were in apparel. In 1950, a half million manufacturing workers were crammed into Manhattan south of Central Park. Today's seven- and even eight-figure lofts with built-in wine coolers and soaking tubs in SoHo and Tribeca are the remnants of a manufacturing district that occupied most of the real estate south of 42nd Street. Virtually the whole of the area bounded by Sixth and Ninth Avenues and 34th and 40th Streets was given over to the garment district. This in the city with uniquely high land and energy costs.[5]

In the five years from 1959 through 1964, New York City lost a hundred thousand

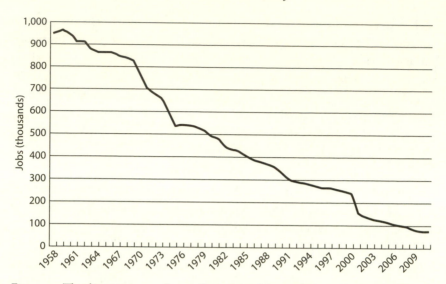

Figure 4.1. The disappearance of manufacturing in New York City. Note that the trend break in 2000 reflects a change in the dataset. New York State Department of Labor, Division of Research and Statistics.

manufacturing jobs under Mayor Robert Wagner Jr. (figure 4.1). During John Lindsay's first term, the loss of manufacturing jobs slowed somewhat, but those were years of a blistering national economic boom, so overflow work kept the city's factories humming. When national growth slowed in 1969, however, urban manufacturing jobs went off the cliff. The job losses slowed a bit in 1972 but plunged again during the very steep recession in 1973–1974.[6] Since the high point in 1959, there has never been an up year.

As Greg David, long-time editor of *Crain's New York Business*, points out in an essay, "The Myth of Manufacturing," every mayor since Lindsay has tried to revive production industries with a variety of schemes and special zones. It was not only a waste of money but has kept great tracts of valuable land undeveloped and off the tax rolls. Artisanal manufacturers, usually with upscale clienteles, can flourish in the city, but New York's days as a major manufacturing center are over forever. What about the immigrants, who used to arrive in New York with limited English and limited skills? Now they get jobs in tourism and health care, probably in roughly the same numbers—although the official statistics don't single out "tourism." Hotel and hospital workers are mostly unionized, and, adjusting for inflation, the wage scales may be comparable with those of their predecessors who sweated in East River foundries or for the garment industry in sewing machine lofts.[7]

The Great Migration

Between 1915 and 1970, some six million black southerners migrated northward and westward in three major streams. African Americans from the seaboard south moved up the coast to the major cities of the Northeast as far as Boston. Deep South cotton-belt migrants gravitated to the great riverine cities of the Midwest, while migrants from Texas and the western edges of the Cotton Belt concentrated in Los Angeles and other California cities. About 1.5 million made the trek from the start of the First World War through the 1930s; 1.6 million in the 1940s, 1.4 million in the 1950s; and one million in the 1960s. The movement slowed and gradually stopped in the 1970s, as returning migrants balanced newcomers. From that point native African Americans joined in a new reverse migration from older Rust Belt cities back to new high-growth regions of the Southeast and Southwest.[8]

The African Americans who made the trek northward, as is usually the case with migrants, were among the most well-educated and most ambitious of the southern black population and at least as well educated as the black populations they were joining.[9] Limited for the most part to entry level service or manufacturing jobs, with little money, and minimally available public assistance, they clustered in the poorest, most crowded sections of the city. The northward migratory flow slowed sharply during the 1930s, and the boundaries of newly black central city areas stabilized. Harlem became a cultural mecca for black artists, literary figures, and musicians, with a smaller scale replica in the Bedford-Stuyvesant area of Brooklyn.

WWII, and the sharp upswing in war-related production, pushed the northward migration into high gear. The exodus of African Americans from the South quadrupled in the 1940s, affecting every major city north of the Mason-Dixon line. The city's black population increased by 137 percent between 1940 and 1960, compared with 197 percent and 193 percent in Cleveland and Chicago, 223 percent in Detroit, and 301 percent in Buffalo. In previously mostly white cities, the relative impact was even greater. Los Angeles's black population increased fourfold, Milwaukee's and Seattle's black population both increased sixfold, Oakland's eightfold, and San Francisco's fourteen-fold.[10] The impact of the black migration was amplified in New York, by a smaller, but poorer, influx of immigrants from Puerto Rico.

Much in the pattern of previous generations of immigrants, the midcentury African American migrants first located in the previous black sections of cities, then as the pressures of new arrivals grew, pushed out their boundaries into the poorest adjacent housing. African Americans who tried to move into white neighborhoods were frequently met with cross-burnings, rock-throwing, arson, and multiple other less violent forms of harassment, including being ostracized from community life.[11]

In New York City, the accumulated resentments triggered a serious riot in Harlem in 1943. Most stores in the main shopping thoroughfares, overwhelmingly owned by whites, were destroyed. The disorders lasted for several days, five African Americans were killed, and some four hundred injured, as were forty policemen. Mayor Fiorello LaGuardia was on the scene virtually the entire time and helped end the confrontations by the promise of emergency deliveries of free milk and food for the area.[12]

Lindsay's Predecessor

Robert F. Wagner Jr.'s first two terms as mayor could fairly be called distinguished. As in most older cities, depression and war had left enormous deficits in New York's housing, schools, street improvements, parks, and other public amenities. The 1940s migrations had left some 140,000 African American and Puerto Rican families squeezed into dilapidated single-room-occupancy tenements. The charge that New York's urban renewal programs were exercises in "negro removal" was never true. Wagner and building czar Moses built far more housing than they tore down, much of it in older and newly minority neighborhoods. The number of minorities in substandard housing dropped substantially, despite the continued rapid influx of poor minority immigrants. And the new housing was accompanied by hundreds of new schools, parks and playgrounds, and five new hospitals. Wagner was also among the first mayors to create forerunners of the federal antipoverty programs, and he made a serious attempt to reorganize his urban renewal programs toward smaller scale projects, emphasizing community participation and greater attention to relocation and other social services.

Wagner's father, the great New York senator, had remade the nation's labor laws, so the mayor was very close to the big New York unions. Cajoling, schmoozing, calling on old loyalties, he managed to execute his big construction programs without giving the city away to the unions and contractors and broke ground in admitting public-employee unionism into the city, while resisting untoward raids on the public purse.

By the middle of Wagner's third term, however, he was tired and losing touch. Leadership of the minority communities had shifted to firebrands who had cut their teeth in the fight for civil rights in the South. Having survived guns, dogs, water cannon, and southern jails to break down the Jim Crow regime in the South, they had no time for Wagner's style of making slow progress without rattling cages. In fact, Wagner didn't have much to give them, for his expansions of social programs had already put the city in the red. And he had lost control of the police, whose rough methods of dealing with the city's newest immigrants hadn't changed much since the Harlem riots. There were more major riots in Bedford-Stuyvesant and in Harlem in 1964 and a number of smaller incidents of serious violence throughout 1965.[13]

To the city's elites, however, Wagner's most unforgiveable sin was to lose control of the city budget. In the spring of 1965, with heavy enrollment pressures in schools, welfare caseload rising by nine thousand a month, and 1,500 new street and transit police hires, the city was more than a quarter billion dollars in the red. Proclaiming that a "bad loan is better than a good tax," Wagner proposed to cover the gap by borrowing. The Citizens' Budget Commission accused him of "incredible fiscal mismanagement."

Enter Lindsay

John Vliet Lindsay came to office with a superb congressional record but no experience in the gritty politics of running a city. He had gained national attention as the floor manager for the 1964 Civil Rights Act, one of the era's landmark legislative accomplishments. But his very success in pushing through such a controversial bill had left him at odds with the old lions of the national Republican Party, who dispensed the choicest committee assignments. With top liberal Republican stalwarts Nelson Rockefeller, Jacob Javits, and Kenneth Keating holding the governorship and both New York senate seats, the 1965 mayoral election seemed to be the only high-profile path out of the House. After much public hemming and hawing, Lindsay finally jumped into the race and ran one of the first of the modern techno-campaigns. With careful polling and voter targeting, he squeezed out a narrow victory over the colorless city Comptroller Abraham Beame by making big inroads in the normally Democratic Jewish and minority sectors of the electorate.[14]

The obstacles Lindsay faced were symbolized by a full-scale transit strike on January 1, 1966, his first day in office. For the next twelve days, the transit workers' leader, an old ex-communist, blackthorn cane–wielding Irishman, Mike Quill, delighted in making Lindsay look naïve and out of touch, with a tin ear for the rituals of public union and administration confrontations. Worse, Lindsay finally made a settlement that cost far more than most experts had thought reasonable and twice the president's national inflation guidelines, drawing sharp criticism from Washington. For all the other city unions, it set a target to be surpassed.

To most city residents, the first Lindsay administration looked like a series of fiascos, with the pattern set by the transit strike. Old-line labor leaders didn't like him and bristled at what they saw as his constant criticisms of city workers and city methods. In addition, many front-line workers, like police, firemen, sanitation men, and welfare case workers felt under siege by the influx of new, poor, and increasingly unruly immigrants and exacted their revenge at the bargaining table. City pay and benefit scales grew very rapidly under Lindsay, although the increases hardly mollified the unions. (Although few New Yorkers were aware of it, newly unionized municipal workers in almost all other major cities were winning pay awards of at least the same magnitude, see below).

The very rapid growth in benefits and new programs for the poor only sharpened union aggressiveness. During Lindsay's first year in office, the city was ground zero in a campaign led by the National Welfare Rights Organization to force much higher acceptance rates of new clients. The radicals were almost certainly correct that the city administration, for partly racial reasons, was turning away large numbers of eligible applicants. Lindsay's first welfare commissioner, Mitchell Ginsberg, drastically streamlined and speeded up the acceptance process. During Lindsay's first term, the caseload more than doubled to about two hundred thousand, and annual spending increased from $400 million to $1 billion. The new federal Medicaid program for the poor soon rivaled cash assistance in its cost to the city and by the 1990s cost far more. Big growth in the city's antipoverty programs merely reinforced the charge that Lindsay was giving away the city to the new immigrants. Almost all the antipoverty money, however, came from the federal government; locally financed antipoverty spending under Lindsay was actually lower than under Wagner.

Lindsay's most notable accomplishment was to establish a new pattern for police management of civil unrest. Most northern cities, including New York, had a long history of using great force to quell civil unrest, whether by strikers or civil rights activists. As civil rights marches—and outright riots—started to flare around the country, even smaller cities were buying half-tracks and machine guns.

The New York strategy, which evolved empirically, entailed flooding a trouble spot with blue uniforms to isolate the disturbances and only then arresting the incendiaries. That was hard for cops to swallow, for it often required leaving looters alone until a tactical area was secured. But on any fair judgment, it mostly worked. New York City's multiple flare-ups never degenerated into the all-out police-ghetto warfare seen in Los Angeles, Detroit, and Newark. By the 1970s, most major cities had adopted variants of New York's approach.

Cities were a primary focus of national policy during much of the 1960s, particularly as Lyndon Johnson pushed through the Civil Rights bill and the creation of his War on Poverty. Lindsay's star-turn role in passing the civil rights legislation, his espousal of the welfare rights movement, and his success in preventing major riots in New York made him something of a national liberal hero—"America's Mayor" to many in the press, one frequently mentioned as a future Republican presidential candidate.[15] Throughout his first term, that impression was enhanced because of apparent success in fiscal management.

Financial Administration under Lindsay: The First Term

Lindsay was not nearly as wealthy as many people assumed, but he was a blue-blooded WASP—his brother Robert was a senior executive at J. P. Morgan and later president of the firm—and the silk-stocking elite provided important electoral support. They tended to be liberal on social policy, but fiscal puritans, and were far more offended by Wagner's loss of budget control than by Lindsay's spending on the poor (see chapter 2). And Lindsay justified their faith by balancing all of his first-term budgets—the first time in forty years that city budgets had been balanced without resort to gimmicks. Along the way Lindsay repaid much of Wagner's last-term debt and deposited $80 million in the city's "rainy day" reserve funds.

How did he do it? First by raising taxes: business taxes were converted to an income basis and a personal income tax was introduced, as well as an income-based "commuter's tax" on nonresidents who worked in the city. More important than taxes, great floods of federal money were available to cover the lion's share of the new initiatives for the poor. Finally, and quite fortuitously, the city was on an economic roll. The mid-1960s saw some of the fastest real economic growth in the country's history. From 1962 through 1967, U.S. GDP grew at a white-hot 5.8 percent annual rate after inflation, and employment in New York City hit its all-time peak in 1969, not surpassed even in the boom years of the 1990s and mid-2000s.

Lindsay took office in January 1966, halfway through the July 1965 through June 1966 city fiscal year, so the July 1966–1967 budget was the first that was his own. Over his first four years, operating spending grew by 49 percent. Spending on social services and welfare payments doubled and overtook public schools as the largest budget item. Higher education was the fastest-growing budget item, increasing by 121 percent, although it started from a low base, while spending on health programs and hospitals grew by 58 percent. Traditional services spending grew more slowly— police and fire by 41 percent and public schools by 39 percent.

As table 4.1 shows, new federal and state aid accounted for well over half of the spending increases, but city tax revenues were also up strongly, at an annual inflation-adjusted rate of 5.2 percent. (Inflation had begun to accelerate in the latter part of the period, with four-year average annual New York regional Consumer Price Index, or CPI, growth of 4.8 percent, very high for the era.) Increases in state aid were roughly split between better education formulas and welfare payments, while federal aid was dominated by welfare and the new Medicare and Medicaid

TABLE 4.1.
Taxes compared with state and federal aid

	FY 1967	FY 1970	Change (%)	CAGR (%)	CAGR-CPI (%)
Real estate taxes	1,409	1,893	34.4	7.7	2.9
State and federal aid	1,248	2,812	125.3	22.5	17.7
Sales taxes*	382	722	89.0	17.3	12.5
Corporate and other business taxes	185	245	32.4	7.3	2.5
Personal income tax**	0	205			NA
Other	554	637	15.0	3.6	−1.2
Total	3,778	6,514	72.4%	14.6%	9.8%
Less state and federal aid	2,530	3,702	46.3%	10.0%	5.2%

Sources: Office of the Comptroller, Annual Reports; Bureau of Labor Statistics, "Consumer Price Index, New York-Northern New Jersey-Long Island, all Items."
Note: FY = fiscal year; CAGR = compound annual growth rate; CPI = consumer price index
*Includes new stock and mortgage transfer tax introduced in 1966.
**Introduced in 1967.

programs. (Medicare helped increase the revenues of city hospitals, while Medicaid became the de facto single payer for welfare recipients and certain other categories of the poor.)

With respect to local taxes, strong growth in real estate values drove a 2.9 percent annual real growth in tax revenues, which accounted for 41.3 percent of the total city tax revenue increase. Most of the rest, or 46.5 percent of the total, came from the new personal income tax and sales tax increases, including a new stock and mortgage transfer tax. Business taxes rose somewhat more slowly than real estate taxes, while "Other," a mélange of interest, rents, fines, fees, water, and other charges, increased more slowly than did the inflation rate.

The spending increases were mostly planned and financed by real aid and explicit taxes, without resort to gimmicks. The city earned small surpluses in each of Lindsay's first-term budget years, even managing to replenish long-neglected reserve funds, so he could plausibly claim that he had put the city on the road to financial health.

It was an illusion, for the city was merely coasting on the thin skin of a Wall Street bubble, arguably the first of the postwar period. City real estate prices rose sharply, while soaring incomes on Wall Street spiked revenues from the new income-based taxes. Stock trading was still mostly paper-based, so Wall Street hired tens of thousands of clerks and runners and greatly expanded brokerage and sales positions. In 1969, the city's unemployment rate was a vanishingly small 3.1 percent, obscuring the steady loss of manufacturing jobs.

Although few people realized it at the time, the restructuring of city revenues embedded some ominous dependencies. For one thing, the city was much more dependent on state and federal aid and so lost its ability to chart its own fiscal course. More important, the Wall Street boom presaged the enormous growth of the financial services industry over the next forty years, to the point where the city would become virtually a one-industry town. And, since Wall Street incomes and collateral spending fluctuated violently with each boom and bust, the city's new income-based tax revenues fluctuated violently as well. In the pre-Lindsay years, real estate taxes accounted for about 60 percent of revenues; since they were based on a five-year moving average of assessed valuations, they dampened the impact of changes in the economy. By 1990, revenues from income-sensitive taxes outstripped real estate–based revenues, and the volatility of the city tax base was raised accordingly. The perverse effects were amplified by the large share of social services in the city budget. Since boom times simultaneously raised revenues *and* reduced social service spending, surpluses were exaggerated, tempting mayors toward new initiatives, while the inevitable busts raised demands for service even as revenues collapsed.[16]

Paying the Piper: City Finance in the Lindsay Second Term

The national recession in 1973–1974 was the nastiest since the Depression, and it hit the city very hard. The rate of decline in the manufacturing sector more than doubled, and the spike in inflation created havoc in bond markets. The effect on the city was devastating. Between 1970 and 1975, the city lost 450,000 jobs, or almost one of every eight, and its unemployment rate more than tripled to 10.6 percent (figure 4.2).[17] To make matters worse, the fastest-growing job sectors were in government and services (government jobs actually increased slightly), but they were the least productive of tax revenues, since neither the government nor the rapidly expanding service sectors, like nonprofit hospitals and health centers, paid property or corporate taxes.

At the same time, city spending pressures were soaring. Much of the cost growth was self-inflicted. In his second term, Lindsay pushed through an "Open Enrollment" program in the city college system, on top of the already big expansions in his first term. Costs ballooned from $84 million in 1965 to $320 million in 1970 and to $613 million by 1975. Other costs were less controllable. Welfare rolls flattened out in the 1970s, but grants levels, which were mostly set federally, rose strongly because of inflation. The twin introductions of Medicare and Medicaid increased access to hospital care but hypercharged the rise in hospital costs. Between 1970 and 1975, municipal hospital budgets more than doubled to $1 billion.

In a normal environment, the city would have been forced to make very steep

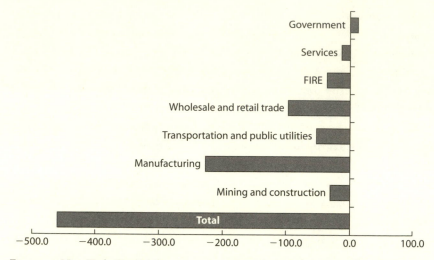

Figure 4.2. New York City job losses, 1970–1975, in thousands. FIRE = finance, insurance, and real estate. New York State Department of Labor, Division of Research and Statistics

budget cuts every year starting at least by the 1971 fiscal year. The service cuts would have been painful, but there would have been no city fiscal crisis. But because the city's accounting systems, run out of Comptroller Abe Beame's office, consistently overstated city revenues, there was no real pressure to make deep spending cuts. When the forecasted revenues inevitably failed to materialize, the comptroller simply booked them as receivables and financed the cash flow shortfalls by short-term borrowing. There is no evidence that it was intentionally deceptive, or that anybody—in the comptroller's office, or in the mayor's office or the Budget Bureau, or among the various city watchdogs and state overseers, or until very late in the game, the bankers who sold the debt—had a clear idea of what was happening.

The Short-Term Debt Bubble

New York City was empowered to issue short-term debt to cover the gaps between revenues being earned and collected or to anticipate the proceeds of authorized but not yet issued bond sales. There were three main categories of short-term debt: (1) tax anticipation notes (TANs), usually issued against unpaid real estate assessments; (2) revenue anticipation notes (RANs), issued against earned but uncollected federal and state aid or other nontax revenues; and (3) bond anticipation notes (BANs), against approved debt issuances (figure 4.3).

The TANs illustrate how the slow rot set in. As large parts of the South Bronx and other sectors of the inner city were simply left vacant or incinerated, city property

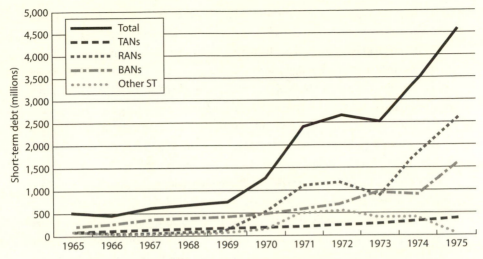

Figure 4.3. New York City short-term debt issuance, in millions. TAN = tax anticipation notes, RAN = revenue anticipation notes, BAN = bond anticipation notes, ST = short-term. Office of the City Comptroller, Annual Reports.

tax proceeds were consistently overestimated. But instead of writing off the excessive tax estimates, the comptroller used the supposed receivables to support the issuance of TANs. When the receivables remained uncollected, the city simply rolled them over—paid them off by issuing new ones. Because the city's account books were huge, very detailed, and mostly manual, accurate reconciliations of revenue forecasts and outcomes were not routinely performed. When the state comptroller examined the city's books after the financial crisis, he concluded that "over 80 percent" of the real estate taxes listed as receivables "were neither readily available nor collectible."[18]

The RANs are the most spectacular example. As the city's fiscal straits tightened about 1970, Lindsay's general strategy was to press for more state aid rather than to make deep cuts in programs. All of the early 1970s budget cycles were political circuses, and all were resolved at the eleventh hour by various gimmickries, which always included generous new estimates of state and federal aid. All parties participated in the charade.

Alarm bells should have rung after the 1970 fiscal year, the first really difficult budget year in Lindsay's first term, for RAN sales jumped from $128 million to $537 million, although there had been no dramatic increases in federal and state aid. But RAN sales were buried deep in the comptroller's accounts, and few outsiders, including senior budget officials, paid attention to them.

By the next year when RAN sales topped $1 billion, it was, or should have been, clear what was happening, since it was almost inconceivable that federal and state aid were that far behind. The excess aid estimates in 1970 had caused big cash flow shortfalls that had been covered by the RANs, and those same aid assumptions were carried forward to the 1971 budget. So RAN issuance necessarily doubled to roll over the half billion in 1970 RANs and add the new half billion for 1971. There was a sharp rebound in GDP in the 1972 and 1973 fiscal years, improving city tax revenues, so the RANs outstanding increased only modestly. But when growth was shattered by the 1973 OPEC oil price increases, revenues collapsed and RAN issuance soared.

Although the 1974 budget was officially Lindsay's last, crafted in the spring of 1973, it was to a great extent driven by Beame. Considered a shoo-in for the up-coming mayoral elections, he quickly and quietly cobbled together a budget with City Council and state officials that included a big staffing increase for the police department. It was part of Beame's electoral strategy of presenting himself as the quiet technician who got things done without the histrionics of the Lindsay years, and he repeated the performance in his first official budget, for the 1975 fiscal year. Figure 4.3 tells the story.

With short-term debt issuance soaring past $4.5 billion in 1975, there was no place to hide. Since most of the city's short-term issuances had six-month maturi-ties, the city had to go to the bond markets for some $9 billion in the 1975 fiscal year alone, accounting for about 40 percent of all the short-term state and local debt in the country. Even the bankers finally noticed, and several major banks advised their good customers not to invest in city securities, although, much as in the 2000s sub-prime mortgage boom, they continued to underwrite and sell them. Markets finally took alarm in 1975, when a state development corporation, for entirely unrelated reasons, defaulted on a bond issue. As investors took fright, the window for buying city debt slammed shut, and the city was exposed as insolvent.

Did Lindsay Drive the Spending Increases?

New York City during the Lindsay era was unique in the wide range of activities that were financed from the municipal budget. No other municipal government financed public education, a complete network of major hospitals, and community and four-year colleges, and no other American city was assessed 25 percent of the total cost of the federal welfare and Medicaid programs for people within its borders.

In order to facilitate comparisons from city to city, the Census Bureau breaks out "common functions" that virtually all cities perform—including police, firefighting, sanitation, roads, sewage, parks and recreation, libraries, and financial administra-tion. Table 4.2 shows the average salaries in those functions in the ten largest cities in

TABLE 4.2.
Average salaries in common functions in the ten largest cities in 1966 and 1973

	1966		1973		
Ranking	City name	Average salary	City name	Average salary	% change
1	Los Angeles	$8,836	Washington, D.C.	$14,668	96.3
2	New York	$8,090	Detroit	$14,137	91.2
3	Chicago	$7,523	Los Angeles	$13,933	57.7
4	Washington, D.C.	$7,511	Chicago	$13,324	77.1
5	Detroit	$7,393	New York	$13,135	62.3
6	Philadelphia	$6,505	Philadelphia	$12,389	90.5
7	Cleveland	$6,123	Cleveland	$11,535	88.5
8	Houston	$5,834	Dallas	$9,559	73.4
9	Dallas	$5,456	Houston	$9,540	63.5
10	Baltimore	$5,453	Baltimore	$8,892	63.1

Source: U.S. Bureau of the Census: *Local Government Finance* for respective years.
Note: Common functions include police, firefighting, sanitation, roads, sewage, parks and recreation, libraries, and financial administration.

1966 and 1973. The pay comparisons, moreover, overstates New York City's generous compensation, since it had the highest cost of living.

Some city fringe benefits, like health care, appear to be more generous than in most other cities, but pension benefits were not, especially since they did not have the guaranteed post-retirement escalators that many cities did. All municipal pension plans were more generous than the norm in the private sector, however. New York City's were distinguished by being among the most conservatively funded.

The story on New York City's pay escalation, in short, is that it was part of a nationwide phenomenon. But because of the city's profile as a de facto national capital and Lindsay's national political ambitions, it received far greater coverage in the national press.

Much the same could be said of the sky-rocketing welfare rolls. The largest, and most criticized program, was Aid to Dependent Children, primarily for single mothers and their children. New York City caseloads began to grow noticeably during Mayor Wagner's last term. This growth accelerated sharply after Lindsay took office but flattened out early in his second term. In the rest of the country, the rolls took off about five years after the first acceleration in New York, then grew steadily for the next decade, without the ups and downs that occurred in New York. But over the entire period from 1960 to 1975, the rates of the national and the city caseload growth were almost identical, roughly quintupling in both cases. The microdifferences in the national and city growth patterns probably relate to the massive New York City welfare actions organized by the National Welfare Rights Organization in the years just before and after Lindsay took office. In New York, moreover, city officials fundamentally agreed with the activists' contention that large numbers of eligible people were being unfairly rejected, as opposed to the high resistance levels in many other jurisdictions.

But, while Lindsay should not be blamed for the jumps in city pay and the soaring welfare rolls, he still bears a substantial responsibility for the ultimate financial collapse. He genuinely believed that city governments should be in the forefront of the struggle to alleviate poverty and achieve greater racial and ethnic equality. To that end, he constantly pushed at the boundaries of the city budgetary limits and was very effective in mobilizing unions and other public pressure groups to the cause of higher spending. Irresponsible as the budget gimmickry was—and it was mostly not concocted by Lindsay—he was a major source of the heat that made the expediencies so attractive. Given the shaky state of both Wall Street and the national economy in the early 1970s, it was folly to push for a major expansion of the city university system, just as it was folly to embark on massive extensions and upgradings of the city hospitals. It was not until the crash ensued that both state and city officials—and city unions—took a realistic view of the city's financial capabilities and began the long process of transferring functions to other levels of government or simply eliminating them altogether.[19]

Crash and Recovery

When the city's insolvency first became evident in 1975, resorting to bankruptcy proceedings was forestalled with an $800 million advance payment of state aid. Over the next three years, amid much Sturm und Drang, the city's finances were effectively taken over by the state. Collections of the city's sales tax and stock transfer taxes were paid to a new Municipal Assistance Corporation (MAC), chaired by the investment banker Felix Rohatyn, which was empowered to issue new debt. An Emergency Financial Control Board (EFCB) was established to approve city budgets and chart future spending growth. City unions committed some 40 percent of their pension funds to support city debts.

Edward I. Koch, a long-time Democratic Congressman, was elected mayor in the fall of 1977, as the work of the MAC and EFCB was still in its formative stage. In contrast to the Beame administration, which had reflexively obstructed state interventions, Koch embraced them. The municipal workforce was cut by some 23 percent—sanitation men by 21 percent, police officers by 23 percent, teachers by 15 percent, and the senior clerical work force (top middle managers) by 22 percent.

The state took over the operation of the city's higher education system, absorbing 75 percent of its costs. In real terms, between 1977 and 1981, the city's expenditures were cut by 30 percent.[20] Perhaps most important, the city's accounting systems were put on a strict GAAP (generally accepted accounting principles) basis, and account processing was brought into the age of modern computers, which was itself a major accomplishment. (While the state forced the implementation of standard accounting for the city's books, it still, as of this writing, resists such a reform in its own books.[21])

Koch went on to serve three terms. Deservedly identified with the city's restoration to financial health, he is still among the most popular of mayors. As the economy recovered after the sharp national recession of 1981–1982, he could boast, in 1983, that the city would end its fiscal year with a $500 million surplus, the biggest in its history, capping a run of three consecutive surplus years. Of the major cities, New York was experiencing the fastest growth in per capita income and the lowest rate of inflation. The income-sensitive taxes were growing half again faster than inflation, and a rapid rise in real estate values allowed the city to dampen assessment increases, making the tax-to-value ratio the lowest in twenty-five years. On the other side of the ledger, city spending growth was the lowest among the largest cities, growing at only half the rate of inflation. The heavy debts from before the 1975 crash had mostly been discharged or funded on much better terms, so debt service was down, while changes in city pension plans were slowing the rise in pension costs.[22]

It was an impressive accomplishment and was achieved well before the 1980s Wall Street boom really took off. However, the city's financial fortunes were on the road to being ever more tightly tied to the fortunes of Wall Street.

David Dinkins succeeded Ed Koch as mayor in 1990, just as Wall Street slipped into a deep funk after the collapse of Michael Milkens's junk bond–fueled leveraged buyout (LBO) binge. Dinkins would have personally preferred to redirect the city's energies toward the alleviation of poverty, but budgets were much too constrained. A crime wave that had really begun during Ed Koch's third term was laid at his doorstep, and he was easily turned out of office in 1993 by Rudolph Giuliani, running primarily on an anticrime platform. Giuliani in turn was succeeded by Michael Bloomberg in the 2001 election.

New York and Its Poor

The city government no longer has the major role in income support for its poorest citizens. The traditional welfare program was transformed into primarily a job readiness program by President Bill Clinton's "welfare reform" in 1997. Although clients may still be paid subsistence grants under the new Temporary Assistance to

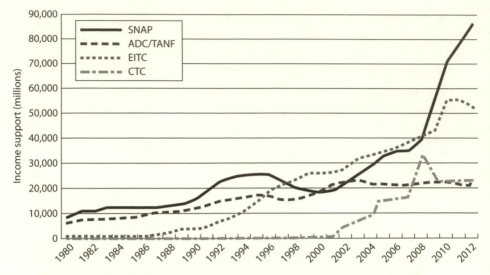

Figure 4.4. Nationwide federal spending for primary income support programs, 1980–2012, in millions. SNAP = Supplementary Nutrition Assistance Program, ADC = Aid to Dependent Children, TANF = Temporary Assistance to Needy Families, EITC = Earned Income Tax Credit, CTC = Child Tax Credit. Fiscal Year 2013, Historical Tables, Budget of the United States Government.

Needy Families (TANF), they are time-limited. Federal funding is made through a single block grant that has barely changed in value over the past decade (figure 4.4). Predictably, the value of the grants has been falling sharply in many states, as funds are diverted to other programs. Since the implementation of the program in 1997, the national welfare caseload has fallen by slightly more than half; New York's rolls, both city and state, have dropped by about 60 percent.[23]

At the same time, under a series of mostly Republican presidents, including Gerald Ford, Ronald Reagan, and George H. W. Bush along with Clinton, the federal government greatly expanded monetary assistance to low-income families. The major programs are SNAP (Supplementary Nutritional Assistance Program) a modernized "food stamp" program, and two credits, the earned income tax credit (EITC) and the child tax credit (CTC). For lower-income families tax credits under both programs are "refundable"—if your tax credits are larger than your tax liabilities, the difference is paid to you in cash. Figures 4.4 and 4.5 show the very rapid growth in those programs, especially over the past decade.[24]

Taken together, the rise in inflation-adjusted income support has been about 1.75 times faster than the rise in real national GDP (figure 4.5). Although the financing has been generous, the restrictions can be harsh. During the recent Great Recession,

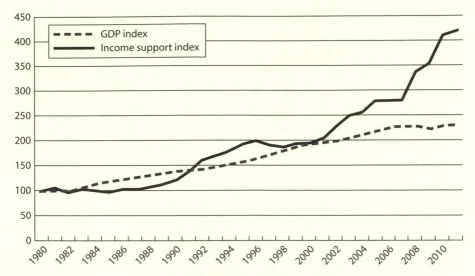

Figure 4.5. Real value of income support versus real GDP, 1980 = 100. Program data, Historical Tables, Budget of the United States Government; GDP and GDP Deflator from Bureau of Economic Analysis, National Income and Product Accounts.

for example, a poor person who became unemployed lost not only his job income but his earned income tax credit grant besides. In principle, many such people could migrate to the TANF program, but field reports suggest that coordination is poor, and enrollments in both the EITC and TANF are considerably lower than the size of the eligible population.

Despite its diminished role in income support, the city government still has important involvements in poverty reduction. Both Mayors Giuliani and Bloomberg, with considerable justice, regarded their respective policy focuses—on crime and education—to be potent antipoverty programs. The city is also a last resort refuge for the unfortunates or incorrigibles who fall between the cracks in the dominant support programs. Mayor Bloomberg has made substantial investment in homeless services, including additional shelters and nonprofit supported housing development for formerly homeless and low-income families. City drug addiction and mental health services are almost de facto focused on low-income people. That said, however, poverty reduction through income support is no longer a primary city responsibility.

The Rise of the Plutocracy

In many ways, the city has had a terrific run, especially over the last twenty years. It is cleaner, safer, better integrated, with busier streets, better services, and fewer slums, a magnet for the world's best and brightest. The parks sparkle, and tourists crowd the subways at night, which would have been inconceivable in the 1970s. Some three decades ago, the Times Square area was a seedy, dangerous waste; now it has been transformed into a kind of "Disneyland East;" the marquees are lit and the streets are crowded at all hours. Young professionals are integrating Harlem and transforming Brooklyn from Williamsburg to Bedford-Stuyvesant. Manhattan's old manufacturing areas are cynosures for the world's glitterati.

The downside is that the city's new socioeconomic profile is forcing out the middle classes. The city Robert Wagner turned over to John Lindsay was still substantially a blue-collar manufacturing city, mostly comprising traditional neighborhoods built around ethnicity and religion—Jews, Irish, Greeks, Poles, Germans—along with the growing influx of new immigrants from the South and Puerto Rico. By 2010, manufacturing employment, nearly a million workers in 1965, had dropped to only seventy-five thousand. The largest employment sectors are professional and business services (e.g., lawyers and accountants), trade, health care, government, and securities. (Conservatives may be astonished that the total of government jobs in 2011 was actually *lower* than in 1970.)[25] Non-Hispanic whites had long since become a minority amid a polyglot population. Some 37 percent of city residents are foreign-born, and half speak a language other than English at home.[26]

The biggest story, however, is the violent wrench in the city's income distribution profile. The well-known researches of the economists Thomas Piketty and Emanuel Saez have shown that by 2007 the top 1 percent of earners in the United States were collecting almost 24 percent of taxable income, against just 10 percent in 1980. New York's Fiscal Policy Institute has replicated the Piketty-Saez study using New York State and New York City income tax returns. In 1980, the top 1 percent of New York City residents took 12 percent of taxable income, but by 2007 their take had ballooned to a mind-numbing *44 percent,* while the top 5 percent of New York City households took *58 percent* of taxable income. So-called "middle income" people, earning at the 50th to the 95th percentile, accounted for 34 percent of taxable income, while the bottom 50 percent divvied up the 8 percent left over.[27] A recent reconstruction of income inequality in prerevolutionary France shows the top 10 percent of the French took somewhere between 40 percent and 50 percent of all income, close to the U.S.-wide distribution of today and not nearly as skewed as in modern New York City.[28]

The share of the top earners rose very sharply through the 1990s, then dropped suddenly during the dot.com bust, before exploding after 2001 (figure 4.6). In New York City, wealth is driven primarily by the financial sector, which enjoyed hypergrowth in the 2000s.

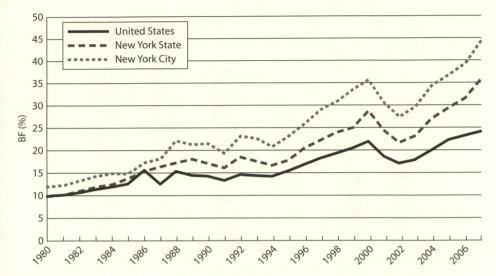

Figure 4.6. The top 1 percent income share in the country as a whole, New York City, and New York State showing a rapid rise since the mid-1990s. Piketty and Saez's analysis of the top 1% income in the United States. http://www.econ.berkeley.edu/~saez/index.html; Fiscal Policy Institute analysis of New York State and New York City personal income data from the Department of Taxation and Finance. Used with permission.

The most high-flying bank of all during the 2000s was Goldman Sachs: the average pay of its top five executives in 2007 was more than $60 million each. The average pay of all of these banks' employees—including clerical and other workers—was $240,000 in 2002 and $385,000 in 2007. (In 2007, Goldman's employees averaged $661,000.) But even those pay scales pale beside those of hedge fund and private equity executives, who routinely reaped pay packages in the hundreds of millions.

The redistribution of income within New York City has sharply narrowed the city's middle class and left a huge bulge bracket of very low earners. A careful study of city poverty in 1999, well before the peak in inequality, showed that it was increasing, even though the usual disposing factors—single-mother families, education levels, and so on—all signaled that it should have fallen. The increase in poverty, it turns out, was almost entirely traceable to the redistribution of income upward.[29] The fact that the bottom half of the workforce captures only 8 percent of earned income suggests a huge lumpenproletariat living on the leavings of the quasi-royalty at the top. (The annual wage of the worker at the 50th percentile of New York City wages in 2007 was only $28,800.) New York City is also one of the few places where the rewards for higher education have been dropping for the non-elite. The real

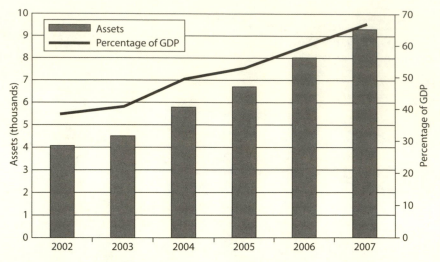

Figure 4.7. Five big banks: Assets in thousands of dollars and as percentage of GDP. To facilitate comparisons, the five banks—Citigroup, JP Morgan Chase, Bank of America, Goldman Sachs, and Morgan Stanley—reflect the crisis consolidations after 2008–2009, so, for example, Bank of America includes the assets of Merrill Lynch, and JP Morgan Chase includes Bear Stearns. Bank annual reports.

income for a twenty-five- to thirty-four-year-old with a bachelor's degree or higher has fallen by 6 percent since 1990.[30]

The heavy dependence of New York City on the financial sector may pose daunting policy challenges for a future mayor. The hyperfinancialization of the New York City economy since 1990 was facilitated by radical deregulation, very large increases in leverage, and misguided attempts to convert extremely risky instruments like subprime-mortgage–backed bonds into bread-and-butter portfolio instruments. There is also a substantial body of evidence that many senior bank executives were quite aware of the risks they were taking, but subordinated ethics and honor to the pursuit of ever higher income.[31]

From the standpoint of city government, the prominence of Wall Street in the local economy greatly increases the degree of financial discipline required, because of the volatility it imparts to revenues.

There is now a real possibility that Wall Street may be entering a new, and pro-longed, downward cycle. Even assuming a strong economic recovery, there is no reason to expect Wall Street to maintain a 2000s level of activity and earnings. In-deed, there is good evidence that a hypertrophied financial industry actually *retards* growth, probably because so much capital gets sidetracked into casino-like specula-tion.[32] The country has had strong recoveries with a much smaller financial sector, without the wild structuring of exotic new instruments, the frenetic, debt-fueled buying and selling of companies, high-frequency trading or exotic leveraged ETFs.

Big banks have almost never been very profitable (figure 4.7). Return on assets typically hovers around 1 percent, far less than the normal cost of capital. (Return on *equity* has been very high, but only because of the banks' outsized leverage.) With capital requirements rising, and with no obvious replacements for the menagerie of securities that fueled the boom and led to the crash, bank earnings are shrinking. To raise capital, banks will have to increase the stream of dividends paid to investors at the expense of the largesse they shower upon their employees.

Over time, that could have a profoundly positive effect if it forces a shift to a better balanced and more broadly distributed economy. But that will not happen without many painful adjustments.

NOTES

1. Robert Hoe, *A Short History of the Printing Press and of the Improvements in Printing Machinery from the Time of Gutenberg up to the Present Day* (New York: privately published, 1902).

2. James T. Patterson, *Grand Expectations: The United States, 1945–1974* (New York: Oxford University Press, 1996), pp. 311–327.

3. New York State Department of Labor, Division of Research and Statistics, "Nonagricultural Employment in New York City, 1958–2000"; U.S. Bureau of Labor Statistics, "All Manufacturing Employees, 1939–2012."

4. Edward L. Glaeser, "Urban Colossus: Why Is New York America's Largest City?" *FRBNY Economic Policy Review* (Dec. 2005): 19–20.

5. Joshua Freeman, *Working-Class New York: Life and Labor since World War II* (New York: The New Press, 2001), pp. 7–13.

6. New York State Department of Labor, "Nonagricultural Employment."

7. Greg David, *Modern New York: The Life and Economics of a City* (New York: Palgrave Macmillan, 2012), pp. 43–50. Elsewhere in his book (p. 17), David singles out the "crushing burden" of Lindsay's business tax increases as a primary factor in the decline of manufactur-ing. But that doesn't pass the "but-for" test—that the future of city manufacturing could have been substantially different if only Lindsay had left taxes alone. (Nationally, after fall-ing sharply in 1970, manufacturing jobs ticked up again in 1971 and 1972 before collapsing in 1973. But there was no uptick in the other northeastern/Midwestern cities for the same reasons as in New York.)

8. Isabel Wilkinson, *The Warmth of Other Suns: The Epic Story of America's Great Migra-tion* (New York: Random House, 2010), pp. 217–218.

9. Ibid., 262.

10. Raymond A. Mohl, "Race and Housing in the Post-war City: An Explosive History," *Journal of the Illinois State Historical Society,* 94, no. 1 (spring 2001): 11–12.

11. Mohl, "Race and Housing," for a rich set of accounts drawn from throughout the country.

12. *New York Times,* August 3–11, 1943.

13. Charles R. Morris, *The Cost of Good Intentions: New York City and the Liberal Experiment, 1960–1975* (New York: Norton, 1980), pp. 17–22.

14. Except as indicated, the account of the Lindsay mayoralty follows, generally Morris, *Cost of Good Intentions.*

15. Sam Roberts, ed., *America's Mayor: John V. Lindsay and the Reinvention of New York* (New York: Columbia University Press, 2010), p. 6.

16. New York City Comptroller, Annual Reports. The city's primary business tax in 1960 was a turnover tax, not strictly speaking, an income tax, but I have treated it as such for the comparison here.

17. New York State Department of Labor, "Nonagriculture Employment."

18. U.S. Securities and Exchange Commission, *Final Report in the Matter of Transactions in the Securities of New York City* (Feb. 5, 1979), "Supplemental Staff Report," 8.

19. For a full discussion, see Morris, *Cost of Good Intentions,* pp. 172–194.

20. Edward Glaeser, "Do Mayors Matter?" *New Republic,* February 12, 2011.

21. There is an excellent account of crisis events in a presentation by Mayor Edward I. Koch to the Senate Finance Committee in 1978, copy in the Baruch University Municipal Assistance Corporation archive. (The cover page is missing; occasion and date is from a handwritten notation.)

22. Edward I. Koch, "Remarks, Citizens Budget Commission Annual Dinner," June 15, 1983. Baruch University Archives.

23. Pamela J. Loprest, "How Has the TANF Caseload Changed over Time," *Urban Institute, Brief #08* (March 2012); "New York TANF Spending Factsheet," *Center on Budget Policy and Priorities* (2012); Ife Finch and Lisa Schott, "TANF Benefits Fell Further in 2011 and Are Worth Much Less Than in 1996 in Most States," *Center on Budget Policy and Priorities* (Nov. 21, 2011).

24. Sources for this section include Fiscal Year 2013, Historical Tables, Budget of the United States Government, for all spending data; and U.S. Bureau of Economic Analysis, National Income and Product Accounts, for economic data. For individual programs: USDA Food and Nutrition Service, Program Data at www.fns.usda.gov/pd/snapmain/htm; "Policy: The Earned Income Tax Credit," *Center on Budget Policy and Priorities* (updated February 2012); Internal Revenue Service, Publication 972, "Child Tax Credit," 2011.

25. New York State Department of Labor, Division of Research and Statistics, "New York City Current Employment."

26. U.S. Census Bureau, "Population Estimates, American Community Survey."

27. Fiscal Policy Institute, "Grow Together or Pull Further Apart? Income Concentration Trends in New York" (Dec. 13, 2010).

28. Christian Morrisson and Wayne Snyder, "The Income Inequality of France in Historical Perspective," *European Review of Economic History,* 4 (2000): 59–83.

29. Mark K. Levitan and Susan S. Wieler, "Poverty in New York City, 1969–1999, The Influence of Demographic Change, Income Growth, and Income Inequality," *FRBNY Economic Policy Review* (July 2008): 13–30.

30. Fiscal Policy Institute, "Grow Together," 6.

31. Charles H. Ferguson's *Predator Nation* (New York: TimesBusiness, 2012) is a highly readable and detailed account.

32. Stephen G. Cecchetti and Enisse Kharroubi, "Reassessing the Impact of Finance on Growth," *BIS Working Papers No 381* (Bank for International Settlements, July 2012).

Mayor Lindsay setting a good example with new refuse bags. The city tried out new paper and plastic refuse bags in order to lighten the refuse collection loads. Bags were being distributed free to the residents of the trial areas. June 13, 1969. © Daily News, L.P. (New York). Used with permission.

CHAPTER FIVE

Management versus Bureaucracy

DAVID ROGERS

John Lindsay was appalled by the filth of the city. Few issues commanded so much of his time and attention or caused as much frustration. Citizen polls conducted in 1969 indicated the need to improve sanitation services was second only to crime among problems citizens perceived.[1] The increased volume of trash in the five boroughs and the department's failures to keep up with it revealed severe problems of low productivity that had existed at least since the late 1950s. As much as a quarter of all the city's garbage got picked up late in 1970. Lagging collections started every Monday of each week and built to a substantial mess by midweek. In June 1970, a small riot over uncollected garbage broke out in Bedford-Stuyvesant, Brooklyn, prompting the mayor to provide 1,500 additional workers to prevent further riots throughout the summer, particularly in poorer areas, where the mess was worst. The department churned through six different commissioners from 1965–1970, reflecting the mayor's and citizens' deep dissatisfaction with trash collection, as basic a municipal service as there was.

But, over the next three years, the Lindsay administration transformed the problem-plagued Sanitation Department. Improvements from 1970 to 1973 included an increase in tons per truck shift from 8.5 to 11.5 and higher in some areas. Truck downtime went from roughly 40 percent a day to less than 10 percent. And street sweeping miles doubled.[2] How did Lindsay do it?

The answer is emblematic of a wide range of management initiatives that Lindsay introduced during his two terms as mayor of New York City. It is a story of many cutting-edge urban management innovations, most of which were used in the dramatic Sanitation Department turnaround. They included appointing a policy analysis staff in a new superagency, the Environmental Protection Agency (EPA), the first of its kind to do such broad-based environmental analysis for an entire city. They also included bringing in several outside consultants—for example, McKinsey, a new Project Management Group in city government, and operations management researchers from the State University of New York at Stony Brook—doing astute diagnoses of the problems, and providing suggestions for implementable solutions. Finally, the reforms involved Mayor Lindsay's taking big risks in appointing two new outside CEOs, Jerome Kretchmer and Herb Elish, whose prior careers were neither in management nor in sanitation but who nevertheless had the skills to orchestrate the contributions of these consultants and introduce several of their own, thereby making such a turnaround possible.[3]

Overview

Despite Lindsay's successes in applying management techniques to seemingly intractable urban problems, history has, for the most part, been unkind to him. After the late 1960s and 1970s, liberalism came under increasing criticism for its optimistic view that government could deal effectively with such urban ills as race, poverty, and crime. The disillusionment with Great Society programs and consequent pronouncements about the "limits of social policy" soon led to the country's turn to the right. John Lindsay's public image correspondingly declined. His reputation as "America's Mayor" and a "leader of urban America" has been replaced by that of a "well intentioned" but "naïve liberal," unaware of how "ungovernable" New York and other big cities really had become.[4] As a result, Lindsay's many management reform initiatives received short shrift in the literature on New York.

Lindsay was a leading figure in applying rational management techniques to managing big city government, and his initiatives in this regard merit closer examination than they have been given in the past.[5] These reforms include the superagency, performance-based budgeting, project management, a productivity program, decentralization, and a talent search for people to implement these initiatives. Never before had such an array of management reforms and able people been brought to bear to improve the workings of any city government. The story of how it worked out in New York deserves to be told for lessons that may be applied in cities across the country, not to mention the New York City of today.

A Culture of Change in New York City

The Lindsay administration's infusion of rational management techniques represented a major cultural shift in municipal government. Before Lindsay, most policy and program decisions in New York City government were made without much analysis of the relation of inputs to performance.[6] Little information existed, nor was it sought, on the relative merits of different ways to deliver needed services. Basically, government agencies were not performance oriented and consequently had no procedures or timetables that held them accountable for results. Low or deteriorating productivity usually went unchecked. The Budget Bureau, for example, where these decisions were initially made, used crude techniques of line item accounting, with examiners keeping track of resources or inputs, to hold costs down; but there was no attempt to ascertain what types and levels of inputs might lead to more effective agency performance. The federal government had begun such efforts in the early Kennedy years, through the influence of Robert McNamara and colleagues he recruited from the Ford Motor Company.[7] They used cost-effectiveness and cost-benefit techniques in decisions on various programs at the U.S. Department of Defense and then spread them to other agencies the federal government. But cities had not been using these approaches at the time of Lindsay's election. The same could be said for such other management techniques as productivity programs and project management. The Urban Institute in Washington and RAND were developing new ways of measuring productivity in the public sector, especially at the federal level, but again, cities had not caught up with these developments.[8]

The Lindsay administration's efforts should be seen, then, as an example of a major attempt at culture change, with the potential to improve in basic ways how New York City government was managed. Thus, the Budget Bureau actually became an Office of Management and Budget under Lindsay, even though its name remained the same. Decisions were to be made, not just on the basis of how they were in the past, or on intuition, but rather through a careful analysis of the potential costs and benefits of different approaches.

Correspondingly, the city and its unions set wages and salaries mainly on seniority before 1970, when Lindsay's budget director, Ed Hamilton, developed a productivity program that based them increasingly on employee performance.[9] This policy also represented a significant change from the old culture.

The Institutional Setting: Innovation under Severe Constraints

As explained in the previous chapters, John Lindsay first won election as mayor of New York in 1965, a time of accelerating demographic, economic, and social changes that converged to produce an urban crisis in cities around the nation.[10] The fact that big cities like New York where the changes were most pronounced were given the greatest responsibility of all levels of government to intervene made the challenge even more daunting. As Fred Hayes, New York City's budget director, wrote: "We needed a new theory of municipal governance."[11]

Soon after his election in 1965, John Lindsay referred to New York City government as a "pile of old rusty junk," and there was much validity to the charge.[12] Though the city had some able senior managers who were holdovers from the La-Guardia years of the 1930s and 1940s, they were nearing retirement, and the ranks were quite thin at lower levels.

When Lindsay took office, New York's municipal government could best be characterized as a "slow change" system, operating more to maintain the status quo than to adapt to the vast changes it was confronting. Several interrelated components had brought about this condition.[13] First, it existed as a monopoly, with little incentive to innovate. In the sanitation case, for example, Emanuel Savas found that private carters collected garbage at roughly one-third the cost of city agencies.[14] Then there were the newly emerging powerful municipal employee unions and a civil service system that proliferated a maze of work rules and procedural requirements. Add to the mix the absence of analytic thinking in program planning, already noted, driven in large part by a lack of information on agency performance. Effective management was further crippled by a dispersion of executive authority among overhead agencies functioning as serial review sites (Department of Personnel, Purchasing, Bureau of the Budget) that led to prolonged delays in implementing programs. Such well-meaning checks and balances—meant to limit nepotism, corruption, and autocratic, centralized authority—ended up paralyzing cities like New York so that they could not adapt to new challenges.

One result of all these obstacles was the consequent absence of a culture of performance evaluation, innovation, or self-criticism. Despite New York City's having a strong mayoral system, these entrenched features of city government provided an inertial drag, stacking the cards against management modernization.

The Superagency

Before Lindsay's election, New York had proliferated more than fifty separate agencies of city government, contributing to considerable overlap, duplication, and waste. There was little coordination among them, leading to poor policy making, diffused accountability, long delays in implementing programs, and an enormous span of control for the mayor.

Lindsay's first major reform was to consolidate this sprawling structure into ten separate superagencies. The new structure was designed to reduce significantly that span of control, minimize duplication, and facilitate the adoption of new approaches to planning, budgeting, and control. Indeed, the reform's advocates argued that without such a consolidation, it would not be possible to incorporate new techniques of rational management in running the city. They also noted that the creation of consolidated agencies at the federal level, for example, at the Department of Health, Education, and Welfare (HEW, now Health and Human Services) and the Department of Housing and Urban Development (HUD), required a similar approach in the city, if it was to be the beneficiary of substantial federal aid. "Before Lindsay's election," wrote David Grossman, former budget director, "agencies almost totally lacked critical overhead functions, such as their own budget analysts, personnel units and management analysis staffs. With the superagency they would have a consolidated base for such functions."[15]

Lindsay consequently appointed a task force to come up with such a restructuring. Its publication was referred to as the Craco Report, named for its chairman, Louis Craco, who had worked in the Lindsay campaign in 1965 and had brought in several public spirited attorneys to serve with him.[16] The report highlighted what it referred to as the "chaotic and fragmented administrative machinery now in use" and proposed a law to consolidate it, citing numerous examples of the dysfunction of the old structure. As an example:

> Three city agencies now have jurisdiction over the paving of city streets. As a result, Cross Bay Boulevard in Queens was paved by the Highway Department until it reached North Channel Bridge. The Department of Public Works paved the bridge. The Highway Department paved the road again until the Cross Parkway Bridge which was maintained by the Triborough Bridge and Tunnel Authority. Thereafter, the road became the Shorefront Parkway and was maintained by the Department of Parks. The length of road, maintained by three city departments and one Authority, is less than ten miles long.[17]

Two line agencies the commission did not group into larger superagencies were police and fire, both of which it regarded as too critical to the safety and security of the citizenry to be subsumed in a larger entity. The city council enacted the legislation in January 1967, omitting as well the Human Resources Administration, the antipoverty superagency, as too complex and politically volatile to be included. The mayor established it anyway, by executive order, following the administration's own superagency study.[18]

While the superagency concept made sense in theory, following such traditional management principles as unity of command and limited span of control, implementing it proved an extraordinarily complex task. Senior managers and staff in the Lindsay administration consequently gave it mixed reviews. All agreed that the rationale for the superagency was sound. They disagreed in retrospect, however, on whether the superagency form was the most appropriate one for restructuring New York City government.

On the positive side, some informants asserted that the superagency did diminish the mayor's span of control and made running the city much more manageable than before. Ed Hamilton, former budget director and deputy mayor, noted: "Any management consultant worth his salt would have noticed immediately that the city's many agencies all reporting to the mayor gave him an impossibly large span of control. We needed a layer immediately below the mayor that made his job tenable."[19]

Other perceived benefits included an enhanced coordination of agencies to improve policy making and to increase the mayor's capacity to monitor the agencies' implementation of programs. Also, the superagency increased the capacity of the city to recruit and retain talented people. One top official who had been recruited as a superagency administrator and was later appointed as a line agency commissioner reported that he would not have been as attracted to a job in the Lindsay administration had his first position instead been as commissioner of a line agency involved mainly in day-to-day "nuts and bolts" service delivery.

Fred Hayes, budget director from 1966 to 1970, concluded: "I now place more emphasis upon the organizational changes. The superagencies are a constant target for political sniping, but they are proving essential to the entire effort as a locus, removed from day to day operations, for efforts at innovation and evaluation that are critical to better management."[20]

A different point of view also prevails, however, acknowledging the importance of functions the superagency's supporters attribute to it but suggesting another form. The critiques emphasize that even though the line agencies subsumed under a single superagency had complementary functions, their histories, cultures, and management systems were too different for them in many instances to be combined effectively. Moreover, critics argued that rather than cutting costs and minimizing duplication, the superagencies did the opposite. Since many line agencies refused to eliminate their management support activities from the past—e.g., budgeting, purchasing, labor relations, auditing—the superagencies, following their mandate, then duplicated those activities. "A superagency structure can easily create another layer of bureaucracy wanting its own staff, creating more red tape, and slowing down decisions," recalled Howard Mantel, a member of the Craco Commission and scholar on public administration.[21]

Several Lindsay staff reported that one reason the superagency was so difficult to implement was that many commissioners felt it would limit their direct access to the mayor. As Nat Leventhal, former housing commissioner and later deputy mayor under Koch, put it: "Some agency commissioners did not want their tie to the mayor interfered with by a superagency head. And it added a whole new level of bureaucracy on top of what was already there."[22]

A senior manager noted that, in at least one superagency, the administrator spent so much time managing conflicts among his commissioners that he was unable to move ahead on critical policy and program issues. Stan Breznoff, former administrator of the Human Resources Agency (HRA), explained:

The concept of the superagency was good but it takes so much will by the superagency head to make it work. The notion of having shared priorities is good, but each agency has its own importance and becomes an end in itself. There have been so many agencies and functions within my superagency, HRA, that I could see it wasn't going to hold. Just keeping the parts together is a full-time job, since the natural tendency is to split. We needed more balance between autonomous agencies and one central superagency.[23]

Jack Krauskopf, former HRA administrator, put together a comprehensive commentary on the superagency, based on his experiences.[24] Admittedly, HRA had more volatile politics than other superagencies. It faced many intense conflicts among its constituent agencies regarding the most appropriate policies for helping poor minority residents become self-sufficient and improve their lives. Nevertheless, many of its implementation problems may well have applied to other superagencies as well.

HRA's volatility caused constituent agencies to keep getting spun off or added on in response to the latest crisis. Each new mayor, in turn, responded to crises in a reactive way. Thus, Mayor David Dinkins set up a Department of Homeless with a new commissioner when that became a hot issue, while Rudolph Giuliani put Children's Services on its own under a new commissioner, after scandals arose there. Several agencies, including Head Start, Manpower Training, and Child Welfare were moved in and out over the years.[25] Even without such volatility, the integration issues made all the superagencies difficult to manage. As a senior manager in another superagency put it, "It takes years to put superagencies together, especially over strong independent agencies."

The need still existed, however, to reduce the mayor's span of control and for coordinated policy making. To fill that need, a new structure has developed since the Lindsay era, focusing on deputy mayors, with each deputy responsible for a different functional area of government. Such a structure emerged in the Koch administration (1977–1989) and under Mayor Michael R. Bloomberg (2001–2013), and the city now has seven or eight deputy mayors, some of whose portfolios, in the words of one informant, "could probably be considered parallel to those of superagency administrators."

Several staff and senior managers from the Lindsay years explained in their judgment why the superagency did not fit the city's political context. While it could be argued that "not fitting" made the superagency form particularly attractive for a New York City reform mayor, it sometimes didn't turn out that way. One former Lindsay manager stated: "Lindsay used up a lot of political capital to develop this organizational chart." Former Deputy Mayor Robert Sweet commented: "Several commissioners had a relationship with the mayor that would not be broken. Those superagency administrators who were recruited from the outside and had no political history in the city could not compete with the commissioners. So there was a political reality that the superagencies did not take into account."[26]

This discussion is not to denigrate the superagency in favor of restoring an old fragmented structure that hampered prior mayors. Rather, it is to suggest that the superagency faced strong political resistance that had to be negotiated over a longer time period than the Lindsay administration gave to the task. As a result, Lindsay's rapid implementation of the superagency form brought mixed results. Peter Goldmark, a senior advisor to the mayor explained:

"You have to sneak in a new form like the superagency by starting with goals and then introduce a structure that goes with the goals, where people will not object because of their focus on the goals."[27]

Planning, Programming, and Budgeting System and Program Analysis

The other early management reform that the Lindsay administration initiated was a new methodology for budgeting and program planning. Though not necessarily thought through that way, the superagencies, at least in theory, created an organizational environment that facilitated such rational planning. The initiative began with Lindsay's hiring Fred Hayes as budget director in August 1966. Hayes had won national acclaim for his leading role in U.S. Bureau of the Budget (now Office of Management and Budget) covering Housing and Home Finance (now HUD) activities, then as assistant commissioner in the Urban Renewal Administration, and finally with the Office of Economic Opportunity (OEO), applying cost-effectiveness analysis from its prior use in the Defense Department. He soon brought in an OEO colleague, David Grossman, as his deputy, hired Carter Bales, a management consultant from McKinsey, to head a Program Planning Department, and set up a New York City / RAND group to do studies on agency policies and operations. All these groups reflected a concerted effort to promote profound culture changes in New York City government by introducing rational management techniques.[28]

Over the next four years, Hayes became the leading figure in the Lindsay administration's efforts at reforming New York City government. He combined a deep understanding of urban policy issues, a strong command of the new methodology of cost-effectiveness analysis, a flexibility in applying it, and significant skills in managing the politics required to be effective in that task. A charismatic figure in his own right, Hayes led a highly successful effort to recruit talented young staff, both from his wide circle of Washington, D.C., colleagues and from around the country.

Hayes pursued management reforms mainly through the New York City Budget Bureau and was particularly effective at getting the "old guard" of budget examiners and engineers to collaborate in new projects rationalizing the management of city agencies, even though they disagreed with many of the reforms he initiated. Two of the leading senior budget managers, Harry Bronstein and James Cavanagh, though not always supportive, nevertheless collaborated on some of Hayes's initiatives, even after he left city government in 1970. This was at least in part an expression of their respect for his nonpartisan professionalism.

Hayes essentially worked through two Budget Bureaus. One was the traditional, line item budget examiners' group that he inherited. The other was a new group of "outsider" management analysts he had recruited. The two groups often collaborated in task forces that also included managers in the line agencies to be reformed, all working on management modernization projects. This approach combined information on how the old system worked, with the analytic skills of the newcomers, and led to more agency "buy-in" than had the Budget Bureau simply tried to impose new approaches more unilaterally.

At the start, most of the new recruits knew little of how city government worked. Some openly expressed more disrespect for old-line agency staff and procedures than might have been politically wise. Their early relationships with civil service employees reflected a conflict of cultures that appeared difficult to bridge. The old-liners wanted to run the agencies as they always had, with little analysis of the costs and benefits of different programs. They prided themselves on their long experience in city government and weren't about to be displaced or made to change their work habits by young outsiders who regarded academic training in management and policy analysis as qualifying them to change the way agencies were managed. Hayes and his top staff were sensitive to these concerns, however, and recruited new young people who could be trained to work collaboratively with the agencies. And as the newcomers learned more about the agencies, they established more credibility with the insiders.

Hayes set the tone for this work, with Lindsay's strong support. His staff revered him, as did Lindsay, and after Hayes died in 2001, his and Lindsay's alumni group set up a Fred Hayes annual award to the city agency employee deemed to have made the most significant management improvement contributions. During Hayes's years as budget director, the mayor called on him constantly for advice. Moreover, Hayes's office served as a gathering place for the many new staff. They became more than just a group of colleagues with shared values and skills. Rather, they developed such close ties with Hayes, with the mayor, his aides, and with one another, that their friendships exist to this day, more than forty years later.

Hayes referred in his writings to "the Lindsay approach to management."[29] The approach basically involved using rational analysis to manage such problems as low productivity, failure to adapt programs to neighborhood needs, workflow break-downs, and prolonged delays in designing and implementing projects.

Carter Bales, Hayes's colleague and accomplished consultant at McKinsey, led much of this management systems upgrade work through a new Office of Program Planning and Analysis within the Budget Bureau that Hayes set up in late 1966.[30] The office was designed to do two things. One was to attack city problems by using what Hayes called "a habit of analysis" to create new, more cost-effective programs or significantly improve existing ones. The second was to develop within the agencies themselves the capability for self-analysis and innovation.

Hayes, Bales, and their colleagues, rather than attempting to imbue city government all at once with their analytic approach, followed an incremental one of adapting their new methodology to particular issues the agencies faced at any given time that were politically sensitive enough to require the mayor's immediate attention. The issues included, for example, poor maintenance of sanitation trucks contributing to the piling up of uncollected garbage, inflexibility in fire department responses to alarms, increasing numbers of drug addicts in high crime areas, increasing air pollution related to poorly functioning apartment incinerators, and limited police presence in high crime areas and at high crime times.

The number of issues far exceeded the city's capacity to respond, so the selection of a limited slate was critical. Several criteria determined that selection: the importance of the program, the feasibility of doing the analysis, the time urgency, and the likely speed in getting early results.[31] As Peter Goldmark, special assistant to the mayor and later New York State Budget Director, recalled:

> I remember one conversation I had with the mayor when I told him: "I see you as having a big pipeline of issues flowing across your desk at any given time. You feel you won't handle them well unless you try to tend to them all. But in fact you will only be effective if you deal with a small number at a time, maybe 5 or 6." That seemed to click with him.[32]

The impacts of introducing an analytic capability throughout city government were quite significant. Before Lindsay's election in 1965 and well into his first term, though there were differences among them, most agencies engaged in limited planning. They had few analytic staff, little senior management support for improvement, much resentment toward the new analysts from the Budget Bureau as overstepping their bounds, and, as a result, poor information regarding program impacts on their clients and the wider community. By the early 1970s, well into Lindsay's second term, many agencies had upgraded their analysis capability considerably. The Sanitation Department, cited in the opening of the chapter, was a dramatic but not unique case. Others included the Health Services Agency, which developed major public health programs, the Environmental Protection Agency, the Housing and Development Agency, which broke a logjam on modifying rent control guidelines, the Police and Fire Departments, which made major improvements in response times to local emergencies, and even the HRA, notwithstanding the latter's political volatility, in cutting ineligibles from the welfare caseload and reducing fraud in its back office operations.[33]

At least two factors accounted for the receptivity of agencies to outside pressures for management modernization. One was their leadership. Some of the senior managers the Lindsay administration recruited were more capable at analysis and more committed to management improvements than others. Jerome Kretchmer and Herb Elish in Sanitation, Gordon Chase in the Health Services Agency, Andy Kerr in Housing and Development, Jule Sugarman and Art Spiegel in Human Resources, and Robert Lowry in the Fire Department are some examples of new managers who initiated or welcomed management improvements. A second was the nature of an agency's service and organization. Police and fire were more paramilitary-style command-and-control organizations, whose impacts and services were more straightforward and measurable than those of other agencies.

Many of the management improvements came in Lindsay's second term, by which time the line agencies had become more accepting of the new methodology of management analysis, and their new managers had developed a better knowledge of how city government worked and which levers to pull to make it work better. It was also a time when Lindsay applied lessons learned from the political turbulence of his first term. This included crippling labor strikes, mainly those of the transit, teachers, and sanitation unions, and a corresponding revolt of the predominantly white working class, many of them municipal union workers, who lived in the boroughs outside of Manhattan. His agenda for the city had by then become more inclusive, from a primary emphasis on racial justice for minorities to a deep concern for the needs of other constituencies as well, through improved city government productivity in all areas of the city.[34]

The Project Management Group

A critical component of the Lindsay administration's success in improving agency management was a new project management group established in 1968. The mayor's senior staff became increasingly aware in his first term that there were serious problems of implementation with their management initiatives. A dramatic event in this regard was Carter Bales's presentation in 1967 to the Policy Planning Council on causes and proposed solutions to the city's air pollution. Applying a technique called "issue analysis," Bales mapped out the main factors contributing to incinerator-driven pollution, suggesting legislation to diminish them. David Grossman, then deputy director of the Bureau of the Budget, remembered it this way: "We were so excited about how Carter analyzed the problem, and how the mayor picked up on it that we went away thinking, 'Ah, we're now moving into the twenty-first century in getting government to work better.' "[35]

A few weeks later, Jay Kriegel, a senior mayoral advisor, met Grossman and asked how the follow up was proceeding. Soon Grossman came back with the answer that little had been done. Lindsay's top staff realized immediately that the incinerator initiative was only the latest example of how slowly the bureaucracy moved and how the city would need a much more organized approach to implementation. City government was overloaded with issues and unable to prioritize them, let alone have different agencies and departments within them collaborate to manage them effectively.

The city then recruited Andrew Kerr, a Harvard Business School graduate and former colleague of Bales at the consulting firm Booz-Allen to head a project management group, ensuring that high priority programs and promising reform did, in fact, get implemented.[36] Senior Lindsay staff referred to him as a "bulldog" and a person with "strong general management skills."

At first, the project management group was set up as a separate entity. Kerr recruited MBAs from such business schools as Stanford and Harvard. He also recruited industrial engineering graduates from colleges in the New York metropolitan area, whose training in operations management was particularly appropriate for the projects the group took on.

Kerr described his group's approach. "We started each project by defining goals. We then carved out a bundle of tasks and did a work breakdown or map of what was to be done. This meant identifying tasks—which ones first and which later."[37] These maps and their milestones for completion provided a mechanism for assigning accountability.

The projects the group worked on usually involved many agencies. Managing air pollution, for example, required housing agencies to press landlords to close down incinerators. It also involved getting the Sanitation Department to clean the additional garbage that resulted from the incinerator shutdowns. The technology of mapping all the tasks highlighted the range of agencies and their interdependence that most projects involved. "Project management showed that problems cut across artificial boundaries of agencies, departments, and levels in the hierarchy," explained Kerr.[38]

The role of the project management group was to facilitate through the project

map the coordination of the many involved agency staff. Through regularly sched-
uled meetings of all participants, the project management approach made it into a
joint activity. While some long-time city officials resisted these efforts, the project
management technique was designed to be "user friendly." Project managers had
been trained not to behave as threats but rather to run meetings on the projects as
collaborative enterprises. Joan Hochman, a project manager, recalled:

> Yes, it was intimidating to some agency people, but they began to see that we
> were there to help them do a job. We allowed them to see connections through
> our maps between their work and our new methodology. The meetings were real
> problem solving, to see where we were on or off target and what we would do
> together when we did not meet a milestone. The meetings were to provide an
> ongoing measure of performance, and, at the end, we would bring in the mayor
> to say "bravo" and let them take the credit.[39]

Kerr and his staff worked on high-profile projects that had been stalled in their
implementation. A sample of such projects included air-pollution abatement, community playground and swimming pool construction, hospital renovations, addict
rehabilitation, parks cleanup, relocating garages for the repair of sanitation trucks,
refining rent control, and interim cleanup and rat control in a Model Cities area
(see chapter 1).[40]

The group's success stemmed in large part from strong support by the mayor,
his Planning Council, and the Budget Bureau. At one point in Lindsay's first term,
James Webb, NASA's administrator, suggested that the city use project management
techniques similar to NASA's to manage unresolved issues in city government. That
conversation likely helped further legitimate the project management group. Early
successes in completing projects then solidified its power base in city government.[41]

There were other ingredients to the group's success as well. The project management senior staff shortcut bureaucratic routines by going directly to agency heads
and the mayor's office when there were slowdowns in projects, which helped a lot.
Even skeptical civil servants began to see project managers as resources for agency
improvements that would make them (civil servants) look good.

The procedures the group used to report on the progress of its projects further
contributed to its effectiveness by making visible the accountability for successes
and failures. Kerr explained:

> We used status reports on all our projects, indicating the names of the people
> responsible for the different tasks, and providing dates for their completion. If
> there was a commissioner who had been dragging his heels on one of our projects,

it would show up immediately; and the mayor would often phone the commissioner right away to say that he was holding up the works. Commissioners got upset when the mayor had a negative perception of them; and that increased our leverage to get things done.[42]

The project management group became so successful that, by the mayor's second term, it moved from managing specific projects to becoming an internal management consultant for the agencies on a longer-term basis. As Grossman noted: "Andy helped make our budget bureau an Office of Management and Budget."[43] For example, in its work with the Sanitation Department, the group started out working on the apartment incinerators problem. Later, as Kerr explained: "The Sanitation Department truck repair function was a critical internal consulting task for us, involving the poor location of local garages. That became a big operations improvement project for us."[44]

Despite their many successes, Kerr and his staff had no formal authority. They were effective to the extent that they built up informal power over time with the mayor, his assistants, and staff in the line agencies. Kerr's reputation for effectiveness grew to such a degree, however, that he was appointed administrator of the Housing and Development Agency in 1972. The project management group was discontinued under Abe Beame, Lindsay's successor, who opposed incorporating modern management techniques into city government. He supported instead the interests of his main constituencies—the political machine, the agency bureaucracies, and the civil service.

Productivity Program

The superagency, program planning, and project management, while important, were preludes to the development in August 1972 of a comprehensive productivity program that built on prior reforms to further support management improvements. Andrew Kerr, then head of the project management group, and his associate John Thomas recommended such a program to Ed Hamilton who, as deputy mayor, then successfully carried it out.[45]

The program was the first of its kind of any public sector jurisdiction in the nation, and Hamilton's timing was good. First, it built on the city's organizational and management systems reforms of the first several years of Lindsay's administration, largely under Hayes's leadership. Without these foundations such a program would not have been possible. As Hamilton wrote in a report to Lindsay introducing the program:

In 1965 New York City was in no condition to mount a systematic productivity effort. The government was fragmented. . . . An almost complete absence of analytic talent in city agencies made it impossible to install the complex management information systems necessary to monitor operations. . . . The city budget was not determined in terms of program categories but in terms of sterile line items, which tell one how many clerks there are in an agency but not what they are doing or how much it is costing the city to have them do it. . . . In short, New York City, like other jurisdictions . . . did not have the raw material to launch a comprehensive productivity effort.[46]

By 1970, however, enough of the infrastructure required to make a systematic productivity program possible was then in place. Other favorable conditions were also present. A nationwide recession had cut into the city's budget to such a degree that staff cutbacks had to be made throughout city government, requiring that remaining staff increase their productivity just to provide minimal levels of services. Moreover, in anticipation of this need to downsize, the mayor had established a Labor Policy Committee in 1970 to limit salary increases to rises in the cost of living and measurable increases in productivity. Finally, the public was increasingly concerned about the need for such a program. As Hamilton wrote to Mayor Lindsay in August 1972: "there is one factor which militates decisively in favor of a program to increase public sector productivity: at long last the public seems to care. . . . Through your own efforts and those of other urban spokesmen, the last three years have brought a refreshing new public awareness of the importance of productivity."[47]

A key ally was the media. Hamilton and the mayor were fortunate that a top *New York Times* reporter, Peter Kihss, publicized this new program with great zeal.

"There aren't 10 reporters in the entire nation who focused on government productivity the way he did," Hamilton recalled about Kihss. "He wrote a big article about our productivity program the day after we inaugurated it. Once he got into it, the *Daily News* and other papers felt they could not ignore it. The program thus attained a lot of visibility, both in the city and around the nation, as news of it spread."[48]

Even City Comptroller Abraham Beame, who was so opposed to Lindsay's management reforms, made complimentary comments about the program.

Measuring productivity in government is a difficult task, especially in view of the fact that the city's traditional culture had militated against that. Hamilton proposed several types of performance measures.[49] First, where output was easily measurable, thereby reducing unit costs and improving responsiveness (parks cleaning, street patching, sanitation vehicle maintenance, and rat control); second, to improve deployment of resources where output is harder to measure (fire response, police dispatch, and sanitation collection); third, improving the organization and processing procedures of government (capital construction, fund processing, and the use of computers); and fourth, technological innovations. Though Hamilton modestly characterized the use of these measures as "primitive" and "only scratching the surface," they were many steps ahead of where city government had been before Lindsay's election in 1965. And the fact that all city agencies have been required to issue reports on their performance since 1972 indicates its sustainability.

One benefit of the program was that some city agencies have not only provided annual reports on their performance since 1972, but some have included data using 1969 as the base year.[50] Here are a few examples: Missed Sanitation Department collections went from a high of 20 percent in 1970 to 2 percent in mid-1971 to 0.1 percent in mid-1973. Collection trucks out of service declined from 36 percent in 1969 to 20 percent in mid-1971 to 9.8 percent in mid-1973. Total tons collected per week (millions) increased from just over 3.1 in 1969 to 3.45 in mid-1971.

Health Services Agency experienced similar successes. Gordon Chase, its new CEO, established many new public health programs and made big increases in the number of clients served by the old ones. As an example, he started a new restaurant food inspection program that involved roughly 10,500 such inspections in 1969 and was already up to over 14,000 in mid-1971. He revived a poorly functioning vital records program where New Yorkers could have access to birth and death information, starting with roughly 315,000 requests processed in 1969 to over 450,000 in mid-1971. Regarding birth records, the agency increased the number of requests processed per day by 23 percent, reduced processing time by 82 percent, and eliminated twelve weeks of unprocessed backlog. Mental health patients served increased from 140,000 during this time period to 150,000; and the agency increased the number of direct patient contact hours per professional staff week by 50 percent. A new hypertension screening program tested 14,000 people at no additional cost.

In response to dramatic increases in fire alarms, the number of emergency reporting system boxes installed by the Fire Department went from none in 1970 to roughly 140 in mid-1971. The number of new firehouses increased from one in 1970 to six in 1971 and another six in 1972, along with twelve in planning and construction in the same year. In addition, a new polymer chemical called rapid or slippery water that a RAND consultant introduced in 1971 and that increased the water pressure in hoses tremendously was introduced to ten engines during the first half of 1971. Before 1970, the department's response to fire alarms always included at least two trucks and three hoses. Following a study by RAND and its work on a simulation model, the fire department developed a much more "adaptive response" to fire alarms, contributing to significant savings.[51]

Parks, Recreation, and Cultural Affairs experienced significant improvements in services and facilities usage during this period, due in large part to efforts by the project management group. The number of cleanup and repair crews increased from none in 1969 to eighty in mid-1971. The number of swimming pools in use increased from forty-six in 1969 to close to a hundred in mid-1971. Attendance at ice skating rinks increased from just under eight hundred thousand in 1969 to an estimated 1.3 million in 1972. And the number of indoor recreation centers went from eight in 1969 to twenty in mid-1971.

During 1971–1972, the Human Resources Administration made significant productivity gains. Previously beset by a high incidence of fraud in the distribution of welfare checks, it established a fraud control program that recovered over $2.4 million from issuance of duplicate checks. Further, the agency began to put into practice an error accountability program and to initiate corrective action. It implemented a new state-mandated work relief program, including referral of over sixty-two thousand employable welfare recipients to the state employment agency for jobs and the actual placement of more than six thousand recipients in work relief positions in city agencies. It also developed and implemented the Emergency Employment Act program under which city agencies hired more than four thousand unemployed persons, and it eliminated a backlog of twenty-eight thousand Medicaid applications, opening ten new application centers, thus eliminating long waiting lines and reducing fraud. And they increased day care capacity by 50 percent, opening 108 new centers providing care for an additional 7,100 children.

All these improvements took place during a time of staff cutbacks in response to an emerging national recession and shrinking tax base for the city. They clearly reflected the cumulative impact of management reforms introduced since 1966. The productivity program not only further encouraged them but also led to the development of the first systematic database on performance indicators for New York City government and likely for its counterparts in other municipalities.

Decentralization: Office of Neighborhood Government

The management reforms discussed above involved strengthening the management of city government from the top down. They were in that sense centralization measures, on the assumption that a more rational central organization would make for better local service delivery. But many limitations of the city government before Lindsay took over related to the agencies' overcentralization, whereby program and policy decisions were often made "downtown," many miles away from the neighborhoods and too often uninformed about local needs. Line agency officials at the local level had no decision making authority to set policy, allocate resources, or innovate. Furthermore, city agencies had no mechanism to work with each other at the local level, despite the fact that most community issues required the collaboration of at least two agencies. As a result, there was a lack of agency responsiveness to local service demands.

Lindsay's agenda from the beginning of his first term was to bring government much closer to city residents than before, and he ended his second term with a significant initiative reflecting that commitment. It had much precedent, moreover, from the early months of his first term. "We found a long list of gripes from community leaders about service issues; potholes, traffic lights that did not work, and there we were at City Hall, ten miles away, with no links to the community," reported Jay Kriegel, a top advisor to the mayor.[52]

The Lindsay administration then set up decentralized administrative centers known as Little City Halls throughout the city as outreach arms where the mayor and his commissioners could give community groups an opportunity to express their grievances directly to City Hall to facilitate the city's response. The mayor's commissioners and other senior staff were assigned local areas to visit regularly to hear complaints about city services. If a locality was not receiving needed services, that problem became visible to senior managers in city government who would act on the information. "This forced commissioners to get out of their cocoons downtown," explained Kriegel, "and increased our responsiveness to what was going on down below."[53]

As a follow up to the Little City Halls, Lindsay declared 1970 the "Year of the Neighborhoods" to indicate his administration's intent on improving service delivery at the local level.[54] Despite the management reforms of Lindsay's first term, New York City residents in the late 1960s still expressed concern about city government being unresponsive to such neighborhood issues as crime, drug use, condition of roads, sanitation and snow removal, abandoned parks, and lack of recreation facilities. This was especially true in the outer boroughs. While committed to making city government more responsive to local needs, Lindsay wanted to avoid the political upheavals that the school decentralization reform of the late sixties had brought. He proceeded cautiously in 1970 and 1971, as various decentralization advocates presented their proposals.[55]

The mayor finally opted for an administrative decentralization program. He established the Office of Neighborhood Government (ONG) in early 1971 to pursue it and appointed Lew Feldstein, previously his liaison to the public schools, to run it. Feldstein and his colleagues set up eight decentralized districts: three in poor minority areas, two in transitional ones, and three in middle-class white ethnic areas.

ONG pursued two main goals: Greater service integration involving increased coordination among agencies working on local service issues and improved responsiveness of city government to local concerns. The ONG design had several components:[56]

1. District service cabinets to be located throughout the city;
2. Administrative decentralization of selected city agencies;
3. District managers appointed by the mayor, to lead the cabinets;
4. Common district boundaries (coterminality) for each participating agency;
5. A single information system and local budget for each district; and
6. Continuous evaluations of district performance.

ONG opted for districts similar in size (125,000–200,000) and boundaries to those of already existing community planning boards. It chose as participating line agencies those that already had field operations and that were strongly managed from the top, including police, fire, sanitation, parks, transportation, in addition to education and other human service agencies. Getting commissioners to empower their field supervisors to participate in district cabinets was a continuing challenge. Some agency heads were more cooperative than others. And even though New York had a strong mayoral system, the mayor proceeded cautiously in pressing the agencies to decentralize, lest he use up too much political capital.[57]

Selecting a district manager was one of the most critical early decisions. The managers' leadership skills were what differentiated the more from the less successful districts. They had to be effective at handling conflicts and getting agency managers and community representatives to collaborate in solving service problems; they had to be good coalition builders; and, in both regards, they had to develop trust among all the participants and not side with any faction that might then alienate others. They also had to be effective advocates for the community in negotiating with senior city officials for more resources, after the cabinets reached agreement on particular programs. As John Mudd noted, they were the catalysts who set the local problem-solving machinery into motion. They were successful to the extent that they were "integrators" of the interests of the agencies and citizen participants. And they had to be effective in all these tasks without any formal authority, much like Kerr and his project managers. Mudd referred to the district managers as "aggressive intermediaries."[58]

Lindsay defined ONG and its district service cabinets as a nonpartisan management program. This perspective matched a federal government initiative to encourage interagency coordination through the Model Cities Program. As a result, New York received a federal services integration grant to help support the experiment.

Though ONG's impacts were not easily quantifiable, a Columbia University research group, headed by sociologist Allen Barton, provides the most systematic data, along with ONG's own reports to the mayor. The Columbia group did surveys of the perceptions of key participants—district managers, cabinet members, and community leaders and residents—along with case studies on the implementation of a sample of sixty-five projects in the eight original districts. One of their main findings was that, despite inevitable problems in securing agency cooperation, ONG worked effectively on many local service issues.[59]

The biggest problems were that some agencies were slow to delegate authority to their local area supervisors and were unwilling to make their boundaries coterminous. Moreover, city council members, seeing ONG as competing with them in representing neighborhood interests, refused to provide needed additional funds to expand the program.

Despite these problems, ONG carried out roughly 125 useful projects in its two years of operation, usually involving hard rather than soft services—relating, for example, to traffic, road repairs, garbage, safety, and parks maintenance. Education, health, and other social services problems were less likely to be addressed. Programs in hard services—such as police, fire, and sanitation—were less complex, the outputs were more measurable and attainable in the short term, and the agencies involved were more amenable to decentralization. The district managers, in particular, were effective in promoting the cooperation among agencies required to ensure the projects' success. The annual cost of setting up the ONG district office and staff was quite modest, roughly $125,000 a year per district.[60]

The Columbia University surveys indicated that over 80 percent of the civil servants participating in the program found the district service cabinets useful or very useful. Almost unanimously, the cabinets favored the program's continuation and expansion. They particularly liked cooperating with staff from other agencies. A few quotes from agency cabinet members illustrate their widespread enthusiasm for the decentralization experiment, in contrast to the skepticism of many in the beginning:

> Before, my contact with other agencies was more complicated; now I can deal with agencies with more sophistication and efficiency, since I know them and understand their practices.
>> Captain John Watters, Police Department, 101st Precinct, Rockaways

> The cabinet has been helpful to me in doing my job. It has introduced me to other service chiefs I would not otherwise have met.
>> C. J. Obregon, Area Housing Director, Crown Heights

> Before I joined the cabinet, the other agency chiefs were just names, no faces. Now I know them and can work with them.
>> Joseph Messardi, Sanitation Department Superintendent, Bay Ridge.[61]

In addition, more than 60 percent of the participating civic and political leaders rated the program as good or very good. Both agency staff and local leaders viewed it as having cut down on red tape and brought racial and ethnic groups together.

As Barton wrote: "In our opinion the program of district managers and district cabinets is one that other cities should seriously consider trying."[62] Support for that view, in addition to the Columbia University group's research findings, came from state legislation in 1972, establishing a Charter Revision Commission for New York City, chaired by State Senator Roy Goodman.[63] The commission was formed to review the structure of city government, including decentralization. It staged a referendum in late 1975, resulting in 55 percent of the voters supporting decentralization with district service cabinets and strong community boards. This new, multiagency decentralized system (ONG) thus demonstrated that it could provide a much more responsive neighborhood government than had existed before and showed promise of even greater future success, if given the political and financial support it required.

Depending on how one defines the term "political," ONG's decentralization initiative was a nonpartisan reform. The mayor did not select district managers based on political party membership. The managers and their cabinets did not follow the agendas of any local party machine or city council member. Rather they filled a vacuum that the machine's decline and the limitations of city government had produced.[64]

Yet, when Lindsay indicated in 1973 that he would not run for a third term, it was clear to ONG that the survival of this program was in considerable doubt. City Comptroller Abraham Beame had already indicated his intention to run for mayor, and his well-known negative views about this decentralization program made it likely that he would close it down. ONG efforts to forestall that included an aggressive expansion from eight to twenty-six districts. The eighteen new ones, however, did not have a district manager or complete service cabinet. But the intent was to build a strong enough support base that the program would survive.[65]

Though the referendum vote in 1975 supported the Charter Revision Commission's recommendations to continue with ONG's reforms and was a reported embarrassment to Beame, he still eliminated most of it and turned the rest into a political patronage operation. He then renamed ONG the Office of Neighborhood Services and political clubhouse presidents, party district leaders, and their relatives began to appear on the payroll in increasing numbers.[66]

A legacy from ONG, despite Beame's politicizing it and paring down its district manager and cabinet, is a citywide community board system. Community planning boards actually date back to 1963, but they were given more powers in 1977, resulting from the referendum conducted by the City Charter Commission discussed above. The boards have an advisory role in land use decisions and an influence in reviewing budget decisions affecting their local areas. They appoint district managers to coordinate services delivered at the neighborhood level, but the current managers don't have the same kind of clout that they wielded under the Lindsay ONG arrangement.

Talent Search

The management reforms described in this chapter would never have taken place without Lindsay's having recruited highly skilled and dedicated young people to carry them out. Hayes estimated that roughly 250 people were brought in as analysts during Lindsay's first term as mayor.[67] That number does not include analysts recruited later, nor does it include senior managers brought in throughout his two terms.

A majority of the new recruits were recent college graduates or people who had completed graduate programs in business (MBAs), public administration, or urban studies. Some started in New York City government as summer interns, staying on after that. Some had recently graduated from law school. Some had worked as management consultants just prior to arriving. Most had skills in the analysis of management and urban problems or a capability to develop them quickly, a capacity to work in a highly politicized environment, and a dedication to public service. They functioned in many respects as a kind of domestic Peace Corps, some having been active before in the civil rights movement.

It was remarkable that so many talented people were attracted to this administration, since both the salaries and the status traditionally attached to working in local government were lower than those in the private sector. Also, New York City's reputation as a place where urban problems were particularly severe may have deterred some people, though Lindsay likely made it attractive to others. As one senior staff person recalled: "This was in the shadow of the Kennedy years, and Lindsay made it ok for people to like working in the city."

In addition to Lindsay's drawing power, the social networks of Hayes and his senior colleagues were a big source. In the early years, much of this recruitment was done informally, but in the late 1960s, Hayes set up a talent recruiting office in the Budget Bureau. Most important, there was no attempt to recruit people based on their political party affiliation. Lindsay, as a fusion mayor, elected by politically progressive and moderate voters, followed the dictum of New York City's prior fusion mayor, Fiorello LaGuardia, that there was no Democratic or Republican way of delivering city services.

Former Sanitation Commissioner, Herb Elish, summarized the recruitment program: "We became a mecca for young people to come to New York City to make a difference. We recruited a high quality of professional people. It is the leader who matters most (Lindsay) and then the people he recruits and puts in place. He completely changed the game in the city."[68]

Several turnarounds of agencies in Lindsay's second term were a result of his recruitment of talented people who became outstanding senior managers. One was Herb Elish, who became deputy administrator in the Environmental Protection Agency and later commissioner of the Sanitation Department. Another was Gordon Chase, administrator of the Health Services Administration.

Elish used studies by analysts from the Environmental Protection Agency, the Sanitation Department's superagency, as well as by McKinsey, the city's Project Management Group, and an industrial engineering and policy analysis group from the State University of New York at Stony Brook, to transform the Sanitation Department.[69] As discussed above, the agency's productivity had been abysmally low for many years, resulting from several conditions: a dysfunctional repair system leading to roughly 40 percent of collection trucks out of use at any given time, poor matching of staff workloads with garbage accumulation, and an informal norm of low productivity in both repair and collection. Even the Sanitation Union's president, John DeLury, was embarrassed by the agency's poor performance.

Immediately following his appointment as sanitation commissioner by Jerome Kretchmer, head of the Environmental Protection Agency and another of Lindsay's highly talented new recruits, Elish established a relationship with DeLury through weekly meetings, informing DeLury that the agency's productivity was unacceptably low and that he intended to change it.

Elish's actions were a combination of "hard" and "soft" management techniques. His weekly meetings with DeLury were highly contentious at first, but over time, they appealed to DeLury's sense of pride in seeing improvements in the agency's performance. Early on, Elish pointed out that the city was paying much more for repair work than private companies were and that he would not allow that to continue. He confronted the mechanics union with these data, fired eight of the most egregiously slow-working mechanics, set much higher productivity standards, and stated that workers would not be paid if they failed to meet the new standards. The mechanics threatened work slowdowns, but Elish won the confidence of DeLury, who became a strong ally.

This alliance with the sanitation men's union, one of the city's most militant, resulted from several Elish initiatives. He increased the wages of sanitation workers when the workers exceeded the higher productivity standards. He showed DeLury that he was sensitive to the pride of the sanitation men and their union in the department. He kept up his weekly meetings with DeLury. And when Elish retired as commissioner in late 1973, DeLury praised Elish's openness, fairness, and nonpolitical style in making personnel decisions for the agency.

Most important, Elish tempered an aggressive style in his early months as commissioner with a more modulated one later on. While he did use recommendations from the outside consultants, he was flexible in implementing them. He did fire some top managers early, but he did not go public with his dissatisfaction, did not propose a major reorganization, and shifted much of the implementation to career insiders. He also pursued it incrementally, district by district, building on early successes. This reduced the insecurity of senior managers and developed trust. The subtle orchestration of outsiders' studies and his aggressive push for much higher productivity on one side and his respect for DeLury and for insider managers on the other contributed significantly to his effectiveness.

The same success of Elish characterized the tenure of Gordon Chase in the health agency. Lindsay appointed him as the administrator of the Health Services Administration in November 1969. Chase proceeded to transform the agency over the next several years.

The Health Department in its heyday had been a showpiece. As the *New York Times* reported: "It set the pattern for research and immunization programs everywhere. . . . In virtually every phase of public health administration, New York City was in the vanguard. Its top health professionals basked in world acclaim."[70] The agency experienced a significant decline, however, in the 1960s, partly due to lack of funding and its low salaries relative to those in the private sector. Lindsay had a different diagnosis, namely that the agency's mismanagement also contributed to its decline.

Chase had no background in health administration or in medical care, and the medical establishment vigorously opposed his appointment. The Academy of Medicine stated: "the Academy considers Mr. Chase professionally unqualified to exercise the enormous responsibility of safe-guarding the health of this vast community."[71] Lindsay was thus taking a high risk in appointing Chase, but it turned out to be worth taking, as evidenced by the list of Chase's many achievements during his tenure (1970–1973), both in expanding existing public health programs and in establishing many new ones. The list included lead poisoning screening, addiction treatment and prevention services, published restaurant inspections, upgrading prison health and mental health services, comprehensive alcoholism treatment, an abortion surveillance program that provided data to enhance the public's safety and inform policy debates, a major rat control program, speeding up access to birth records, and chairing a new Health and Hospitals Corporation. Particularly significant is the fact that Chase pursued many of these programs despite strong arguments from physicians in the health agencies that they couldn't be done.[72]

Chase's management style, which was critical to his success, had several components.[73] One was to confront status quo groups directly, who claimed that particular projects were not feasible, but then pair those groups, often medical professionals, with new outside managers. In brief, he both faced down the medical establishment and appointed physicians to key senior management positions.

A second was his insistence on quantifying resources and program performance to establish baseline data, raise standards, assess implementation, and establish accountability. One of his principles in that regard was "if you can't measure it, it hasn't happened."

Chase also focused relentlessly on ascertaining the health needs of various populations and then searching for resources to meet those needs, emphasizing fast delivery but not sacrificing quality. This involved taking risks, as with a methadone maintenance program about which there was much controversy. It also involved building a new infrastructure, when needed, as with the Housing Department in the lead poisoning screening program.

In a word, Gordon Chase, like Elish, used both confrontational approaches where he saw a tremendous need for new or expanded programs, and participative, coalitional ones, where he realized he needed political support from status quo groups. While he believed in rapid implementation, especially given his strong "social conscience," he also maintained open-mindedness and "heeded the experts" when they had well taken substantive arguments about "going slow."[74]

Chase's success was driven by relentless follow-up efforts to ensure timely implementation of his various reforms. Nat Leventhal, a former colleague from their work together in Washington, explained: "One thing I learned working for Gordon was that in the public sector, when you give a directive to somebody, chances are they won't do it. He made a carbon copy of every memo he sent to his staff and then he asked me to follow up. It turns out that 90 percent of the memos were not responded to."[75]

As was the case with Elish and Kretchmer, it would not have been possible for Chase to do all that he did without Lindsay's support. Lindsay was taking a big risk in appointing Chase, given the strong resistance by the medical establishment, but he was willing to do so and to give Chase the autonomy to pursue so many changes.

Lindsay in Retrospect

This chapter has reviewed the many initiatives of John Lindsay in bringing management techniques to bear in modernizing New York City government. It is a remarkable legacy, with New York City leading the way for many other cities in embarking on this strategy. The results were not always as successful as the mayor and his cadre hoped they would be, but that is not surprising, given the many constraints they faced. Limited resources (funding, staff, and time), civil service and union resistance, bureaucratic inertia, and at times crippling impact of checks and balances within city government, state and federal regulations, and the impact of new mayors with different agendas, all made Lindsay's efforts to modernize city government a herculean task. Top these constraints off with the fiscal crisis in 1975 that brought the city to near bankruptcy, and one gets a strong sense of how hard it was to make the changes that Lindsay aspired to. Nevertheless, he and his staff accomplished a lot.

One final question in assessing Lindsay's impact on the city is how skilled he was as a manager. On the positive side, he established a vision for the city that restored its attractiveness as a welcoming haven for many poor minorities. His push to make city government much more responsive to the needs of the neighborhoods, to restore and build parks and other amenities, including many cultural institutions, to open opportunities for minorities in city government and higher education, even to open public schools to more parent and community input, notwithstanding the negative politics that resulted, are all examples.

His other, related push to modernize city government so that all New York City residents might be provided better services more efficiently, faster, and with more accountability than in the past was also critical. This involved recruiting many talented people who accomplished much during his tenure as mayor. Not only did he delegate many critical tasks in policy making and implementation to these people, but he also still spent much time keeping himself informed on the details of agency policies and programs. When the Sanitation Department held critical meetings on new procedures to expedite truck repairs and garbage collection, Lindsay was often present, even if he didn't fully understand all the technical issues involved. When conflicts arose in various neighborhoods, he not only sent in his trouble-shooters, but on many occasions he went there in person to reassure the citizenry. In particular, he spent much time as the city's chief executive in pursuing the details of implementation of services and new programs. John Lindsay was in all those respects an activist mayor.

A big part of being an effective manager, however, is developing alliances or coalitions required to get a new vision and new programs implemented.[76] In this regard, Lindsay probably could have helped himself more than he did in getting his agenda of management reforms put into practice. In his first term, he maintained a no-compromise, moralistic posture on many occasions that, while expressing his commitment to move the city in a more productive direction, only increased the determination of municipal employee unions to resist his efforts to reform their agencies. He referred to their leaders pejoratively as "power brokers" whose aggressive pursuit of their members' economic interests helped diminish the quality of life in the city. One result was transit workers, sanitation workers, and teachers strikes that had devastating effects on the city. He also appeared at times to neglect the needs of neighborhoods in the outer boroughs, thereby needlessly incurring their wrath and contributing to a white backlash that likely further increased their resistance to his reforms.

As a result, by not having a big enough political base, Lindsay diminished the prospects of generating more acceptance and sustainability for his agenda. Building such a coalition was admittedly a formidable task. To Lindsay's credit, in his second term he set up a more sophisticated labor relations department and showed more sensitivity to the needs of those communities who had felt like "forgotten outcasts" in his first term. Also in his second term, he successfully linked wage improvements to productivity standards that municipal employees regarded as fair. Thus, much of the sophisticated analysis of the first term got implemented in the second in ways that significantly improved the performance of city agencies.

In a word, John Lindsay had strengths and weaknesses like most leaders. My overall judgment is that his weaknesses paled in comparison to what he was able to accomplish. He was a man of courage, willing to take risks for what he felt were "right" public policies, even if done at times in clumsy ways. Furthermore, like most great leaders, he learned a lot from mistakes of his early years. His second term and the legacy of his eight years as mayor demonstrated many improvements in the city's management that deserve to be studied in even greater depth. Future mayors in New York City and elsewhere would do well to build on what Lindsay was able to accomplish in his two terms there. Rather than succumbing to the antigovernment, antiliberal rhetoric of recent years, we should take another look at what a progressive government may accomplish. John Lindsay, even with his limitations, has provided an important example.

NOTES

Note on methods: This chapter is based on two sets of data. One is in-depth, qualitative interviews with senior managers and staff in the Lindsay administration, including outside observers and critics. The interviews, in person or by phone, ranged in length from roughly 30 minutes to 2 hours. The average length was 90 minutes. I conducted twenty-eight such interviews. A second source is archival material, particularly agency reports, media coverage, and studies. Jay Kriegel, former mayoral advisor, generously gave me access to his voluminous files.

1. This summary statement was taken from an unpublished report by Frederick O'R. Hayes, *Change and Innovation in the N.Y.C. Sanitation Department 1970–1973,* June 30, 1974.

2. Ibid.

3. Ibid.

4. Vincent Cannato, *The Ungovernable City: John Lindsay's New York and the Crisis of Liberalism* (New York: Basic, 2002).

5. David Rogers, *The Management of Big Cities* (Beverly Hills, CA.: Sage, 1970). See chapter 2 for an early discussion of Lindsay's management initiatives.

6. Author interviews with Budget Bureau staff.

7. Fremont J. Lyden and Ernest G. Miller, eds., *Planning Programming Budgeting: A Systems Approach to Management* (Chicago: Markham, 1968).

8. Harry P. Hatry, "Measuring The Quality of Urban Services," pp. 39–63, in Willis D. Hawley and David Rogers, eds., *Improving the Quality of Urban Management* (Beverly Hills, CA: Sage, 1970).

9. Edward Hamilton, "Productivity: The New York City Approach," *Public Administration Review,* November/December 1972, p. 786.

10. Rogers, *Management of Big Cities*, pp. 16–20, 154–159.

11. Fred Hayes, unpublished book on Lindsay and NYC government, chapter 1, "A New Effort in Public Management," p. 22.

12. Ibid., p. 14.

13. Rogers, *Management of Big Cities*, pp. 16–17.

14. Emanuel Savas, "Municipal Monopolies versus Competition in Delivering Urban Services," *Urban Analysis*, 2 (1974): 93–116.

15. David Grossman, e-mail communication, August 30, 2012.

16. *The Mayor's Task Force on Reorganization of New York City Government,* Report and Proposed Local Law, December 1966.

17. Ibid., p. 12.

18. Ibid., pp. 33–35.

19. Author interview with Edward Hamilton, June 15, 2011.

20. "Creative Budgeting in New York City: An Interview with former Budget Director, Frederick O'R. Hayes," *Urban Analysis*, 1 (1973): 150.

21. Author interview with Howard Mantel, January 27, 2012.

22. Author interview with Nat Leventhal, December 8, 2011.

23. Author interview with Stan Breznoff, October 10, 2011.

24. Jack Krauskopf, *Recommendations on Human Services Policy for the Next New York City Mayor and Council*, Working Paper Series, the Aspen Institute, November, 2001.

25. Author interview with Jack Krauskopf, November 17, 2011.

26. Author interview with Judge Robert Sweet, January 24, 2012, and November 28, 2012

27. Author interview with Peter Goldmark, September 6, 2011.

28. For discussion of New York City / RAND Institute's contributions to reforming New York City government, see Peter Szanton, *Not Well Advised* (New York: Russell Sage Foundation, 1981), pp. 81–98.

29. Frederick O'R. Hayes, unpublished and untitled book on New York City, chapter 1, pp. 23ff.

30. Carter F. Bales, "The Progress of Analysis and PPB in New York City Government," in *New Tools for Urban Management: Studies in Systems and Organizational Analysis*, edited by

Richard Rosenbloom (Boston: Division of Research, Graduate School of Business Administration, Harvard University, 1971), chapter 3.

31. Ibid., p. 80.

32. Author interview with Peter Goldmark, September 6, 2011.

33. Bales, "Progress of Analysis," pp. 100–102.

34. Charles R. Morris, *The Cost of Good Intentions: New York City and the Liberal Experiment, 1960–1975* (New York: Norton, 1980), pp. 159–170, 203–214.

35. Author interview with David Grossman, June 21, 2011.

36. Author interview with Carter Bales, July 7, 2011, and Andrew Kerr, November 9, 2011.

37. Author interview with Andrew Kerr, November 9, 2011.

38. Ibid.

39. Author interview with Joan Hochman, February 22, 2012.

40. New York City Project Management Staff, Harvard Business School Case HP705, 1969, pp. 19–21, prepared by Martin Charns and Paul R. Lawrence.

41. Author interview with Kerr.

42. Ibid.

43. Author interview with David Grossman, June 21, 2011.

44. Author interview with Kerr.

45. Edward K. Hamilton, "Productivity: The New York City Approach," *Public Administration Review* (Nov.–Dec. 1972): 784–795.

46. Excerpts from Edward Hamilton's introductory memo to Mayor Lindsay on the citywide productivity program for FY 1972–1973, p. 4, August 7, 1972.

47. Ibid., p. 4.

48. Interview with Hamilton.

49. Hamilton, "Productivity," pp. 787–794.

50. Productivity data cited in this section come from each agency's annual report in the document referred to in note 46.

51. Szanton, *Not Well Advised*, pp. 86–90.

52. Author interview with Jay Kriegel, May 26, 2011.

53. Ibid.

54. John Mudd, *Neighborhood Services* (New Haven: Yale University Press, 1984), p. 65.

55. Ibid., chapter 3.

56. Ibid., p. 70.

57. Ibid., p. 94.

58. Ibid., p. 89.

59. Allen H. Barton et al., *Decentralizing City Government* (Lexington, MA: Lexington Books, 1977), p. 254.

60. Ibid., p. 253.

61. Excerpted from *The District Service Cabinet: A Two-Year Appraisal*, no author, no date, pp. 7–8.

62. Barton et al., *Decentralizing City Government*, p. 253.

63. Mudd, *Neighborhood Services*, pp. 153–157.

64. Author interviews with John Mudd, October 20, 2011, and Lewis Feldstein, November 7, 2011.

65. Office of the Mayor, City Hall, Press Release, July 24, 1973, p. 1.

66. Mudd, *Neighborhood Services*, p. 152. . A history of the ONG program, including its

demise under Beame, appears in Stanley Heginbotham, "The Evolution of the District Manager Experiment," chapter 2 in Barton et al., *Decentralizing City Government*, especially pp. 47–49.

67. Frederick O'R. Hayes, "Creative Budgeting in New York City," in *Change and Innovation in the N.Y.C. Sanitation Department 1970–1973*, p. 120.

68. Author interview with Herb Elish, February 6, 2012.

69. Summarized from Hayes, *Change and Innovation*.

70. John Sibley, "Health Department Seeks Lost Glory," *New York Times*, December 3, 1969.

71. Taken from PowerPoint presentation of Joan Lieman and Jerome Kagan, "Health Panel Initiatives in Lindsay Administration," Public Management Symposium, sponsored by Baruch College, September 30, 2010.

72. Jerome Kagan, memo to the City Council of New York, *A New York City Health Services History: 1969–1973*.

73. Author interviews with Joan Lieman, November 28, 2011, and James Kagen, February 8, 2012.

74. From PowerPoint slides covering a lecture entitled "Management Principles Governing HAS under Chase's Leadership," given by Joan Lieman at International Center for Advancement of Addiction Treatment, n.d.

75. Author interview with Nat Leventhal.

76. See Jeffrey Pfeffer, *Managing with Power* (Boston: Harvard Business School Press, 1991).

Lindsay with David Rockefeller (*second from the left*) and other city planning commit-
tee members presenting the designs that they created as part of the Lower Manhattan
Development Plan. April 12, 1974; photographer Dick De Marsico. John Vliet Lindsay
Papers (MS 592). Manuscripts and Archives, Yale University Library.

CHAPTER SIX

A Design-Conscious Mayor

The Physical City

PAUL GOLDBERGER

If the most famous image of John Lindsay as mayor of New York is the photograph of him in shirtsleeves, walking the streets of Harlem in the hope of providing a calming presence while riots broke out in many other cities, surely the pictures of Lindsay riding a bicycle through Central Park and of him standing with David Rockefeller looking at plans for a revitalized Lower Manhattan are nearly as familiar. They underscore Lindsay's consistent interest in the physical form of the city and his belief that, whatever the physical condition of New York was when he became its mayor on January 1, 1966, better planning and design could turn it into a pleasing, even an uplifting, environment. Lindsay, more than almost any public official of his time, believed in the power of planning and design to improve the quality of urban life, and his administration was marked by a consistent determination to put this belief into effect. Design, Lindsay believed, was not an aesthetic frill but a critical element of public policy.

As with many initiatives of the Lindsay years, the results of his planning and architectural efforts were mixed, but, if they did not transform life for all New Yorkers, in many ways they set the tone and direction for planning and urban design in New York for the succeeding generation. Incentive zoning, special zoning districts, air rights transfer as a historic preservation tool, and encouragement of mixed use buildings, active street life, and pedestrian zones all have their roots in the Lindsay administration, at least as matters of assertive public policy. Before Lindsay became mayor, government agencies and public authorities built public works in New York City and the private sector built private property, and the two had little to do with each other. Zoning laws governed the overall height, bulk, and use of buildings, but that was as far as they went—even the complete overhaul of the city's zoning code in 1961 did not represent the kind of conceptual rethinking that drove planning during the Lindsay years.

Perhaps the most lasting Lindsay innovation was a blurring of the public and private realms through incentive zoning, a process in which private developers were given bonuses of additional rentable space in exchange for including public amenities in their commercial projects. While the practice did not have its origins with Lindsay, before he took office its applications were limited—and modest. He used the concept zealously, turning it into a tool to promote a wide range of planning goals, from maintaining the Broadway theater district to keeping Fifth Avenue alive with shops. At a 2010 symposium discussing the impact of the Lindsay administration on urban planning, Amanda Burden, chair of the New York City Planning Commission under Mayor Michael Bloomberg, spoke of the Lindsay years as providing the conceptual basis for the proactive planning efforts of the Bloomberg administration, which did not begin until more than a quarter century after the end of Lindsay's mayoralty.[1] John Lindsay's influence on public policy regarding design and planning in New York remains strong, forty years after he left office.

Lindsay signaled that the form of the physical city would be a priority for him during his mayoral campaign. In July of 1965, several months before the election, he arranged for a helicopter tour of the city with the architect Philip Johnson and the landscape architect Robert L. Zion. It was, for the most part, a gloomy vista of slums, dirty streets, crumbling piers, poorly maintained parks, and dreary public housing—far from the glamorous New York of midtown skyscrapers or even the workaday New York of middle-class neighborhoods. But it gave the candidate an overview of the urban environment in decline that millions of New Yorkers experienced every day. "My enthusiasm for the city's potential far outstrips my depression over smog, decay, absence of greenery and missed opportunities," Lindsay said after the tour to Ada Louise Huxtable, who was covering the trip for the *New York Times*. He went on: "There is great hope for New York. But it will require bold action, sweeping vision and daring plans. This is the day for long-range planning and the use of experts. And you've got to be tough about it. Our city management has been 'un-modern' for too long."[2]

Lindsay's choice of Johnson and Zion as his tour guides was revealing. Both men were established, high-profile designers whose work was generally considered modern, if no longer cutting-edge. Neither Johnson nor Zion had ties to the political or planning establishments in the city, and both could be viewed as representing the kind of high aesthetic standards generally thought to be absent in municipal projects. Johnson was even blunter than Lindsay in his evaluation of what he had seen: "The only green we saw in Brooklyn was for the dead, in the cemeteries. It was a very sad trip."[3]

The flight, which Huxtable described as the "first step toward the formulation

of a Lindsay campaign platform for urban design," covered portions of all five boroughs and emphasized potential development challenges such as the lower Manhattan waterfront, Governors Island, the site designated for the Lower Manhattan
Expressway, the Brooklyn Navy Yard, Flushing Meadows Park, Roosevelt (then Welfare) Island, and the site planned for Co-op City in the Bronx. Lindsay described
the waterfront as "being so far gone that there's hope to start all over again," and said
that Governors Island should become a park and the Lower Manhattan Expressway
should be cancelled. "If it can't be stopped legally, change the law," Lindsay said.[4]
Even though it would be several months before Lindsay would issue any formal
position paper on planning, it was clear from his comments that his approach would
be anything but modest. Everything about that day in July showed that he favored
activist, large-scale planning gestures and that he envisioned his administration as
both creating and executing bold, sweeping plans.

Lindsay began to put his ideas into practical form in his first year as mayor. In the
spring of 1966 he established a blue-ribbon panel to study the condition of design in
New York City and asked William S. Paley, chairman of CBS, to head it. Johnson and
Zion were both appointed to the task force, along with I. M. Pei, Robert A. M. Stern,
Jaquelin Robertson, Joan K. Davidson, Eli Jacobs, Walter N. Thayer, and Vera List,
among others. It was an exceptionally sophisticated group of members of the business, philanthropic, and design establishments, and Lindsay presumably hoped that
its stature would give it a degree of authority that would buttress his own.

The report, officially titled *The Threatened City: A Report on the Design of the
City of New York* but generally known as the Paley report, was not delivered to the
mayor until February of 1967.[5] It was, and remains, an extraordinary document, at
once an indictment of the city's past policies and an eloquent, even passionate, case
statement for the potential of urban design to improve the quality of life in New
York. The report pulled no punches in its analysis of the current state of the public
realm in New York. The subway system, it said, is the "most squalid public environment of the United States: dank, dingily lit, fetid, raucous with screeching clatter,
one of the world's meanest transit facilities."[6] The Staten Island ferry slip built in the
1950s, the report said, "says that imagination and desire for achievement have died
here; that New York no longer cares about itself."[7] New midtown office buildings
happened "almost by accident, without any plan at all. . . . It remains economics in
the raw, a missed opportunity."[8]

Seeking a New Way to Plan

Lindsay became mayor of New York at a moment when attitudes toward planning,
architecture, and design, not just in New York but also nationally and internation-

ally, were on the cusp of significant change. For most of the post–World War II era, the cure for cities in trouble—of which there seemed to be more and more—was the drastic surgery of "urban renewal," which generally meant wholesale demolition of large swaths of old buildings, even entire neighborhoods, and their replacement with new buildings, often towers spaced widely apart and removed from traditional city streets. In New York, Robert Moses oversaw the process of urban renewal, and he had little patience for community input. Plans were dictated from the top, and they were almost always based on the notion that the new was better than the old, that wide boulevards and highways were better than narrow city streets, and that the traditional city was a mess that could only be improved by, in effect, replacing it, one section at a time. And the presumption was that professionals, if not politicians, knew best and that the public would be told what a plan would be, not asked what it should be.

John Lindsay wanted to be seen as a politician who saw the process as well as the product of city planning differently. He argued from the beginning for greater community participation in planning, and a key element of his campaign was based on his concept of Little City Halls around the city that would house community planning boards, among other functions of city government, decentralizing a process that had been highly centralized. "Citizens seldom have any idea how and when important decisions are made, much less any knowledge of how to influence them. . . . The first intimation that many a local resident has had of an impending highway or housing project has been the arrival of the surveyors—or an eviction notice," Jonathan Barnett has written in *Urban Design as Public Policy.*[9]

The effort to broaden public participation in the planning process would prove exceptionally difficult for Lindsay, in part because of opposition from City Council members who viewed the Little City Halls as the equivalent of Lindsay political clubhouses and sought to prevent the mayor from expanding his power base. The purpose of the council was to represent community interests, and its members did not welcome the suggestion that the mayor's office could do it better.

But there were other reasons, less directly connected to local politics, that Lindsay's efforts to bring the public into the political process were slow and halting. For a long time, the notion that the city needed to be "cleaned up" and that tall towers standing in open space could guarantee a better quality of life for their occupants went largely unchallenged, even by liberals who took issue with many of Moses' tactics and design choices but who believed that the form of the city needed, in a sense, to be reinvented. The widespread recognition that the ambitious urban renewal model had generally not worked would come only years later. Jane Jacobs' celebrated book, *The Death and Life of Great American Cities,* was published in

1961, the first, and the most important, shot across the bow of urban renewal, and a book that challenged almost all of the precepts under which city planning had been operating in the postwar era.[10] Not the least of Jacobs' arguments was that planning "experts" had failed and that it was time for planners and politicians to listen to the people, who often knew better, she believed.

But it would take a decade before Jacobs' book would be accepted as gospel. Many of the most sweeping bulldoze-and-rebuild projects in New York, like the World Trade Center and Lincoln Center, came in the 1960s, after the publication of her book. Jacobs may have been the pioneering voice of a new attitude, but she was not alone. At around the same time as *Death and Life,* in his book *The Urban Villagers* the sociologist Herbert Gans came to the conclusion that the so-called slum of Boston's West End, slated to be removed in a large urban renewal project, was in fact a vibrant, healthy neighborhood,[11] and in 1966, Robert Venturi's *Complexity and Contradiction in Architecture* extended the critique of modern planning to the realm of aesthetics, arguing that modern architecture failed to appreciate the value of most of the ordinary, everyday buildings that make up traditional cities.[12]

John Lindsay may or may not have been aware of these books, but the people he surrounded himself with as advisors on the subject of the physical city undoubtedly were. While they did not always endorse Jane Jacobs' skepticism about professional planners—most of them were, after all, planners and architects themselves, and they were joining Lindsay because they believed in ambitious governmental engagement with the city—they were well aware that the top-down approach represented by Robert Moses did not work. Like Lindsay, they believed, at least in theory, that there was a role for the public in the planning process. But the planners and architects who advised Lindsay and carried out his policies tended to embrace community planning in principle more than in practice. They understood, by and large, the need to look at the city with a finer grain, to see its parts as well as its whole, and that the existing urban fabric of neighborhoods was a strength of the city, not a weakness. But they, and Lindsay, presumed that these perceptions would be sufficient to convince the average citizen that they could be trusted not to plan the city in arrogant, Moses-like fashion and that they would make decisions that represented each community's interests. The positions Lindsay took during his mayoral campaign, such as his initial opposition to the Lower Manhattan Expressway, a project Moses favored that would have all but obliterated the area now known as SoHo, seemed to confirm that his planning views were in line with those of citizen activists.

Yet at the same time, Lindsay never lost his respect for the great, sweeping gesture, the kind of large-scale project that citizen activists are most likely to oppose. Underscoring his unwillingness to give up the "big picture" view, a key accomplishment of his planning commission was the publication of the six-volume *Plan for New York City* in 1969, a document so wide-ranging it might be said to have been of little practical use.[13] But if the master plan represented a broad vision, Lindsay was genuinely eager to prove that the big planning and design gestures he advocated be compatible with viable, healthy neighborhoods, that historic buildings be preserved where possible, that the interests of each community be taken into account, and that the urban form of the city not be reimagined wholesale. As he began his mayoralty, he seemed to believe that urban planning could be practiced in a manner as ambitiously and determinedly as by Robert Moses and as benignly and discreetly as by Jane Jacobs.

It would not take long to prove how difficult this synthesis was to achieve. During his campaign for mayor, Lindsay seemed certain that the Lower Manhattan Expressway was a mistake. Viewing the impact of the elevated Prospect Expressway on Brooklyn neighborhoods during his 1965 helicopter tour only "made it imperative to re-examine expressways and what they do to cities," Lindsay the candidate said.[14] He joined with Jane Jacobs, whose protests against Moses' urban renewal plans for the neighborhood of Greenwich Village he had also supported, in arguing that the expressway plan should be abandoned. Once in office, however, he was less certain. Labor unions demanded construction jobs, and the arguments that the expressway could revive an economically unproductive area of the city seemed too strong to refute. Lindsay held to his opposition to Moses' plan but spent much of 1966 and early 1967 commissioning alternative schemes—combinations of tunnels and open roads; a narrow, double-decker alternative that would have stacked lanes and required less demolition; a skyway that would have risen up eighty feet and would have been so high that it would presumably have had minimal effect on the street and the existing buildings and would also have required minimal demolition.

Finally Lindsay settled on a plan, announced in March of 1967, that would place the highway in an open, cut trench, over which new buildings could be built. The new, submerged road would require the demolition of 650 homes and four hundred commercial buildings, the Lindsay administration claimed, whereas Moses' plan called for demolishing two thousand residences and eight hundred buildings and replacing many of them with huge, futuristic buildings on top of the highway. One version, designed by the architect Paul Rudolph, envisioned enormous, pyramidal structures over the highway, a Buck Rogers vision that seems, in hindsight, to be both exhilaratingly romantic and utterly naïve, not to mention inordinately complex.[15] It would take more than two years and ongoing public opposition for Lindsay to concede that his original position had been correct and that the expressway was not only a public relations disaster and politically untenable but would also run the risk of inflicting permanent damage on the very Lower Manhattan neighborhoods whose growth it was supposed to stimulate. In July of 1969, finally bowing to the citizen activists whose position he had initially shared, Lindsay declared the project dead "for all time."[16]

The off-on-off position Lindsay took on the Lower Manhattan Expressway was in sharp contrast to the tone his administration set with the Paley report, which discussed the city's urban design in lofty terms that barely acknowledged, let alone reflected, political expediency. "The gleaming towers from the Empire State up to Central Park are a mountain range of the mind, an uncanny array of individual designs, a vision of power filed neatly into thousands upon thousands of desk drawers, and a beautiful thing," the report proclaimed in a section called "Grandeur,"[17] part of a chapter that set out to explain the city's strengths. Other sections were titled "Diversity,"[18] "Coherence,"[19] "Style" and "Human-ness,"[20] a collection of characteristics to describe New York that was both prescient and sophisticated.

It is difficult, nearly fifty years after the Paley report was written, to improve on its observation that "style is visual wit. There is a New York style in dress, in advertising, in conversation, but not, strangely, in the hardware with which New York surrounds us."[21] In "Diversity," the report celebrates both ethnic and architectural diversity, and notes:

> Obviously, we are going to lose some of this diversity to advancing technology: the flavorful old Fulton Fish Market is fading, for example, because more and more of the city's seafood now is shipped in frozen. But is all technology irreversible? In our city the real thief of diversity seems to be a real estate technology whose formula produces tall, expressionless buildings, almost always totally empty of character. . . . The sense of place is being eroded by a slowly advancing glacier of these buildings. . . . We should guard even our rundown areas from this mindless monotony. But can we? Yes. The most prominent proof in New York is probably Greenwich Village, where environmental diversity is not fading but flourishing again, perhaps because the Villagers understand particularly well that people are not yet delivered frozen.[22]

While observations like this, at once breezy and sophisticated, could give Lindsay protective cover when he endorsed positions that were closer to those of Jane Jacobs than Robert Moses, as well as buttress his support of the city's Landmarks Preservation Commission, only a year old and still lacking political clout, the real significance of the Paley report lay in its specific recommendations. It suggested that the city look into the establishment of a third business district to complement Midtown Manhattan and Wall Street, that it build new residential and commercial neighborhoods on platforms over rail yards, that the city's waterfronts be redeveloped for residential use and as public space, and that public transportation be improved and expanded to include rail links to airports. Most important, it urged that design quality become a priority, and it suggested that the city had the power to enforce a higher level of design in private as well as public projects.

While much of the report was devoted to elegiac praise of New York, it did not shy away from more detailed analysis of laws and policies governing planning and construction. It urged the mayor to expand the authority of the City Planning Commission and recommended specific changes in the operation of the capital construction budget that could result in giving a higher priority to design quality. The report suggested twelve specific actions for the new mayor to take. Lindsay's determined embrace of the fourth recommendation—"The Mayor should direct the Planning Commission to complete the long-overdue master plan of the city"—and the fifth—"The Mayor should direct the Chairman of the City Planning Commission to create within the City Planning Department an urban design force of trained professionals of the highest competence, to be headed by an architect-planner of proven ability and personal force"—would come in many ways to define his administration's attitude toward the built environment.[23]

Urban Design as a Political Tool

Donald H. Elliott, a partner in Webster and Sheffield, Lindsay's former law firm, with an expertise in land use regulation, played a major role in the 1965 election campaign. During the campaign, five young, ambitious, progressively minded, Ivy League–educated architects—Jaquelin T. Robertson, Richard Weinstein, Giovanni Pasanella, Myles Weintraub, and Jonathan Barnett—called on Elliott in the hope that Lindsay would be receptive to some of their ideas. Elliott "had the imagination to try us out and see if we came up to our own valuation (as we were then in our late twenties or early thirties, there was little evidence for Donald to go on)," Barnett would later write.[24] Elliott asked the group to produce position papers on planning and design. After the election, they were appointed to official study groups, and Robertson, along with a recent graduate of the Yale School of Architecture, Robert A. M. Stern, were named to the Paley commission.

By the time the Paley report was issued, Elliott, who had become counsel to the mayor when Lindsay was inaugurated, was named chairman of the City Planning Commission, and he moved quickly to establish the specialized urban design task force the report had called for. He did not have to cast the net wide to staff the new operation: he convinced four of the five architects who had joined the campaign to go to work for the city, and in April of 1967 they became the founding members of the Urban Design Group. While Pasanella chose to remain in private practice and Weintraub would return to private practice after a short period with the city, Robertson, Weinstein, and Barnett would become pillars of the Lindsay administration and, along with Donald Elliott, the key shapers of the Lindsay policies on urban planning.

Lindsay underscored his seriousness about design by announcing the urban design task force in a speech before the annual convention of the American Institute of Architects in May of that year. The group would "advance the cause of aesthetics in every area the Planning Commission can influence—from street signs to skyscrapers," the mayor said. Barnett defined urban design somewhat differently, calling it "designing the city without designing the buildings."[25]

The Urban Design Group may have been motivated by a desire to improve the aesthetics of the city, but the tool they would ultimately use turned out to be one only tangentially associated with aesthetics: zoning. Zoning laws, first created in New York in 1916 and eventually the mainstay of physical planning in almost every city in the country, generally regulate the height and bulk of buildings and the uses to which they can be put. The city's original zoning ordinance gave New York City the stepped-back, "wedding-cake" look of many office and apartment towers from the 1920s through the 1950s, for example, and revised zoning laws after 1961 encouraged a new generation of slab towers by offering a bonus of 20 percent more floor space in exchange for setting a building back from the street and building a public plaza at its base. Zoning, Barnett wrote, "had always seemed a very dreary subject, of little relevance to any creative endeavor [but] we came to realize that zoning could be made into one of the basic methods of designing cities."[26]

A project planned for Times Square would prove to be the Urban Design Group's first test. Sam Minskoff & Sons, one of the city's major developers, had purchased the venerable Astor Hotel on Times Square before Lindsay became mayor and had already embarked on plans to demolish the hotel and take advantage of the 20 percent bonus option by building a tall office building behind a triangular plaza. Times Square and the theater district needed neither a bland glass office building nor an awkwardly shaped pedestrian plaza, Lindsay's architects concluded, and they suggested that constructing a new legitimate theater as part of the project might be more beneficial to the city than a plaza. The developers dismissed the idea as impractical, unprofitable, and naïve and took their case to the mayor, who backed his urban designers. The survival of Broadway theater was difficult enough, Lindsay felt, without the pressure of redevelopment looming over the theater district; combining new theater construction with new office construction might be a way for the city to encourage growth and economic development without losing one of its great cultural assets.

The Minskoff organization, recognizing that it would probably not be able to avoid building the theater, came up with a new version of the building that included an elaborate theater, public arcade, and rooftop restaurant but also increased the office space to roughly twice what the zoning would normally allow. Elliott and the Planning Commission ultimately managed to negotiate the office tower back to the same 20 percent over normal zoning that was permitted under the plaza bonus, and the city passed legislation creating the Times Square Special Zoning District, allowing any office tower in the area that contained a new theater within it to have a 20 percent bonus in allowable space. After the completion of the building on the Astor site—whose theater, not surprisingly, was initially named the Minskoff—several other new theaters, both large, traditional houses and smaller, experimental houses, were constructed within new office complexes.

Neither the Minskoff building, called One Astor Plaza in feeble recognition of the landmark hotel that was demolished to make way for it, nor any of the subsequent skyscrapers erected under the provisions of the Times Square Special Zoning District were particularly distinguished as works of architecture. The premises under which Lindsay's planners worked may have seemed highly assertive to developers unaccustomed to such intense engagement by city planners, but there was no specific provision for aesthetic review. The members of the Urban Design Group by and large believed that their mission was to focus not on the particulars of any building's design but on its relationship to its surroundings and the way in which it would impact on the public realm. Adding a theater to reinforce the theater district or assuring the continued presence of retail space on a shopping street threatened by the presence of too many banks and airline offices thus seemed an appropriate exercise of urban design to Robertson, Weinstein, Barnett, and Alexander Cooper, an architect who joined them in 1969 and came to lead the Urban Design Group (and who in private practice would design the master plan for Battery Park City in 1979 and later would become Robertson's partner in the private firm of Cooper Robertson). Dictating the pattern of a building's windows, or its external skin, or choosing its materials or the nature of its top, however, was the work of the architect, and when it came to those decisions, the Lindsay team thought, the urban designer had an obligation to stand aside.

While it is hard to argue with the logic of this position, not to mention the admirable restraint it represented, it resulted in the paradox of a city administration preoccupied with architectural aesthetics able to bring forth relatively little architecture of note. The office towers that contained the vaunted new theaters were generally mediocre, and the new Broadway theaters themselves tended to be large and banal, their ample lobbies and plentiful rest rooms the only elements that marked them as superior to the older Broadway houses. Outside the theater district, where

The park was also in serious physical decline, and neither Hoving nor his successor, August Heckscher, would have the resources to do much about the fact that Frederick Law Olmsted and Calvert Vaux's masterwork was crumbling. Still, Central Park in the Lindsay era had a new energy, a buzz, and it underscored the Lindsay administration's view that urban activity was a fundamental good. If the nation had turned, both culturally and socially, away from cities during the 1950s, either trying to make them more suburban through urban renewal developments that favored the automobile or literally abandoning cities for the suburbs, Lindsay wanted to prove that the city could offer many of the pleasures that people sought without requiring them to go outside the densely built urban core, that it could still provide elements of the good life—indeed, that under the best of circumstances New York could offer a pleasure and exhilaration never possible in the suburbs.

If that belief led to occasional gaffes like his phrase "fun city"—a line that, in its seeming indifference to New York's high levels of crime, poverty, and general physical disarray would haunt Lindsay forever—it nevertheless reflected Lindsay's recognition that New York could be a magnet for young, sophisticated, energetic professionals who sought a livelier, more diverse, and more creative environment than the suburban world to which their parents had escaped. It would be another decade or more before urban gentrification would be a widespread enough phenomenon to be meaningful, but Lindsay's focus on livability was a sign that he envisioned such possibilities for the city, even though he could do little to bring them about.

While few people differed with Lindsay in his hope that Central Park would become known more for bicycle riding than mugging, the administration's efforts here risked appearing naïve. Worse still, they made Lindsay seem, to some, disconnected from the profound, not to say urgent, problems the city faced: the mayor's upbeat celebration of the potential of urban life would mean little if he were perceived as bicycling while Rome burned. Sidewalk cafes and bicycle rides in the park were not going to save a troubled, crime-ridden city so far as its business and real estate community was concerned. Even what might be considered Lindsay's greatest success in making daily life pleasanter for New Yorkers—getting the New York City Transit Authority to begin air-conditioning its fleet of subway cars—came at a time when the subway system itself was coping with a rising tide of graffiti and dirt, which meant that the subway was widely perceived as suffering from the same physical decline as the rest of the city. Cool, comfortable air in the summer was not enough to offset the sense of many New Yorkers that the mayor was not able to fix the broken physical environment.

Lindsay's credibility with business leaders did not rise as a result of his support for the city's historic preservation efforts, which the real estate industry often viewed not as a harmless distraction, like bicycling in Central Park, but as a genuine threat to its interests. The Landmarks Preservation Commission was created under Lindsay's predecessor, Robert F. Wagner Jr., in part in response to the outcry after the demolition of McKim, Mead & White's great Pennsylvania Station. The loss of Pennsylvania Station was hardly the origin of the city's historic preservation movement, of course; it had been growing steadily through the 1950s as more and more well-liked architecture seemed to give way to new buildings that were hardly liked at all. In many ways the culture of historic preservation paralleled, and benefited from, the growing disenchantment with the bulldoze-and-rebuild style of urban renewal. In each case, the old seemed to be tossed aside with cavalier indifference to any potential value it might have in the evolving city, as if improvement in the urban environment could come only by wholesale replacement of the buildings that had once defined it. As Lindsay tended to make common cause with opponents of traditional urban renewal, he supported many of the efforts of the historic preservation movement, and the fledgling Landmarks Preservation Commission expanded its reach, slowly but steadily, during his administration, placing more and more of the city under its protection.

As he did with most of his planning efforts, Lindsay approached historic preservation less as an ideologue than as a politician seeking to balance conflicting interests. The city did not try to stop the demolition of the old Metropolitan Opera House in 1967 after the Met moved to its new home in Lincoln Center, and neither did it prevent the replacement of the Savoy-Plaza Hotel on Fifth Avenue with the General Motors Building in 1968. Both cases involved landmarks that, however critical to the city's history and identity, were not viewed by the Lindsay administration as having greater value than the commercial priorities of the real estate industry. But there was no hesitation about the 1967 designation of Grand Central Terminal as an official city landmark, which would have been unforgivable after the loss of Pennsylvania Station just four years earlier. And in 1969, when the Penn Central Railroad, the station's owner, proposed to build a fifty-five-story tower by the architect Marcel Breuer atop the terminal, the city denied it permission on the grounds that it would be tantamount to destroying the landmark.

The Lindsay administration offered the railroad an inventive alternative along the lines of the complex zoning tradeoffs it had been developing elsewhere in the city. Penn Central could transfer the air rights above Grand Central to adjacent sites it owned around the terminal, thus allowing it to build larger office towers on those sites than the zoning would otherwise permit. The city claimed that it was not taking away the economic value of the air space over the landmark terminal, merely transferring it to nearby sites. The railroad rejected the argument, claiming that landmark designation compromised its rights as a property owner despite the offer of transferable air rights, and took the city to court. The Lindsay administration defended the suit vigorously and lost in state court. In 1978, nearly a decade and two mayors later, the United States Supreme Court decided the case in the city's favor, upholding the position the Lindsay administration had taken in favor of protecting Grand Central Terminal and, by implication, upholding the constitutionality of New York City's landmarks preservation law—a legal triumph with ramifications for the entire historic preservation movement around the country.[29] It was a battle that had begun during Lindsay's mayoralty, which established the legal arguments behind the principle that protecting a privately owned landmark building could be considered a public good—an argument that still prevails.

Architecture, Community, and the Long-term Future

Lindsay was eager to increase both the quantity and the quality of housing in the city, but here, as in so many aspects of the physical city, the administration's successes seemed to play out against a backdrop of overall decline. Enormous projects consisting of multiple towers on superblocks, a staple of the Moses era, were not what the Lindsay administration wanted, and it embarked, instead, on a program of scatter-site housing, smaller projects that would neither have the stigma nor the cost of earlier projects (see chapter 3).[30] The City Planning Commission and the mayor also made clear their intention to retain and rehabilitate numerous older apartment buildings, integrating new ones with them in what might be called Lindsay's post–urban renewal sensibility, a goal that aligned with the priorities of historic preservationists as well.

Here, too, good intentions could carry Lindsay only so far. The mayor's Housing and Development Administration tended, by and large, to favor new construction and resisted putting substantial funds into rehabilitation. But the city did not have the wherewithal to build on a scale even remotely close to its ambitions. As crime grew in the late 1960s and early 1970s, housing abandonments increased, and reductions in funding of key federal housing programs only made the situation worse. So did a rapid escalation of construction costs. By 1971 the Lindsay administration had spent more than $150 million on acquiring and clearing land for potential housing sites—enough to construct a hundred thousand units, according to Alex Garvin[31]— but the city could afford to build little.

Many of the most ambitious new projects created during the Lindsay years were actually developed by the New York State Urban Redevelopment Corporation (U.D.C.), an agency established by Governor Nelson Rockefeller, a sometime ally and frequent rival of Lindsay, and run by Edward Logue, a brilliant, driven administrator who shared Lindsay's fondness for architecture. The U.D.C. was behind the two largest residential developments to begin during the Lindsay years, Roosevelt Island on the former Welfare Island in the East River and Battery Park City on landfill just west of the World Trade Center site in Lower Manhattan. Both projects had high architectural ambitions that were severely compromised as they moved forward. Battery Park City, based in part on a powerful, if wildly futuristic, design by the architects William Conklin and James Rossant, commissioned by the Lindsay administration as the centerpiece of its Lower Manhattan Plan of 1966, sputtered and died after the construction of a concrete tower that bore little resemblance to the Buck Rogers original. (It would come to life again after 1979, with a very different plan by Alexander Cooper and Stanton Eckstut that extended the Manhattan grid across the landfill and sought to create traditional city blocks—a plan that was more consistent with the Lindsay administration's design philosophy than the futuristic original was.)

Still, there were some important successes. An Urban Design Group study made recommendations for publicly assisted housing on a cluster of housing sites in the West Tremont area of the Bronx, called Twin Parks, and several superb structures were built in accordance with the proposal, most notably two by Giovanni Pasanella, who had been one of the architects who originally approached Lindsay during the campaign. Richard Meier, then also at the beginning of his architectural practice, built other sections of Twin Parks, as did Romaldo Giurgola. All were thoughtfully integrated into the context of the old neighborhood and stood as a clear testament to the design and planning philosophy that the administration hoped to be known for. The Twin Parks housing was built with an unusual level of consultation with the community, although much of the community input had to do with where the new housing would be located rather than its actual design, according to Jonathan Barnett.[32] And when plans were drawn up, they were displayed not only at community meetings but in special storefront exhibits to assure that residents who did not attend meetings would still have the chance to see what the new housing would look like. But the success of Twin Parks was not wholly a result of the Lindsay administration's attempt at community outreach—or even of the Lindsay administration at all. While the city initiated the project and set its parameters, it was the New York State Urban Development Corporation that actually got Twin Parks built.

Three of the most important publicly assisted housing complexes of the Lindsay years, Riverbend Houses in Harlem, East Midtown Plaza on East 23rd Street, and Waterside on the East River at 26th Street, were the work of the firm of Davis Brody and Associates. Each broke the red-brick tower mold in a different way: Riverbend and East Midtown Plaza both were woven deftly into complex urban contexts, while

Waterside stood as a sculptural beacon at the edge of Manhattan, opening a portion of the waterfront to new public use. Collectively, however, the three complexes created a critical mass of forward-looking housing that became a key part of Lindsay's architectural legacy, a reminder that his administration was not only willing to work with private developers to raise the city's standards of architecture and urban design, but it was also capable of doing so in an effective and meaningful way.

Perhaps the most important contribution to improving standards in housing design during the Lindsay years, however, came at the very end of Lindsay's second administration: a new set of zoning provisions, with the candid title of "Housing Quality: A Program for Zoning Reform," put together by the Lindsay urban design team under the direction of Alex Cooper.[33] The Housing Quality system replaced traditional zoning with a point system under which proposed apartment complexes were given credit for amenities such as the layouts of individual apartments, natural light in corridors, and sunlight in outdoor open spaces. The program, which applied to luxury, market-rate housing built by developers, also encouraged placing buildings at the street line, a deliberate rebuke to the 1961 zoning ordinance that called for towers set back behind plazas, and it discouraged the insertion of high-rise towers in the midst of low-rise neighborhoods: in sum, Housing Quality was a call for respect for context.

In this sense, the Housing Quality program encapsulated the Lindsay administration's general means of going about planning and design. Lindsay and his team wanted to be seen as representing a newer, more neighborhood-based attitude toward planning and a more urbanistically sensitive view of architecture and urban design, which to a significant extent it did. The Housing Quality program summed up many of the urban design objectives that the Lindsay administration had had from the beginning. Yet it was an initiative driven by planning and design professionals and did not emerge from community participation, underscoring the way that the administration's enlightened planning and design initiatives were often separate and distinct from the high levels of citizen engagement that Lindsay aspired to, even though they often embraced values similar to those of community-driven programs. Ironically, since it took until the very end of the administration to bring the Housing Quality program to fruition (and even then, it did not become official city policy until just after Lindsay left office), technically it is a policy not of the Lindsay administration but of the Beame administration, which had little if any of Lindsay's respect for design.

The document about the physical form of the city that John Lindsay is likely to be most remembered for, however, is not Housing Quality or the Paley report or even the briefs written to argue the Grand Central landmarks case. It is the *Plan for*

New York City, which previous city administrations had never bothered to produce but which the Lindsay administration managed to complete, under the leadership of Donald Elliott, in 1969.[34]

The plan, published in huge, portfolio-size volumes, is essentially a position paper arguing for New York's continued strength and relevance at a time when not only the rest of the United States but many New Yorkers themselves were questioning the value of cities in general and of New York in particular. The plan, like the Paley report, did not deny the magnitude of the problems.

"It is obvious enough that there is a great deal wrong," the second paragraph of the Introduction stated. "The air is polluted. The streets are dirty and choked with traffic. The subways are jammed. The waters of the rivers and bays are fouled. There is a severe shortage of housing. The municipal plant is long past its prime.

"Greatest of all is the problem of the slums. Traditionally they have offered a route to something better in life, but no longer do they seem to. The blacks and Puerto Ricans who are crowded in them have been finding the way blocked in a way groups before did not."[35]

The rhetoric was blunt, especially for an official document produced by the City of New York, and notable for its willingness to connect the problem of social mobility to the city's physical problems. But save for the omission of crime as a factor in New York's troubles, the observations were hardly unusual; everyone knew how difficult things were. The plan opened with an almost conventional litany of problems.

What was startling was the nature of its solution. The common response to New York's problems in the postwar era was to consider crowding to be a key part of the issue: New York, the common wisdom in the 1950s and 1960s had it, is too dense to function, and people are falling all over themselves. "Even if midtown business building were to halt for a dozen years, that would hardly give time enough to relieve the congestion that already exists," Lewis Mumford said in the *New Yorker* in 1955,[36] describing New York's condition as "creeping paralysis."[37] Mumford went on to worry that, if the city "ceases to be a milieu in which people can exist in reasonable contentment instead of as prisoners perpetually plotting to escape a concentration camp," then the quality of architecture and design would hardly matter.[38]

Mumford was convinced, like so many others, that the city was literally choking itself to death and that the only solution lay in breaking up the dense center. "To some observers this great concentration of activity is what is most wrong," the plan stated, as if in reply to Mumford. "They are appalled by the traffic jams, the crowded sidewalks. . . . To do away with the congestion, they would do away with the concentration. The planners in a number of the world's capital cities have embraced this same philosophy. The thrust of their plans is to stop the growth of the center, split up its activities and relocate them in outlying subcenters and new towns."[39]

The *Plan for New York City* took an entirely different stance: "Concentration is the genius of the city, its reason for being, the source of its vitality and its excitement. We believe the center should be strengthened, not weakened, and we are not afraid of the bogey of high density. We hope to see several hundred thousand more office workers in the business districts in the next ten years, and we think the increase desirable and helpful."[40]

These were radical words in 1969, and to many people, they seemed not just misguided but nearly delusional. Crime in New York was on the rise, businesses were leaving, the tax base was shrinking, and the financial future of the city was grim. It would get far worse in the 1970s, after Lindsay left office, as financial commitments made by the city during his term proved harder and harder to keep with what seemed like an ever-smaller tax base. What was the point of a plan that was rooted in the notion that the city's congestion was its strength and that its density should be made greater still? Why was this plan talking about the city getting bigger and stronger when it seemed barely able to hold on to what it had? What was the point of calling Manhattan's business district a "national center"[41] when businesses seemed to be fleeing from it? And, most troubling of all, did it make sense to produce, at great expense, a master plan that did not outline clear steps to solve the problems the city faced?

Of course even the most enlightened urban planners could not use the tools of their discipline to turn the New York of 1969 into the New York of the twenty-first century. The *Plan for New York City* seemed, for all its ambitions, to recognize this. Uncharacteristically for an urban plan, it was written with an understanding of the limits of physical planning. It acknowledged the need for economic opportunity, better medical services and education, and all but suggested that if the city could not respond to these social needs, any rethinking of its physical form, no matter how skillfully wrought, would have scant effect.

The plan recognized, too, the rapid pace of change and how many factors that were sure to influence the city over the next generation were unknowable. "We have not made elaborate trend projections, nor have we specified phase one and phase two goals or any ultimate grand design," the plan's introduction stated. "That would be paper boldness. It would also be intellectually presumptuous. Our plans are going to be influenced by forces that the City can neither forecast nor control."[42]

The plan's hesitation to make specific recommendations about how the city's physical form should evolve gave it an air of vagueness and disconnection from the painful realities of its moment. Yet in some ways the master plan was the most radical document the Lindsay administration produced on the subject of the physical city—a blueprint for what Hilary Ballon would call the "democratic urbanism of the Lindsay administration."[43] By the normal standards of city planning, the plan was almost a subversive text, undermining the very principle of traditional master plans, and a testament to the futility of creating a master plan for a city like New York.

In the end, it was more of a case statement for New York, an argument, written from a remarkably knowing and wise understanding of the nature of urban life, of the long-term value of the city. In the immediate aftermath of the Lindsay administration, as the city fell deeper into financial, social, and physical disarray, its optimism about New York's long-term potential seemed so naïve as to render the plan all but irrelevant, and it was not the center of discussion and debate that Lindsay and Donald Elliott had hoped it would be. But it turned out, over time, to be largely correct. The city did come to embrace density as the plan had urged; its business districts grew vastly larger, new neighborhood subcenters developed, and it began once again to invest in the public realm. It just took another full generation, and major shifts in technology and the global as well as the local economy. And as the plan predicted, it would be factors other than the ideas of planners and architects that would shape the growth of the city in the decades after the Lindsay mayoralty.

It can seem somewhat paradoxical that a mayor as committed to architecture and urban design as John Lindsay was would produce as the legacy of his administration a plan that might seem to diminish, rather than enhance, the role of physical planning. But the lesson of the *Plan for New York City* was not that at all. Like all of the Lindsay administration's planning and design efforts, it emerged out of a deep and committed belief that, while the physical form of the city can have a profound effect on the quality of life, it is never unrelated to the life lived within it and that planning and design can never be viewed in isolation—a message as true now as in Lindsay's own time.

NOTES

1. The event was a panel discussion without prepared remarks, which included Donald Elliott, Alexander Cooper, and Carl Weisbrod, as well as Burden, and was moderated by the author. Burden referred to the activism of the Lindsay years as an inspiration for her own career as a planner. She began to study city planning after Lindsay left office.

2. Ada Louise Huxtable, "Lindsay Surveys City from Copter," *New York Times,* July 24, 1965, p. 8, is the source for this and subsequent quotations from participants in the helicopter tour.

3. Ibid.

4. Ibid.

5. William S. Paley and the Mayor's Task Force on Urban Design, *The Threatened City: A Report on the Design of the City of New York* (New York: City of New York, 1967).

6. Ibid., p. 12.

7. Ibid.

8. Ibid., p. 15.

9. Jonathan Barnett, *Urban Design as Public Policy: Practical Methods for Improving Cities* (New York: Architectural Record, 1974), p. 86.

10. Jane Jacobs, *The Death and Life of Great American Cities* (New York: Random House, 1961).

11. Herbert J. Gans, *The Urban Villagers: A Study of the Second Generation Italians in the West End of Boston* (Boston: Center for Community Studies, 1959).

12. Robert Venturi, *Complexity and Contradiction in Architecture* (New York: Museum of Modern Art; Distributed by Doubleday, Garden City, N.Y., 1966).

13. *Plan for New York City, 1969: A Proposal* (New York: New York City Planning Commission, 1969), 6 vols.

14. Huxtable, "Lindsay Surveys City from Copter," p. 8.

15. The Rudolph scheme, commissioned by the Ford Foundation in 1967, was reexamined in a major exhibition at the Cooper Union in 2010, which contained a spectacular model. By then, with the comfort of knowing that it would never happen, his design could be appreciated for its heroic grandeur and visionary ambition.

16. Maurice Carroll, "Mayor Drops Plans for Express Roads across 2 Boroughs; Mayor Abandons Plans for Expressways across Brooklyn and Lower Manhattan," *New York Times*, July 17, 1969.

17. Paley, *The Threatened City*, p. 26. No writer was officially credited with the text of the Paley report, but the task force included Walter McQuade, an admired writer and editor at *Fortune;* Robert A. M. Stern, who would go on to write several well-received books about New York City; and Philip Johnson, one of the city's most articulate architects. So it was not surprising that the prose rose above the level of the average bureaucratic report.

18. Paley, *The Threatened City,* p. 21.

19. Ibid., p. 25.

20. Ibid., p. 27.

21. Ibid.

22. Ibid., p. 21–22.

23. Ibid., p. 46–47.

24. Barnett, *Urban Design*, p. 7.

25. Ibid., p. 28.

26. Ibid., p. 23.

27. Van Ginkel Associates Ltd, and New York Office of Midtown Planning and Development, *Movement in Midtown: A Summary of a Study Prepared in Cooperation with Office of Midtown Planning and Development, Office of the Mayor, City of New York* (New York: City of New York, 1970).

28. Murray Schumach, "Feud Intensified over Park Roads; Plan for Cycle Race Turns into a Battle between Hoving and Barnes; Scooters Also Issue; Parks Chief Wants Public to Note Cut in Air Pollution and Noise during Race," *New York Times,* May 7, 1966, p. 45.

29. The majority opinion in the decision was by Justice William Brennan, who wrote:

"Underlying the opinion is the notion that aesthetic values, particularly historic preservation, are important public interests that justify restrictions on private land."

30. Steven R. Weisman, "Housing Unit Reports Progress on 'Scatter-Site' Goals for City," *New York Times,* November 28, 1971, p. 51.

31. Alexander Garvin, "Recycling New York," *Perspecta: The Yale Architecture Journal,* vol. 16, 1980, 73–75.

32. Barnett, *Urban Design,* pp. 94–97.

33. Urban Design Council of the City of New York, *Housing Quality: A Program for Zoning Reform* (New York: City of New York, 1973).

34. *Plan for New York City,* vol. I., p. 5.

35. Ibid.

36. Lewis Mumford, *From the Ground Up: Observations on Contemporary Architecture, Housing, Highway Building, and Civic Design* (New York: Harcourt, 1956), p. 207. Mumford's comments on the congestion problem were made in a series of articles he wrote for the *New Yorker's* "Sky Line" column in 1955. These articles were then collected a year later for his book, *From the Ground Up,* and turned into chapters: "Is New York Expendable?" "The Two-Way Flood," "Restored Circulation, Renewed Life," and "From the Ground Up." As the city grew denser in the 1950s, he grew increasingly frustrated by it and came to consider planning, which in his case meant an advocacy of the garden city, far more important than architecture.

37. Ibid., p. 209.

38. Ibid., p. 210.

39. *Plan for New York City,* vol. 1, p. 5.

40. Ibid.

41. Ibid.

42. Ibid., p. 6.

43. Hilary Ballon, "The Physical City," *America's Mayor: John V. Lindsay and the Reinvention of New York* (New York: The Museum of the City of New York and Columbia University Press, 2010), p. 132.

Scene at the redeveloped Brooklyn Navy Yard as John and Mary Lindsay christened the 1,094-foot-long supertanker *Brooklyn* during a send-off attended by five thousand officials and shipyard workers. June 30, 1973; photographer Meyer Liebowitz. *The New York Times*/Redux. Used with permission.

CHAPTER SEVEN

Governing at the Tipping Point
Shaping the City's Role in Economic Development

LIZABETH COHEN AND BRIAN GOLDSTEIN

Upon his inauguration as New York City's mayor on January 1, 1966, John V. Lindsay acknowledged the daunting situation he inherited: "New York City represents all that is exciting about our cities and everything that threatens to destroy them." But beyond this assertion, Lindsay's inaugural address gave relatively little attention to the fundamental transformations under way in New York City's economy, such as rising rates of poverty and joblessness, neither probing their root causes nor offering potential solutions. "The fight for new and better employment," as Lindsay termed his task, was just one among the many challenges he listed on the day he moved into City Hall.[1]

Yet, if Lindsay gave New York's economic instability only modest mention at first, it would quickly become a major preoccupation of his administration during his two mayoral terms spanning from 1966 to 1973. At the time of Lindsay's election, in the mid-1960s, New York found itself at the center of turbulent economic trends. Manufacturing, long New York's financial backbone, had declined at an increasing pace in the years preceding Lindsay's mayoralty and continued its precipitous drop during his administration. By 1975, industries that had employed more than a million New Yorkers in 1950 provided paychecks to barely half that many. While officials looked to the city's white-collar sectors to fill the gap, increasing departures for New York's suburbs by many of the best-known corporations shook confidence in the city's survival as the business capital of the nation. And as the city's middle-class families likewise departed for new suburban homes and schools, they left behind a residential population that was younger and older—and poorer, with blue-collar job skills increasingly obsolete in the city's rapidly transforming economic landscape.[2]

New York City faced crises common to many major American cities during Lindsay's eight years in office, but as the nation's largest city with a long-established industrial economy, New York witnessed the structural transformations commonly known as deindustrialization at an unprecedented scale. Likewise, while policy makers nationwide pursued job and revenue creation as a means of buoying declining urban centers, an arena that came to be known as "economic development," Lindsay's administration—given the visibility of New York—played for especially high stakes as it pursued those goals. Economic development became a realm of increasing importance both to cities and to the country as a whole in the late 1960s and early 1970s, but one that historians have largely overlooked in assessing the two-term mayoralty of Lindsay.

By no means the originator of the concept of economic development policy for cities, Lindsay served as New York's chief executive at a crucial time in the field's definition. The public sector in America, including at the municipal level, had played a role in stimulating private economic growth as early as the eighteenth century, by planning for the use of resources and by seeking to attract industry to new markets. But the term "economic development" had most frequently been used in the context of American interventions abroad. Not until the mid-1960s did it increasingly appear in the domestic urban realm, prompted by the unprecedented shifts under way in the American economy. The national Public Works and Economic Development Act of 1965, for example, established the Economic Development Administration as a federal office under the Department of Commerce, responsible for grant making to support job expansion projects in designated areas of high unemployment. Likewise, state and local governments adopted economic development as a widely used phrase and standard responsibility in their toolkit of governance by the early 1970s. During the era of Lindsay's mayoralty, economic development moved into the mainstream work of urban public officials, who believed that they could reshape the character of local employment at a time of great change. Lindsay shared this belief.[3]

Lindsay's tenure at such a pivotal moment in the history of American capitalism reveals much about his approach to policy making as well as his vision of economic development itself. While mention of economic development today often brings to mind generous tax giveaways to corporations threatening departure or incentive-laden negotiations to attract new business, in this chapter we argue that Lindsay's approach offered a broader, more democratic vision of the possibilities of economic growth. In an era of transition from an industrial- to a service-based economy, Lindsay brought confidence that government, acting in the public interest, could manage such transformation by working in three major realms. First, in seeking to retain New York's increasingly footloose corporate headquarters, Lindsay pursued collaborative partnerships with the private sector, in whom he encouraged faith in the distinctive qualities of New York City. Second, in attempting to counteract rampant deindustrialization, he aimed to use spatial redevelopment to benefit New York's working-class residents. And, third, in aspiring to bolster the city's economy in new ways, he expanded and enhanced the commercial and creative sectors that made New York unique. All three components of this approach to economic development grew fundamentally from Lindsay's faith in the ameliorative power of the state and in the intrinsic value of dense, urban places at a moment when many in the country saw New York City as epitomizing all that was going wrong with America.

Lindsay's mayoralty has proven imperfect in retrospect, and his policies ultimately insufficient to stem broad shifts that reshaped the city long after his term. He achieved only mixed results in his campaign to give a new economic profile to New York. If his vision was marked by overconfidence that the city could navigate increasingly rough seas, however, his shortcomings were due in great part to the fact that the city's economy was becoming a cog in a global economic machine that he could only fix with the limited tools of a mayor. Where Lindsay succeeded best was in the cultural realm, in which New York could be its own boss, with fewer constraints imposed by the workings of an international economy.

Stemming Corporate Flight

New York City had gained an increasingly white-collar character in the years preceding Lindsay's election, a transformation that continued apace upon his assumption of the city's top office. The new economy of New York became a point of pride for city officials, who envisioned the city's transformation into a dense metropolis distinguished by its concentration of corporate headquarters, blue-chip law and advertising firms, and major commercial banks. Consequently, Lindsay's administration largely stood aside as private investors transformed Midtown and Downtown Manhattan into skyscraper canyons, often marveling at the seemingly miraculous transformation such new development wrought in a city previously characterized by an aging, industrial-era streetscape. Yet the go-go commercial real estate market of the Lindsay era hid threatening fractures. Just as the city's economy came to rest on an office-based foundation, many of the city's best-known corporations were fleeing its bounds. If such departures were in part a repudiation of the city's urban qualities, Lindsay responded by celebrating that very urbanity. Corporations, he argued in almost moralistic terms, thrived best in the cities whose density had birthed them, and he invited their leaders to share in improving the city.

In the early 1950s, a visitor to New York City was three times more likely to see a factory worker or a seamstress on the city's streets than an insurance salesman, stockbroker, or government employee. A decade later, he or she would have still found more than twice as many employees in manufacturing as in finance, insurance, and real estate and 50 percent more than in service industries. By 1970, halfway into Lindsay's term, however, a greater share of New York's workers claimed employment in services such as law and advertising than in the city's declining blue-collar industries. Wall Street employees had more than doubled in the preceding twelve years. Fifteen percent of employed NewYorkers worked for local, state, or federal government, a sector that would eclipse manufacturing employment a mere five years later. New York's employed residents increasingly spent their workdays in modern offices, not in aging factories.[4]

Indeed, the streetscape of white-collar New York began to look dramatically different. As sheer glass skyscrapers took over block after block in Midtown and Downtown in Lindsay's first term, hyperbolic descriptions rang true. "A survey of Manhattan office building construction shows that more office space will be completed this year in the midtown area than has ever been built in one year in the entire borough," claimed the *New York Times* in 1968. The nearly seven million square feet finished that year would double the next year, when developers completed nearly fourteen million additional square footage. Those twelve months, the city's Economic Development Administrator said, made the city the site of 25 percent of the commercial development in the entire country.[5]

As the strong economy of the late 1960s propelled companies to expand, developers could not build fast enough to keep up with the ambitions of the city's business tenants. In January 1967, for example, the city's businesses had already leased nearly all the space slotted for completion in the following twelve months, yielding absurdly low vacancy rates. In the Midtown blocks between 50th and 60th Streets, vacancy had dipped to 0.4 percent, while citywide vacancy dropped to half a percent, spiking commercial rents. A loosening credit market in the last years of the decade facilitated commercial construction on an increasing scale, and city officials largely stood aside as developers snatched up empty parcels, replaced existing buildings, and refurbished existing space to meet robust demand.[6]

New York officials had long maintained a relatively hands-off approach to real estate development in Manhattan, depending on zoning as a regulatory tool but largely allowing the private market to determine the shape of the city's central business district. This attitude persisted into the Lindsay administration, which created neighborhood development offices to reduce bureaucratic red tape and invented new zoning techniques to promote certain land uses (discussed later in this chapter), but nonetheless still permitted private developers to build aggressively. Policy makers approved of the torrid pace of construction, hoping it would preserve New York's importance as the business, commercial, and cultural nerve center for the rest of the country. They formalized this aspiration in the 1969 *Plan for New York City*.

Describing New York's function as a "National Center," the City Planning Commission, the plan's author, boasted that "this growth is the reason why New York City has not had to use public funds to subsidize the redevelopment of its business district." Members of the commission predicted continued growth and thus greater economic returns. "This is the most dynamic kind of growth to have," they argued. "It will multiply job opportunities. By strengthening the City's economic base, it will make the City better able to tackle its weaknesses."[7]

But this celebration of New York City as a national center for commerce obscured a disturbing trend that worsened over the course of Lindsay's mayoralty. As many of New York's leading companies built new headquarters in the city center, many others began looking to the city's outer reaches, to other regions, and particularly to suburban enclaves that eschewed the density that Lindsay and his planners celebrated. Suburbanization of offices away from New York City had been under way since the end of World War II, long before Lindsay took office. But outmigration of the city's largest businesses reached a new scale in this era as residential suburbanization mushroomed. Assessments of the trend were often based on *Fortune* magazine's yearly index of the five hundred largest American industrial companies, the "*Fortune* 500," a list that New York City had long dominated with pride.

While the precise number of New York corporations on the list changed year-to-year due to moves, mergers, and varying economic fortunes, the city had claimed around 135 *Fortune* 500 firms each year during the decade preceding Lindsay's first term. At that time, departing firms were generally replaced by incoming entities. Soon after Lindsay took office, however, the pace of departures increased, and numerous mergers further diminished the city's hold on the *Fortune* 500. Whereas there were 139 *Fortune* 500 members located in New York in 1967, only ninety-eight remained at the close of 1974. Forty firms had moved out of the city in those seven years. Most damning, perhaps, four of the seven headquarters to move to New York between 1968 and 1971 departed within a few years.[8] A 1971 study by the office of then–New York City Congressman Ed Koch uncovered the extent to which corporate headquarters in his Midtown district were considering departure. Forty-five percent of sixty-one respondents acknowledged that they were at least entertaining the option, while eleven of those twenty-seven were already in the midst of planning moves.[9]

Although corporate headquarters departed at a quickening pace under Lindsay's watch, his administration hardly bears the sole blame. Indeed, executives gave a range of reasons for their departures, from the personal to the professional. Some wished to live closer to their homes, to escape long commutes, or to find cheaper housing for themselves and employees. Schools and New York City's reputation for crime motivated others, who saw greener pastures in suburban New York's Westchester and Nassau Counties, in Greenwich and Stamford, Connecticut, or in Englewood Cliffs and Parsippany, New Jersey. Many executives claimed that they could more easily recruit employees to new suburban campuses or could draw from a more desirable, better-trained pool of potential workers. The very density that city planners celebrated ironically spurred many such moves. Once New York's vacancy rate approached zero, rent costs and space limitations prompted expanding firms to look farther afield.

But Lindsay's changes to the city's tax code in 1966 contributed to departures too, introducing the city's first income tax as well as a commuter tax, a price that companies could avoid by moving closer to executives' suburban homes. Lindsay argued that the new taxes were necessary to finance the broad range of services the city provided to its residents and workforce, but such costs offered an easy excuse to firms already predisposed to departing, a fact that competing hamlets preyed upon. "Pick Conn[ecticut] for your headquarters," one advertisement in the *New York Times* beckoned (figure 7.2). "Enjoy the tax advantages and 'the Connecticut way of life.' "[10]

Corporate departures undermined the city's hopes that its white-collar employers would take up the slack in declining manufacturing sectors. One evaluation estimated that departing companies took with them as many as ten thousand jobs each year in the early 1970s. With headquarters representing as much as half of the city's office employment, departures from that sector seriously harmed the city's bottom line. But even more problematic, the departure of national headquarters deeply embarrassed the city, threatening its reputation as America's greatest city for business. Departing firms included many of the country's biggest and best-known enterprises, and their announcements made front-page news. PepsiCo broadcast its exit to Purchase, New York, in 1967. American Can Company began constructing a sprawling modern campus in Greenwich, Connecticut, in the same year. Olin Mathieson, Shell Oil, Chesebrough-Ponds, and General Telephone were just a few of those that followed. Even the city's landmark institutions publicly entertained flight. The New York Stock Exchange contemplated departure in response to Lindsay's proposal to increase the tax on stock transfers. The Yankees, too, considered departing, a move that the city thwarted with its purchase and renovation of Yankee Stadium. The Giants football team, however, did follow many of the city's corporate headquarters to New Jersey, where that state built them a new stadium in the Meadowlands.[11]

Lindsay publicly attempted to save face amid such visible departures, often pointing to the firms that were arriving in the city as others were moving out. But

Pick Conn. for your headquarters.

Olin's Chemicals Group did.

New headquarters for the Chemicals Group, Olin Mathieson Chemical Corporation, in Stamford.

Connecticut is in the news headlines as management makes strategic plans for new corporate headquarters. Four of the major reasons for choosing Connecticut are taxes, location, labor and living. Look into Connecticut. Start by writing for your free copy of "Connecticut's Favorable Tax Climate".

Enjoy the tax advantages and "the Connecticut way of life."

CONNECTICUT DEVELOPMENT COMMISSION
Room 100, State Office Building, Hartford, Conn. 06115

Advertisement placed by the Connecticut Development Commission in the *New York Times*. April 9, 1967. Reproduced with permission of the State of Connecticut Department of Economic and Community Development.

as companies left at a quickening pace during his two terms, he implemented more concrete measures intended to stem the ongoing bleeding.[12] Lindsay's approach to corporate flight encompassed interrelated strategies. First, his administration publicly articulated a defense of the fundamental qualities of the city in response to departures, asserting the value of New York's density for business success and underlining the deficiencies of a suburban location. A self-described "one man chamber of commerce," Lindsay served as the city's most enthusiastic cheerleader. Minutes after the announced departure of Chesebrough-Ponds in 1971, for example, Lindsay addressed a lunchtime audience. "This is the city dynamic," he said. "It has more diversity, competitiveness, energy and toughness than anywhere else."

The Lindsay administration promoted the city's size and density as its greatest attributes, not its liabilities. "We start out with the concept that the city is a good thing—a workable form of social organization," explained Donald Elliott, Lindsay's top planning official. "Concentration is the genius of the City, its reason for being, the source of its vitality and its excitement," planners similarly wrote in the 1969 blueprint for the city. In contrast, officials criticized the limitations of suburbia. "The outlying areas," Lindsay said in 1966, "are not geared for [handling] the kind of racial tensions that the big cities are." And not only were they poorly equipped to meet the challenges of a diverse American society. "There is a lack of mass transportation," the mayor argued, "there is overlapping taxation and an unavailability of suitable labor in many of these satellite centers." Those who fled cities looking for utopia, Lindsay claimed, would find similar conditions and no means to repair them. "Politicians who think cities should be avoided are making a big mistake," he warned.[13]

Not all corporate leaders wanted to flee the city. Some of those who stayed joined Mayor Lindsay in his pro-urban crusade. Under his second strategy, Lindsay sought alliances with New York's corporate executives on the premise that the city's public and private sectors shared equally in the city's gains and losses. If such public-private cooperation has now become common, at the time Lindsay's interest in uniting city hall with corporate boardrooms seemed novel. "The city needs the help and support of the business community more than at any time before," Lindsay said in 1967. "If we were as small as Pittsburgh, the Mellons could do it all. . . . But we are huge. Everyone has to come in." His work with New York's Economic Development Council embodied this sentiment. The council, formed in 1965 on the eve of the mayoral election that ushered in Lindsay, included representatives of the city's major corporations, including the board chairmen of Chase Manhattan Bank, Equitable Life Assurance, and R. H. Macy and Company, and the president of the New York Central Railroad.[14]

Lindsay met regularly with the members of the Economic Development Council. They, in turn, assisted him with efforts to retain fellow corporations through suasion and personal connections. Clarence Francis, the council's president and a former chairman at General Foods, joined Lindsay repeatedly in appealing to wavering executives to maintain their headquarters in New York. Together they approached twenty-five such corporations in the year preceding April 1967, keeping departures to only five. Other members served as an alert system for the city government, devising a process by which employees of associated banks and utilities would notify leaders if they detected a company contemplating departure, at which point the information would be passed along to officials so they could intercede.[15] Moreover, Economic Development Council members joined Lindsay's administration in promoting a pro-urban vision, resulting in a clever 1967 and 1968 ad campaign that promoted New York as a matchless place. The city's major papers ran the spreads, each of which closed, "New York is New York. Is there anywhere else?" One poked fun at those who sought to leave the city behind. "Let's all 8 million of us move to L.A.," it proclaimed. Add a subway, skyscrapers, apartment buildings, great restaurants, museums, and a grand park in the center of it all, the ad proposed, and "it will be even better." "Yeah, it's going to be great in L.A. when we get there," the copy concluded. "Because we, the most dynamic 8 million people on earth, could take any place and turn it into New York City. The most dynamic place on earth."[16]

Public relations, partnerships, negotiation, and personal appeals by a famously charismatic mayor made up the "soft" tools of economic development policy. In part such strategies derived from the circumstances in which Lindsay governed. At the time, state law prohibited the city from offering the kinds of public incentives to private entities that would later become customary in retaining fugitive corporations, such as tax abatements or benefit packages designed to compete with other cities. The Lindsay administration's tactics also responded to the reality of the situation. As one major assessment of corporate flight explained, the city's means were "really quite limited." Once a corporation began to discuss leaving New York, executives had already determined the benefits they would glean and had often selected a site for a new campus. By then, Lindsay's entreaties that New York's density offered amenities no other place could match fell on the deaf ears of executives anticipating a shorter commute from home to their executive suite.[17]

Yet Lindsay's relative restraint in responding to corporate departures also grew from his faith that the city's explosive growth would continue indefinitely. Lindsay often comforted himself with the thought that the loss of one company would mean little in a city with hundreds more. A *New York Times* reporter who asked the mayor about departing businesses in 1973, near the end of his mayoralty, was met with "obvious irritation." "What you guys don't report is businesses moving into the city. We're putting up more offices in this downtown area—and renting them—than the next 10 largest cities combined," Lindsay boasted.[18] But, by the mayor's second term, the tight office market of the late 1960s had loosened considerably. The recession that hit at the turn of the decade constrained firms' ability to afford expansion within the city, new technology enabled offices to accomplish more in less square footage, and corporate departures gained momentum. It had taken years to build the huge, often block-filling skyscrapers that developers had planned in the midst of the go-go 1960s, and then, when space finally became available, the demand was not there to fill it. Almost 14 million square feet of office space joined the city's inventory in 1969, and another 16 million became available in 1971, including the first portion of the World Trade Center. Developers completed even more square footage the following year. As a result, commercial vacancy, just half a percent in 1967, stood at 14 percent in October 1973. "Thirty million square feet of office space stand empty," the City Planning Commission fretted, "more than all the occupied offices in Boston, Philadelphia, and Houston combined."[19]

In the midst of this crisis, the city's "soft" approach of collaborating with the private sector but allowing it to develop projects largely unfettered seemed too limited. As planners wrote, "The City heretofore assumed that the construction decisions made and carried out by the private sector were unqualified benefits to the City . . . and furthered the objective of developing new jobs. In the face of the negative aspects of the building cycle, the City Planning Commission now questions whether measures might be taken to even the pace of office development." Planners began to advocate that the city take a stronger regulatory role in controlling the pace and nature of future development, perhaps even going so far as securing the power to approve or deny future construction to minimize booms and busts.[20]

But planners' assumptions that there would even be robust commercial construction to regulate now looked overly optimistic. Early in Lindsay's first term, the Regional Plan Association (RPA) had forecast that Manhattan would add half a million jobs in the city's headquarters and supporting offices by the year 2000, a projection that had served as the basis for the City Planning Commission's vision of the island as a booming "national center." The very different reality that presented itself by the end of Lindsay's tenure led the RPA to scale down its prediction. It now suggested that demand was so slack that the city would not need to build another new office tower for the next twenty-five years.[21] As the city's commercial market bottomed out and corporations continued to depart, Lindsay's confidence in the city's enduring preeminence as America's white-collar capital increasingly appeared as overconfidence.

Creating Space for Industry

The Lindsay administration may have kept its regulatory distance from the corporate leadership it was putting so much faith in, but it intervened in a more hands-on way to preserve the city's industrial economy. Officials understood the loss of blue-collar jobs as a spatial crisis—literally, a lack of space in the city for manufacturing to expand—and responded with spatial solutions. While Lindsay's staff pictured central Manhattan as a vibrant commercial center, they balanced this conception by seeking new space in the city's outer boroughs to employ working-class laborers: new shipping terminals on the waterfront, expanded factories, and state-of-the-art industrial parks competitive with the suburbs. This goal was consistent with Lindsay's dual hope that residents' employment problems could be solved within the city limits and that the power of government could help New York's most disadvantaged populations. In an era of deindustrialization, suburbanization, and technological change, however, this commitment proved an especially Sisyphean task.

If the departure of prominent corporate headquarters captured the headlines, the less remarked upon but simultaneous closure and migration of New York's industries had a far more devastating impact on the city's economy. Such firms once numbered in the tens of thousands, and each typically employed a modest workforce. Their increasing disappearance from the landscape of New York took place gradually, not in massive blows, but the damage added up quickly. In 1960, the city housed almost thirty-six thousand manufacturing firms. By 1966, the year of Lindsay's election, there were fewer than thirty-one thousand firms. Four years later, the number had diminished to just over twenty-six thousand, with an average of twenty-nine employees each. With each year, fewer longshoremen broke bulk on the waterfront. Fewer garment workers and printers produced clothing and books. Fewer New Yorkers clocked in and out at sugar refineries and candy companies.[22]

The causes of this industrial decline varied. New York's ports, long the East Coast's major shipping center, met crippling obstacles in the decades preceding Lindsay's term. The city's piers had deteriorated over the postwar era while officials sparred over who should take responsibility for their improvement. Labor strife, corruption, pilfering, and mob control helped drive up the costs of shipping into New York City. Meanwhile, regional, national, and international competitors gained ground, and the city even faced new competition just across the harbor. In the 1950s, the Port Authority of New York, rebuffed by New York City officials who wished to maintain control of the city's ports, began to develop Port Newark, a nearby waterside site that avoided the complicated shipping maneuvers and congestion involved in bringing goods into New York City.[23]

Port Newark and its soon-to-be-built southern neighbor, Port Elizabeth, were already major threats to New York by the early 1960s, when technological developments further threatened the city's aging harbor. Air travel made passenger shipping rapidly obsolete and the transformation of cargo shipping from break bulk to containerization had an even more devastating impact on the profitability of New York's port. Where longshoremen had once loaded and unloaded goods by hand in small bundles, now massive cranes lifted standardized shipping containers and trucks easily transported them, vastly reducing the human labor necessary for operations. Manhattan's docks simply could not sustain the scale of infrastructure required as containerization became the expected standard. But the Port Authority, deeply invested in its less constrained New Jersey ports, rapidly upgraded them to accept containers. While the New York–New Jersey area remained a major shipping destination in whole, New York City's role in that industry plummeted, as did the number of residents who made the docks their workplace and who supported the shipping industry as wholesalers and transporters.[24]

New York's decline as a port reverberated in the factories whose goods had begun their voyage to the world's markets from the city's docks. Its shipping and manufacturing dominance had long been intimately connected. Factories in Brooklyn or Manhattan, usually operating at a small scale, could easily and quickly move their goods from shop floors to far-flung destinations from the shipping piers that surrounded much of the city until the mid-twentieth century. Propinquity played a major role, as suppliers passed material to neighboring factories and single longshoremen moved finished goods onto nearby ships. Containerization totally changed the game. With the low cost of transporting a standardized shipping container, the convenient proximity of shop to pier ceased to be a meaningful consideration, freeing companies to move where trucks could easily access factories by highway and to where space and labor were cheaper—often out of the city.[25]

Containerization joined other factors to diminish industrial New York. Indeed, manufacturing plants could point to as many reasons for their departure as could corporate headquarters. Factories moved to suburbs and to the American South and West to avoid organized labor, to obtain lower energy costs, and, like their front office counterparts, to escape high taxation. Additional problems were distinctive to particular industries. The garment trades in Manhattan, for example, felt constrained by dense traffic on the streets of their historic district. Other factories were displaced by the city's own plans. Urban redevelopment schemes throughout the city forced out businesses as well as residences. Institutional, housing, and highway construction uprooted tens of thousands of jobs. One city official estimated in 1963 that redevelopment had demolished nearly six million square feet of manufacturing space just in the first three and a half years of the decade. And most, if not all, industries who left sought to gain more space for their operations. New York's factories, often in aging buildings in congested neighborhoods, with little room to expand, hailed from the era of small-scale production that looked less and less profitable in the era of the container. With broad highways connecting the urban periphery to lucrative markets, factories large and small departed New York City's center.[26]

New York's industrial landscape declined just as the city's workforce was changing in ways precisely unsuited to the city's new white-collar economy. In the decades preceding Lindsay's mayoralty and continuing during his two terms, New York's population expanded with new arrivals who had skills more appropriate for blue-collar employment than for service-sector jobs. Officials explained this twist in the labor market in the 1969 *Plan for New York City.* "The number of good jobs in the City has been increasing," they wrote. "But there is a cruel mismatch between jobs and men. The growth sector of the City's economy is in white-collar and skilled blue-collar work. The growth in the labor force is in people who cannot qualify for either." Factories had once offered New Yorkers entry into a solid middle class through trades that provided secure employment, but such opportunities had diminished tremendously. "They cannot get a good job because they do not have the education, or the skill. They are the high school dropouts, the unskilled migrants or the people whose skills become outdated or irrelevant," planners wrote. Deindustrialization disproportionately affected New York City's minority population, particularly growing numbers of underskilled African Americans and Puerto Ricans. "Most of the poor are white," the 1969 plan explained, "but hardest hit are the younger low-skilled blacks and Puerto Ricans and their numbers are increasing every year." The city's total population had remained essentially stable from 1950 to 1970, increasing only from 7,892,000 to 7,895,000. But the African American population in New York increased by more than 900,000 in that span, to 1,668,000, and the city's Puerto Rican population expanded by 600,000, to 847,000, making these new, often working-class job seekers an ever-larger presence in the city.[27]

Faced with this mismatch between job growth and labor market, Lindsay articulated an economic vision for New York that aspired to provide more opportunity to the city's most disadvantaged residents. As recounted in earlier chapters, Lindsay famously showed great concern for the city's minority population. Likewise, in the realm of employment, Lindsay explained early in his administration, "Our goal is nothing short of offering every New Yorker the chance at a decent job." In an era when New York's population was shifting dramatically, Lindsay sought strategies to employ new residents. "There is a social as well as an economic imperative," the City Planning Commission explained. "The City needs more and better blue-collar jobs and it needs them now."[28]

But effecting economic growth in sectors that were rapidly declining was not easy, as it required challenging trends not contained within the city's physical limits and economic control. Deindustrialization was a regional, national, and international phenomenon. Although many factors drove it, each suggesting particular local remedies, the Lindsay administration fixed on the crisis of space as the major factor precipitating departures. "A study we did some time ago revealed that the Number One cause these companies give for leaving the city is lack of space for expansion," explained Lindsay's commissioner of Commerce and Industrial Development in 1966. That diagnosis suggested a solution. He went on, "Our main job is finding space that our own industry can expand to." Whereas Lindsay celebrated the city's density as an attraction for the white-collar economy in Manhattan, ironically that very density was proving a liability for industrial operations in the outer boroughs, whose ambitions were constrained by the city's concentration. If the city could provide space within its bounds to enable expansion and relocation of industry, Lindsay reasoned, the city could achieve its goal of a decent job for all of its residents. "We have to provide land for buildings with capacity to match the production and profit levels required for full employment at satisfactory earnings," he explained. "We are not doing that today."[29]

Public Action

As Lindsay faced the daunting task of creating more space for industry, he envisioned the public sector as the key player, not the public-private collaboration that he had employed in the corporate arena. The mayor had commissioned a study of the city's urban redevelopment policy early in his administration, an effort led by Edward Logue, at the time the chief of redevelopment in Boston. The study, called "Let There Be Commitment," criticized the strategies and outcomes of urban renewal in previous administrations, especially the program's narrow focus on residential construction. "An overall area of agreement is that, in its hectic rush to narrow the housing gap, New York has blinded itself to other areas of physical need," the report contended, criticizing the city's neglect of such realms as schools, parks, community facilities, and industrial sites. With this report under Lindsay's belt, urban redevelopment would gain variety that it had largely lacked in preceding decades, when Robert Moses directed the city's renewal program. Lindsay displayed new sensitivity to the city's historic buildings, more interest in an inclusive process of planning, and greater desire for an innovative approach to developing city land, in order to create jobs for the city's growing blue-collar population.[30]

Lindsay's administration expressed confidence that public intervention could slow—if not reverse—seemingly inevitable economic shifts. This belief reflected Lindsay's liberal commitment to the power of government. "The City's economy has its own dynamics and there is only so much the government can do to shape it," the 1969 *Plan for New York City* acknowledged. Yet, regardless of those limitations, the public sector still maintained a crucial role. "That margin is critically important," the authors continued. "If the City uses its points of leverage it can generate a large number of jobs—and good jobs, jobs that lead to advancement."[31] To this end, soon after taking office Lindsay established a semipublic agency, the Public Development Corporation, sanctioned to take control of city-owned land and to issue bonds to finance tax-exempt industrial development projects. State legislative approval enabled the Public Development Corporation to lease land to private entities for long terms at modest rates, a measure intended to make space for industrial expansion available to firms looking for land within the city limits. Lindsay likewise established an Economic Development Administration as part of his broader reorganization of city government into superagencies, a bureaucratic change that demonstrated the administration's commitment to facilitating industrial expansion in the city (see chapter 5).[32]

Lindsay's vision for the growth of New York's blue-collar economy imagined a geographic differentiation of labor markets in the city. Manhattan's central business district would become the "national center" of corporate America, while industry would rise in northern Manhattan and the outer boroughs. Thus, an industry like Manhattan's garment trade, long the seat of apparel manufacturing in the United States, found that city officials were decidedly ambivalent in providing needed assistance to keep it in its central location. "I think there is merit to any disillusionment that the garment industry may feel about the city's lack of progress in the last year in helping it to solve its problems," admitted Richard Lewisohn, then Lindsay's commissioner of commerce and industrial development, in 1967. Lindsay himself expressed both pride in New York's famed garment district and frustration with the impact it had on the surrounding Midtown commercial area. "The whole thing is like real handicraft industry—like making the cuckoo clock in Switzerland or going to Rheims and seeing the champagne and wine cellars, the grapes at one side and the bottle of wine at the other," the mayor told an interviewer. "They do business on the street, up and down corridors, over a hamburger and a cup of coffee. But what it does to us in congestion!"[33]

Officials proved enthusiastic about blue-collar expansion outside of the dense city center, however, pursuing a range of strategies with that outcome in mind. At the smallest scale, the Lindsay administration helped relatively modest industrial operations grow beyond their existing facilities. In partnership with the state, the city provided low-interest loans to small manufacturers early in Lindsay's first term. Katina Gianopoulos, for example, owned a thirty-year-old coffee roasting company in Brooklyn that hoped to double its workforce—from four to eight—and quadruple its square footage, an expansion that became possible by borrowing $30,000 from the city. With the establishment of the Public Development Corporation, the city could more directly assist manufacturers in need of greater space. Lindsay introduced a vest-pocket industrial program to this end, an initiative that reflected the smaller scale common in much of his redevelopment policy. Officials helped amass parcels to support the expansion of existing factories and to enable new businesses to enter the city. The S&S Corrugated Paper Machinery Company had made its home in Williamsburg, Brooklyn, for fifty years when it purchased a twenty-acre site in suburban New Jersey in the mid-1960s, looking to leave New York behind. But, before its executives took the next steps, the firm responded favorably to an offer of aid from the city, which provided a parcel adjacent to the S&S factory. The Public Development Corporation leased the Williamsburg plot to S&S for twenty-five years and closed streets adjacent to the factory, allowing the plant to remain in the borough and to add 96,000 square feet to its operation. That the new parcel had been the home of a hundred low-income families, however, proved controversial—and suggested the priority the city put on retaining industry.[34]

Such efforts paled in comparison to the most ambitious plans the Lindsay administration undertook: to salvage the city's place in the region's shipping network and to spur large-scale development in vast industrial parks. Officials acknowledged that the city would never return to its former glory as the heart of worldwide shipping, but they nonetheless sought to retain at least a foothold in the transportation of goods. "Containerization caught the City government asleep," the 1969 plan admitted. Officials forsook Manhattan, once the jewel in the Port of New York's crown, but hoped that peripheral waterfront development could support the new technology that had transformed shipping. "The Manhattan waterfront cannot compete for containership freight. There is not enough back-up space," planners wrote. "New container freight terminals within the City should be in Brooklyn and Staten Island."[35]

The city pushed for a "showcase" container port for the northeast corner of Staten Island in Lindsay's first year as mayor, a 135-acre plan that entailed the replacement of old piers with a new wharf to be leased to private concerns. Then Jakob

Isbrandtsen, a prominent shipping magnate, offered the city a vastly larger 550-acre site in northwest Staten Island a few months later for an additional container port, a project that Isbrandtsen developed with enthusiastic administration support. In Lindsay's second term, officials extended their effort with a proposal to begin yet another container port in Red Hook, Brooklyn. In urging Board of Estimate approval, Ken Patton, then the leader of Lindsay's Economic Development Administration, reminded officials of New York's "once unchallenged preeminence in maritime commerce." This plan would "create 500 new waterfront jobs and 2,200 jobs in such directly allied activities as trucking and warehousing," Patton claimed, while "four thousand existing jobs would be preserved." Whether the city could sustain enough berths to restore lost luster remained a question for the future, but the opening of these new ports certainly blessed Lindsay with glowing publicity. Lindsay gleefully dedicated the largest container crane ever built at the opening of the Brooklyn port in July 1973, breaking a bottle of New York State wine on its wheels. Soon after, the mayor proudly announced that the northwest Staten Island port, which the city planned to purchase, had attracted the United States Lines, a major shipping operation, back to New York City from Port Elizabeth, New Jersey.[36]

The development of industrial parks likewise aimed to preserve and restore blue-collar work in the city. Such parks were not a Lindsay invention. His predecessor as mayor, Robert F. Wagner Jr., had initiated several plans to designate large areas within the city limits for industrial development, but Wagner's efforts had languished amid bureaucratic dithering. The Flatlands Industrial Park, for example, a 96-acre plot in Brooklyn, had been designated for development in 1959 but only received Board of Estimate approval in the last weeks before Lindsay took office. Likewise, the Wagner administration had considered projects for College Point in Queens and for Staten Island in the early 1960s but made little progress moving them from paper to reality. This history of slow action prompted an Urban Land Institute study of industrial development in New York to come down hard on the city's record. The city, the institute's analysts wrote in 1968, had not only contributed to departures by prioritizing housing development but had also made tardy and ineffectual responses to industrial flight. The city had land to offer yet had not done so on a meaningful scale, a conclusion that Lindsay shared when he promoted the city's industrial park program. "We have to provide land for buildings with capacity to match the production and profit levels required for full employment at satisfactory earnings," Lindsay responded to the Urban Land Institute report. "We are not doing that today."[37]

By the midpoint of Lindsay's first term, he had activated industrial park projects in each outer borough: on Staten Island, at Flatlands and the Navy Yard in

Brooklyn, at College Point in Queens, and at Hunts Point in the Bronx, a site that would become the city's center for food wholesaling. Though not the largest park, the plan to transform the Navy Yard from a military installation into an industrial campus marked the most symbolic effort to make new space available to address the loss of the city's blue-collar sectors. The Navy Yard had occupied its Brooklyn site since the eighteenth century, growing into its role as one of the largest employers in the borough and the largest navy shipyard in the nation. But the yard and many of its counterparts elsewhere fell victim to defense cuts in the mid-1960s. Closure brought the loss of as many as fifteen thousand jobs, especially affecting workers in surrounding Brooklyn neighborhoods. The shattered property was well suited for development, providing not just vast acreage on the waterfront but also extensive existing infrastructure for industry, including a number of large buildings, piers, dry docks, and rail connections, all of which the city purchased from the federal government.[38]

Officials expressed ambitious hopes for the future of the Navy Yard, a site that Lindsay characterized as ideal for "badly-needed, high wage, steady jobs" that some-day would employ tens of thousands of New Yorkers. "Eventually as many as 40,000 jobs may spring from that one enterprise, not to mention the 'multiplier' effect around the surrounding neighborhoods," Lindsay wrote in his 1970 book, *The City*. Such goals set a high bar, but New York's newspapers shared the administration's optimism that they were achievable. "Thousands of Jobs to Open at Navy Yard Site," the *New York Amsterdam News* announced in early 1969. "Brooklyn Navy Yard Starting to Hum Again," the *New York Times* claimed a few months later. Two years later, the *Times* offered a paean to the resurgent Navy Yard. "Navy Yard Revives on a Grand Scale," the headline proclaimed. "The battleship *Arizona*, now resting on the bottom of Pearl Harbor, was built there, as was the *Maine*, whose destruction in Havana harbor in 1898 touched off the Spanish-American War. The battleship *Missouri*, on whose deck Japan surrendered in 1945, was built in the yard." The yard's historic importance would continue deep into the twentieth century, the writer explained. "Now a giant tanker, twice the size of the largest ever built in this country, is taking shape." Indeed, by the close of the 1960s, the Navy Yard included a manufacturer making commercial ovens and pollution control equipment, a book bindery, and a factory producing scales, among others. Seatrain Shipbuilding Corporation restored the yard's original trade, an effort that was soon to turn 1,500 tons of steel into one of the largest crafts ever to set sail from American shores.[39]

Seatrain called its new tanker the T. T. *Brooklyn*, a name commemorative not just of the factory's location but also of its 2,700-person workforce, 1,800 of whom called the borough home (see figure at the beginning of the chapter). Lindsay presided at the tanker's debut (July 1973 was apparently a banner month for christenings), and, while Mary Lindsay missed in smashing the champagne against the ship, the mayor remained buoyant at the joyful occasion. The Navy Yard, he remembered, once full of workers during his service as a Navy man in World War II, was a windswept landscape by the time he returned as mayor. Now, the revitalized Yard and the T.T. *Brooklyn* built there were signs of the "enormous vitality and viability of New York City," the mayor announced, evidence that the city could slow or reverse its blue-collar decline.[40]

Even with successes at the scale of a supertanker, some observers still wondered whether the administration's industrial development efforts were actually bailing out a sinking ship with a thimble. One assessment by the City Planning Commission at the close of Lindsay's mayoralty noted that even the city's efforts to provide land at low cost often proved insufficient for firms looking to expand. "After costing actual building plans, many firms found that expansion was too expensive," staff wrote. "The renewal program has not offered gross rents that make new construction in the City competitive with other locations." Industrial parks and assistance with land acquisition at small sites helped some firms expand their operations, but aggregate manufacturing employment continued to decline throughout Lindsay's second term. Another four thousand firms left the city between 1970 and the end of 1973. "The returns in terms of increased employment have been disappointing. It is time to decide whether the program can and should be made to work, or whether it should be discontinued," the Planning Commission reluctantly acknowledged.

Planners wondered whether the city should instead turn to more aggressive incentives, such as the tax abatements that were common in the city's residential market and would become ubiquitous in economic development after Lindsay's tenure, or take a new tack entirely. At stake were fundamental philosophical questions about the role of government in the city's changing economy. Was the city wasting money by subsidizing the declining manufacturing sector, or did it have the responsibility to provide a raft for its working-class citizens amid rough economic seas? For Lindsay, even if the outcomes were not always as significant as hoped, or as long lasting, the answer to the latter question was an unequivocal "yes." Others were not so sure, recognizing perhaps more presciently than Lindsay that New York's loss of blue-collar jobs was part of a major global, not simply regional, restructuring of the location of industrial production.[41]

A Livable City

Lindsay's most lasting success in economic development came not from these efforts to stem the departures of white-collar and blue-collar businesses but out of the experimental mode that marked his administration even at its darkest hours. "Fun city" was born as a phrase ridiculing the mayor's optimism amid the crippling transit strike that began his mayoralty, but the spirit of invention that marked the two Lindsay terms—of "happenings," artistic performance, and public spectacle (discussed more fully in the next chapter)—proved his most visible legacy as well as an economically profitable one.[42] Lindsay's exuberance for celebrating the city's intrinsic qualities, often the very qualities that seemed to motivate departures from it by business and industry, foreshadowed a future in which New York's economic base would rest increasingly on its identity as a cultural icon and retail paradise. It was in this realm that Lindsay proved most perceptive, building on the city's assets rather than attempting to resist unrelenting economic transformations. In this sense, Lindsay anticipated the direction that economic development policy would take in subsequent decades. New York City's economic future, like that of many other American cities, would come to depend on profits from culture and consumption.

These efforts took three major forms and achieved their intended ends to varying degrees. First, officials recognized the value of economic development at the smallest scale, in the daily transaction between consumers and the merchants whose businesses had long lined the city's sidewalks. They set out to enhance such retail commerce. As Donald Patton explained, this scale of business bore impacts far exceeding its seeming modesty. "The city has an obvious stake in expanding New York as a corporate headquarters and in keeping industry from moving away," Patton said in 1970. "But to an even greater extent the greatness of the city depends upon the small-business man. We want to help bring back to him the neighborhood residents who have wandered off to the big central stores or the suburban shopping centers." Stores faced new challenges in the Lindsay era, from burgeoning malls on the urban periphery, unfocused development within the city limits, and a general shabbiness that emerged in many shopping districts. "Main Street, N.Y.C. has fallen on hard times," the *New York Times* explained.[43]

Patton contended that simple coordination between the city Economic Development Administration and the many other agencies that worked in neighborhoods—such as the police department and sanitation—could do much to upgrade shopping districts. "Operation Main Street," as officials called the program that launched in late 1969, began with small improvements on fifteen streets throughout the five boroughs. On Richmond Avenue in Staten Island, for example, the city installed new streetlights, added free parking, increased police patrols, and picked up trash more frequently. On Merrick Boulevard in Queens, the city planted new street trees. Such efforts met both approving and skeptical responses. A Bronx bank manager applauded the greater police presence on Bainbridge Avenue. "We had quite a drug problem here a while ago, but now the police are right on top of it," he told a reporter. Others cited "brighter" streets and "fewer broken windows" outside their shops. But some noted that the city's efforts rarely extended beyond Main Street itself, into neighborhoods that suffered from many of the same problems, and that the city's window dressing often amounted to just that.[44]

If the Lindsay administration's trademark enthusiasm sometimes missed its mark, it nonetheless demonstrated the mayor's willingness to experiment with new modes of enhancing the city. Operation Main Street expanded to include temporary street closings in mid-1970, for example, an effort intended to transform traditional shopping streets into outdoor festivals. The temporary closing of Madison Avenue on a September evening attracted crowds with free drinks, gifts, outdoor dining, and live music. The city continued the program the following spring under the banner of the "Madison Avenue Magic Promenade," but the Tuesday closings were not magical for many of the avenue's high-end merchants, for whom the events were perhaps too successful in drawing an audience eager for amusement. The crowds came for the festivities, they complained, not for shopping. "We only get browsers," one merchant lamented. Efforts to make closings permanent eventually failed. But the Lindsay administration's vision of outdoor entertainment and spectacle as a complement to urban shopping would become increasingly common in American cities, particularly in the "festival marketplaces" that New York and many of its counterparts looked to as development strategies in the following decades. New York's South Street Seaport, which Lindsay's design team had laid the groundwork for and developer James Rouse eventually built, was among the earliest such examples when it opened in the early 1980s.[45]

A second, more immediately successful, effort was the administration's endeavor to bolster one of New York's signature resources: the endangered theater industry. The rapid commercial development of Midtown had threatened the theaters of Broadway as construction moved west toward Times Square. As the value of land far exceeded the potential profits of even successful theaters in the area, demolition of historic playhouses increased to make way for modern skyscrapers. The number of theaters had already declined from forty-seven in 1940 to thirty-four in 1967, a total that would further diminish as office construction reached a fever pitch.[46]

As Paul Goldberger notes in chapter 6, the city opposed the destruction of theaters not only because their loss threatened the city's cultural preeminence but also because the Lindsay administration recognized Broadway's contribution to the broader economy of New York City. "We recognized that the legitimate theater is not only an important institution in its own right, but a critical element in the City's national center function as well," the City Planning Commission wrote. "Hotels and restaurants depend on the continued existence of theaters. The theater is a key part of the communications industry, and a very significant attraction in bringing corporate headquarters to the national center." The loss of Broadway would also mean the loss of one of the city's unmatched economic engines.[47]

With the relatively loose land use tools that New York's zoning laws provided, officials had few remedies with which to oppose the impending destruction of the city's theater district. Yet the administration's openness to experimentation offered an avenue to an ingenious strategy that turned profit-oriented commercial construction on its head. Initially, through a concession negotiated by the city's planning staff with a single developer, and eventually through a formalized Special Theater District that stretched over Times Square and the surrounding area, officials modified the city's zoning code to allow the Planning Commission to grant developers the right to build larger buildings if they incorporated theaters in their plans. Aficionados celebrated the 1967 announcement of the rule with gusto. "This news which, for devotees, is comparable perhaps to the disclosure of a miracle drug able to conquer the common cold, came to light the other day," wrote the *New York Times* theater critic.[48]

The innovation proved to be remarkably effective, even for developers who wondered if the cost of building a theater would be worth the additional space they were allowed to construct. In addition to the initial project that inspired the strategy, One Astor Place, the Lindsay administration saw the completion of two new theaters: one in the Uris Building at 1633 Broadway and a fourth, the American Place Theater on West 46th Street. Their success motivated the creation of similar incentive zoning districts elsewhere in New York City, including a Fifth Avenue district that aimed to prevent the loss of the retail that made that area one of the city's most distinctive commercial axes as well as an economic asset. As the country descended into a prolonged recession in the mid-1970s, the revitalized theaters of Broadway offered one of the city's few economic bright spots. The unexpectedly high profits of the Great White Way—$57 million in the 1974–1975 season, a 24 percent increase over the preceding year—suggested that the Lindsay administration had been wise to ensure the district's survival.[49]

Lindsay's third effort to capitalize on the city's cultural influence for the purpose of economic growth—promoting the film industry—was perhaps the simplest, but it delivered the greatest results. Though long America's best-known city, in the postwar era New York appeared in popular films only rarely. The city had made little effort to be hospitable to Hollywood during the Wagner administration, frustrating those who wished to film in New York with a warren of permitting requirements, bureaucracy, and interference. Lindsay, however, recognized both the prestige and the income that would derive from opening the city to filmmakers. Within his first year as mayor, he announced innovations designed to vastly simplify the byzantine approval process, including streamlined permitting, fewer fees, dedicated police units at film locations, and an end to the arbitrary censorship that officials had applied to films they disliked. Lindsay promised new efforts by his office to free directors from annoying constraints. Indeed, the mayor himself interceded to overrule city officials who attempted to prevent the shooting of *Up the Down Staircase* in 1966 because they felt it would cast the city's schools in a bad light. Lindsay likewise negotiated with the city's unions to make sure that wages in New York City matched those in Los Angeles, a barrier that had frightened filmmakers away in the past.[50]

In making it easier to film in New York City, Lindsay welcomed artists both to use the city's unique urban landscape as a set and to become a vital part of the city's economy. If filmmaking aligned with Lindsay's broader project to enliven the city in new ways, so too did it align with his desire to tap the city's intrinsic qualities for economic development. The mayor was not subtle on this count, making the economic goal of his experiment quite clear at the June 1966 press conference announcing the film initiative. "These productions will spend anywhere from $1-million to $3-million each in the course of their filming," Lindsay told the audience. "That's more than double the activity of this period a year ago." Mayors, of course, speak in hyperbole, but if anything Lindsay's projections proved too limited. In 1965, crews made only two major films in the city. In contrast, directors shot twenty-seven films during 1966, Lindsay's first year in office, and forty-two in his second. Lindsay's commissioner of Commerce and Industrial Development estimated that those films generated a $40-million economic impact in 1967, through salaries, supplies, and other expenses. The following year of 1968 brought forty-three films to the city, and 1969 yielded forty-five more. New Yorkers became accustomed to seeing Dustin Hoffman, Harry Belafonte, Barbra Streisand, and Ingrid Bergman on location in their neighborhoods. It was a "New Outdoor Sport: Watching Filmmakers," wrote the *New York Times*. Starstruck reporters and residents were not the only ones to heap praise on Lindsay's efforts to turn the city into a film capital. So too did local union leaders who touted the initiative's contribution to the city's job base. "There is full employment in the motion picture crafts here, thanks to the Lindsay program and his personal efforts," said Steve D'Inzillo, secretary-treasurer of the East Coast Council of Motion Picture Operating Unions, "the only major city in the United States where such conditions exist."[51]

The eleven thousand workers in D'Inzillo's unions could feel secure in their employment by the close of Lindsay's mayoralty. Indeed, Lindsay's experiment would boom in the decades following his time in office. A city commissioned study in 2012 estimated that filming accounted for over $7 billion in annual spending and employed 130,000 New Yorkers, many in well-paying jobs.[52] In the new century, New York would vie with other cities in North America for film crews as well as retail magnets, cultural institutions, and other "clean" jobs that it had pioneered in the Lindsay years. Lindsay's recognition that culture and consumption could provide dependable building blocks for economic development would prove remarkably prescient.

Taking Measure

Hindsight teaches us lessons that Lindsay could not yet have known. Today we can look back and see that Lindsay governed at the very tipping point that brought the ascendance of a new economy in New York City. If at the time officials despaired over the vast stretches of office space that lay vacant at the close of the Lindsay mayoralty, we now know that those very offices would fill with workers in emerging white-collar economic sectors during the following decades. New York's economy would come to depend less and less on the corporate headquarters that Lindsay-era officials hated to lose, as finance, insurance, real estate, and legal and other business services grew in importance.[53] Lindsay's hopes to retain blue-collar industries in New York would prove less triumphant, as the movement of production to suburbs, to the South, and to the developing world became unstoppable. Despite the divergent fates of New York's economic sectors, however, a city seemingly on the path to decay managed to right itself over the next quarter century, boasting a prosperity few could have predicted in 1973.

Faced with huge economic challenges and limited resources, Lindsay experimented—by partnering with likeminded executives, by supporting industrial expansion both small and large, by aiding neighborhood shopkeepers, by revising zoning regulations, and by promoting New York as a movie set. Not all his innovations succeeded, but he nonetheless made several influential and lasting contributions both through bolstering declining economic sectors and building new sectors that have remained vital to the present day.

His most important contribution may have been that when many left New York City for dead, Lindsay insisted that a dynamic city was still a project worth pursuing. Urban centers, he argued, could thrive once more and the very qualities that made them unique could fuel their future prosperity. Moreover, in an era of declining faith in the role of the public sector in the economy, from both the political left and right, Lindsay remained committed to government's responsibility as a stabilizing force shielding its citizens from the turbulence of economic transformation. If Lindsay's uneven success resulted from the enormous challenges of a globalizing economy—leading to larger gains where the city had greater control over its fate, such as in the realm of culture and consumption—his persistence nonetheless reflected an adamant conviction that municipal policy could make a significant difference in the city's economic future.

But, while New York can now point to a strong economic foundation that owes much to Lindsay's decisions, it has also developed to be a profoundly unequal one, whether defined in demographic, financial, or spatial terms. Lindsay's approach to economic development—a vision that encompassed the city's skilled and unskilled residents, old and new economies, and center and periphery—had aimed to create a more equitable city with jobs for New Yorkers of all types, throughout the city's five boroughs. Unfortunately, all of these high hopes for New York's economy did not come to fruition during his service as mayor, nor have they in the years since. Another story awaits telling of economic development after Lindsay. But as New York mayors continue to confront structural economic transformations, joblessness, and persistent poverty, John Lindsay's idealistic ambition that a city like New York can and should house and employ a diverse population—and that government-led economic development can make that possible—remains inspiring today.

NOTES

1. Text of Lindsay's Inaugural Address at City Hall, *New York Times*, January 2, 1966, p. 56.

2. Temporary Commission on City Finances, *The Effects of Taxation on Manufacturing in New York City: Ninth Interim Report to the Mayor* (New York: Temporary Commission on City Finances, Dec. 1976), p. 4; Temporary Commission on City Finances, *Economic and Demographic Trends in New York: The Outlook for the Future: Thirteenth Interim Report to the Mayor* (New York: Temporary Commission on City Finances, May 1977), pp. 76–77, 85; Barry Gottehrer et al., *New York City in Crisis* (New York: David McKay Company, Inc., 1965), pp. 1–36; Joshua B. Freeman, *Working-Class New York: Life and Labor Since World War II* (New York: The New Press, 2000), pp. 251–252.

3. Peter K. Eisinger, *The Rise of the Entrepreneurial State: State and Local Economic Development Policy in the United States* (Madison: University of Wisconsin Press, 1988), pp. 15–17; *Public Works and Economic Development Act of 1965*, Public Law 89–136, 89th Cong., 1st sess. (Aug. 26, 1965). The increasing movement of the term "economic development" from international realms to the domestic urban policy realm is apparent in a review of its use in the *New York Times*. See ProQuest Historical Newspapers: *The New York Times* (1851–2008). The use of the phrase "economic development" in English-language publications increased in frequency in the 1950s and 1960s and peaked during Lindsay's first term, 1966–1969. See "Google Books Ngram Viewer" (search for phrase "economic development"), http://books.google.com/ngrams.

4. Temporary Commission, *Effects of Taxation*, p. 7; "City Gains in Securities Jobs, with 132 Percent Rise from 1958–70," *New York Times*, September 10, 1972, p. 44.

5. Glenn Fowler, "News of Realty: Offices Set Mark," *New York Times*, December 9, 1968, p. 78; Alan S. Oser, "A Major Company Will Leave City," *New York Times*, October 16, 1970, p. 1; Regina Belz Armstrong, *The Office Industry: Patterns of Growth and Location: A Report of the Regional Plan Association* (Cambridge, MA: MIT Press, 1972), p. 134–41.

6. Thomas W. Ennis, "Building Goes on But Space Is Rare," *New York Times*, January 8, 1967, p. 311; New York City Department of City Planning, *Economic Development in New York City: Manhattan Office Development, Comprehensive Planning Workshop* (New York: New York City Department of City Planning, 1973), pp. 7–8.

7. New York City Department of City Planning, *Economic Development*, p. 10; *Plan for New York City, 1969: A Proposal* (New York: New York City Planning Commission, 1969), 6 vols., vol. 1, p. 31; Mariana Mogilevich, "Designing the Urban: Space and Politics in Lindsay's New York" (doctoral dissertation, Harvard University, 2012), pp. 252–254.

8. Seth S. King, "American Can Co. Will Leave City," *New York Times*, February 16, 1967, p. 1; Wolfgang Quante, *The Exodus of Corporate Headquarters from New York City* (New York: Praeger Publishers, 1976), pp. 42–44. Quante's study provides the most thorough analysis of the city's corporate departures at this time.

9. Michael Stern, "Rep. Koch Finds 27 Major Companies in Midtown Area Are Weighing a Move from City," *New York Times*, November 3, 1971, p. 65. See Quante, *Exodus of Corporate Headquarters*, pp. 192–198, for full results of the survey.

10. Quante, *Exodus of Corporate Headquarters*, pp. 81–131; New York City Department of City Planning, *Economic Development*, p. 9; John Mollenkopf, "The Politics of Change," in *America's Mayor: John V. Lindsay and the Reinvention of New York*, edited by Sam Roberts (New York: Museum of the City of New York and Columbia University Press, 2010), p. 106; Vincent J. Cannato, *The Ungovernable City: John Lindsay and His Struggle to Save New York* (New York: Basic Books, 2001), p. 552; "Pick Conn. for Your Headquarters" (advertisement), *New York Times*, April 9, 1967, p. 149.

11. Quante, *Exodus of Corporate Headquarters*, pp. 69, 181–183; Martin Arnold, "Westchester Cites Industrial Goals," *New York Times*, February 20, 1967, p. 39; Richard Reeves, "Mayor Tried to Halt Move," *New York Times*, February 11, 1967, p. 1; King, "American Can Co. Will Leave City," p. 1; Glenn Fowler, "Lindsay Cautions Runaway Concerns," *New York Times*, February 25, 1971, p. 1; Oser, "A Major Company Will Leave City"; Lee Silberman, "Big Board Move?" *Wall Street Journal*, April 5, 1966, p. 16; Maurice Carroll, "With Votes on Yankee Stadium Lined Up, Mayor Is Ready to Start Pushing Project," *New York Times*, September 20, 1971, p. 26; "Yankee Stadium Purchase Approved by Rockefeller," *Wall Street Journal*, July 7, 1971, p. 18; Ronald Sullivan, "Football Giants to Leave City for Jersey after 1974 Season," *New York Times*, August 27, 1971, p. 1.

12. Seth S. King, "New York—Fun City for Business," *New York Times*, March 12, 1967, p. 202.

13. Fowler, "Lindsay Cautions Runaway Concerns"; John H. Allan, "Investors Wooed by the City Turn Bullish About Future," *New York Times*, October 21, 1972, p. 35; Isadore Barmash, "Mayor to Use TV to Spur Apparel," *New York Times*, September 26, 1966, p. 72; *Plan for New York City*, vol. 1, p. 5; Murray Schumach, "Lindsay Extols Virtues of Downtown Manhattan," *New York Times*, August 8, 1973, p. 41.

14. Seth S. King, "Business Leaders Joining Officials on City Problems," *New York Times*, April 17, 1967, p. 1; "Lindsay Asks Business Group to Help Him Stop 50 Companies from Leaving the City," *New York Times*, November 11, 1965, p. 54.

15. King, "Business Leaders Joining Officials," p. 1; Murray Illson, "Bank-City Team to Aid Business," *New York Times*, February 4, 1966, p. 1.

16. Philip H. Dougherty, "Advertising: City in Drive to Lure Industry," *New York Times*, September 8, 1967, p. 54; "Let's All 8 Million of Us Move to L.A." (advertisement), *New York Times*, October 17, 1971, p. 25. Other ads in the campaign appeared in the *New York Times* on October 2, 1967, January 24, 1968, February 23, 1968, March 22, 1968, and April 5, 1968, featuring the boroughs of Brooklyn and Queens, the attractions that New York offered for free, and the city's educational resources, among other themes.

17. New York City Planning Commission Economic Development Section, *Summaries and Transcripts of the Economic Development Workshop—Industrial Development Workshop*, October 17, 1973 (New York: New York City Planning Commission, 1974), pp. 17–18; Quante, *Exodus of Corporate Headquarters*, p. 148.

18. Schumach, "Lindsay Extols Virtues," p. 41.

19. Armstrong, *Office Industry*, p. 141; New York City Department of City Planning, *Economic Development*, p. 8.

20. New York City Department of City Planning, *Economic Development*, p. 10.

21. Quante, *Exodus of Corporate Headquarters*, pp. 132–136; Armstrong, *Office Industry*, p. 154.

22. Temporary Commission on City Finances, *Effects of Taxation*, p. 11.

23. Freeman, *Working-Class New York*, pp. 161–162; Marc Levinson, *The Box: How the Shipping Container Made the World Smaller and the World Economy Bigger* (Princeton: Princeton University Press, 2006), pp. 76–86.

24. Marc Levinson provides the most comprehensive account of the transformation of New York's port in this era, especially as a result of containerization. Levinson, *The Box*, pp. 76–100; Freeman, *Working-Class New York*, pp. 162–165.

25. Levinson, *The Box*, pp. 8, 99.

26. Freeman, *Working-Class New York*, pp. 145–161; Levinson, *The Box*, p. 99; Gottehrer et al., *New York City in Crisis*, pp. 92–102.

27. *Plan for New York City*, vol. 1, p. 17; Temporary Commission on City Finances, *Economic and Demographic Trends*, pp. 65, 85, 88. Joshua Freeman further notes that a discriminatory housing market worsened the mismatch between labor supply and jobs, since minority New Yorkers were often unable to move closer to suburbanizing factories due to residential restrictions. See Freeman, *Working-Class New York*, p. 144.

28. Thomas P. Ronan, "Lindsay Proposes Aid for Business to Bar Its Flight," *New York Times*, February 20, 1966, p. 1; *Plan for New York City*, vol. 1, p. 65.

29. Lawrence O'Kane, "City Is Fighting to Keep Industry," *New York Times*, January 16, 1966, p. R1; Charles G. Bennett, "City Said to Drive Industries Away," *New York Times*, January 8, 1969, p. 94.

30. Institute of Public Administration, New York, Study Group on New York City Housing and Neighborhood Improvement, *"Let There Be Commitment": A Housing, Planning and Development Program for New York City* (New York: Institute of Public Administration, 1966), p. 5; Hilary Ballon, "The Physical City," in *America's Mayor: John V. Lindsay and the Reinvention of New York*, edited by Sam Roberts (New York: Museum of the City of New York and Columbia University Press, 2010), pp. 132–146.

31. *Plan for New York City*, vol. 1, p. 17.

32. Homer Bigart, "New Unit to Push Job Development," *New York Times*, March 26, 1966, p. 13; William M. Beecher, "Clay to Head New Agency to Revitalize City Industry,"

New York Times, May 26, 1966, p. 1; Charles G. Bennett, "New Agency Hits Snag in Council," *New York Times*, November 2, 1966, p. 32; Charles G. Bennett, "Felt Will Head Public Development Corporation," *New York Times*, August 4, 1967, p. 33; Charles G. Bennett, "Mayor to Appoint Aide on Industry, *New York Times*, April 11, 1967, p. 50; Charles G. Bennett, "City Economic Agency an Entity Today," *New York Times*, July 22, 1968, p. 39.

33. Barmash, "Mayor to Use TV," p. 72; Isadore Barmash, "Help for Garment Industry Slow," *New York Times*, July 5, 1967; Israel Shenker, "Fun City Revisited: Lindsay Glances Backward," *New York Times*, December 6, 1970, p. 116.

34. O'Kane, "City Is Fighting"; Will Lissner, "City Reports Aid to Small Firms," *New York Times*, August 28, 1966, p. 38; "Brooklyn Machinery Plant Cancels Plans to Leave City," *New York Times*, September 9, 1969, p. 45; Alan S. Oser, "Industry Finds Room for Growth in the City," *New York Times*, November 28, 1971, p. R1. The city similarly assisted the Supreme Equipment and Systems Corporation, which tripled the size of its Brooklyn-based workforce with help from the Public Development Corporation. The PDC purchased a $3-million, two-block property from developer Harry Helmsley, which it in turn leased to Supreme. See "Company Returns to City from Scarsdale," *New York Times*, March 23, 1973, p. 461.

35. *Plan for New York City,* vol. 1, p. 17.

36. George Horne, "City Plans Containership Terminal," *New York Times*, October 26, 1966, p. 1; "Stapleton Picked as Terminal Site," *New York Times*, April 18, 1966, p.58; George Horne, "S.I. Land Offered City for Ship Use," *New York Times*, January 19, 1967, p.1; George Horne, "S.I. Containership and Oil Terminals Urged," *New York Times*, January 27, 1967, p.196; Richard Phalon, "Container Facility on S.I. Now Set to Open in May," *New York Times*, April 22, 1972, p. 66; "Area Residents Protest Plan for Brooklyn Piers," *New York Times*, August 6, 1971, p. 62; "City Planners Urged to Back a Container Port in Red Hook," *New York Times*, March 2, 1972, p. 77; "World's Largest Container Crane Dedicated at Brooklyn Waterfront," *New York Times*, July 14, 1973, p. 29; Max H. Seigel, "U.S. Lines Will Return to City From Container Port in New Jersey," *New York Times*, September 12, 1973, p. 51. The city's waterfront redevelopment did not wholly bypass Manhattan. The Lindsay administration also planned a passenger terminal on Manhattan's west side, which opened in 1974. See "Midtown Terminal for Liners Backed by Estimate Board," *New York Times*, November 22, 1968, p. 92; Robert Lindsey, "City Opens Six-Liner Terminal," *New York Times*, November 24, 1974, p. 1.

37. Urban Land Institute, *A Review of Industrial Land Use Patterns and Practices in New York City: Prepared for the City of New York City Planning Commission* (Washington, DC: Urban Land Institute, Aug. 1968), pp. 4–5, 18, 21–22; Bennett, "City Said to Drive Industries Away," p. 94. For the initial proposal for a Staten Island industrial park, see Lockwood, Kessler & Bartlett, Inc., *Proposed Staten Island Industrial Park: Feasibility Study* (New York: City of New York Department of City Planning, 1962). On the initial plans for College Point, Queens, see Paul Crowell, "College Point Site in Queens Planned for Industrial Park," *New York Times*, August 22, 1960, p. 1.

38. Charles G. Bennett, "City's Economic Picture Mixed," *New York Times*, June 8, 1968, p. 33; Warren Weaver Jr., "Cut of 5,000 Jobs at Navy Yard Reported Planned by June, 1965," *New York Times*, March 6, 1964; *Plan for New York City,* vol. 1, p. 67; Urban Land Institute, *Review of Industrial Land Use*, p. 23.

39. John V. Lindsay, *The City* (New York: Norton, 1970), pp. 80–81; Charles G. Bennett,

"City Is Negotiating to Take Over Navy Yard for Industrial Center," *New York Times*, July 7, 1966, p. 1; "Thousands of Jobs to Open at Navy Yard Site," *New York Amsterdam News*, February 8, 1969, p. 23; Peter Kihss, "Brooklyn Navy Yard Starting to Hum Again as 8 Manufacturers Bring New Life and Hope to Area," *New York Times*, May 11, 1969, p. 67; Robert A. Tomasson, "Navy Yard Revives on a Grand Scale," *New York Times*, October 3, 1971, p. A19; Werner Bamberger, "Shipbuilding Growing in Brooklyn Again," *New York Times*, November 22, 1970, p. 84.

40. Paul L. Montgomery, "A Supertanker Christened in Brooklyn," *New York Times*, July 1, 1973, p. 169.

41. New York City Department of City Planning, *Economic Development in New York City: Industrial Redevelopment, Comprehensive Planning Workshop* (New York: New York City Department of City Planning, Oct. 1973), pp. 14–15, 20–22; Temporary Commission on City Finances, *Effects of Taxation*, p. 11. Even Seatrain would soon experience disappointment. Amidst the world oil crisis in 1975, the firm laid off its three-thousand-person workforce, leaving the Navy Yard with only 2,200 employees. The *Times* noted that once again the site felt like a "ghost town," but Seatrain was able to rehire most of its workers a few months later with federal assistance. See Grace Lichtenstein, "Seatrain, Builder of Tankers, Lays Off 1,800 at Brooklyn Yard," *New York Times*, January 23, 1975, p. 66; Grace Lichtenstein, "Navy Yard Dream Now a Nightmare," *New York Times*, February 9, 1975, p. 24; Joseph P. Fried, "Navy Yard Rebirth Brings Joy to Area," *New York Times*, May 18, 1975, p. BQLI94.

42. James Sanders provides an excellent overview of this aspect of Lindsay's policy making. See James Sanders, "Adventure Playground," in *America's Mayor: John V. Lindsay and the Reinvention of New York*, edited by Sam Roberts (New York: Museum of the City of New York and Columbia University Press, 2010).

43. Glenn Fowler, "City Works to Freshen Up Its 'Main Streets,'" *New York Times*, May 17, 1970, p. 296; Craig Whitney, "Supermarkets and Fears Shut Small Stores Here," *New York Times*, September 29, 1969, p. 49.

44. Fowler, "City Works to Freshen Up," p. 296; Richard Phalon, "City Giving Neighborhoods First Aid," *New York Times*, August 20, 1970, p. 37.

45. Nancy Moran, "City Plans to Close Fifth Ave. and 18 Other Streets on Some Saturdays," *New York Times*, June 16, 1970, p. 15; Lawrence Van Gelder, "A Mile of Madison Ave. Becomes a Mall for the Night," *New York Times*, September 23, 1970, p. 1; Fred Ferretti, "Madison Ave. Closings Stir Dissent," *New York Times*, May 13, 1971, p. 47; Sanders, "Adventure Playground," pp. 96–97; Mogilevich, "Designing the Urban," pp. 272–277. On festival marketplaces, see Alison Isenberg, *Downtown America: A History of the Place and the People Who Made It* (Chicago: University of Chicago Press, 2005).

46. Lewis Funke, "New Theaters, New Hopes," *New York Times*, October 15, 1967, p. 117.

47. *Plan for New York City*, vol. 1, p. 32; Ballon, "Physical City," pp. 140–141.

48. Funke, "New Theaters, New Hopes," p. 117; Ballon, "Physical City," pp. 140–141.

49. David A. Andelman, "Web of Steel Holds Fate of the Stage," *New York Times*, June 21, 1970, p. 252; Milton Esterow, "City Proposes More Theaters to Revitalize Midtown District," *New York Times*, October 1, 1967, p. 1; McCandlish Phillips, "Broadway Adds a New Face— The Uris," *New York Times*, November 20, 1972, p. 45; Ada Louise Huxtable, "American Place Theater Finds a Cozy Home Under New City Code," *New York Times*, December 21, 1971, p. 39; Louis Calta, "4 Office Theaters Are Taking Shape," *New York Times*, August 3, 1971, p.

22; Ada Louise Huxtable, "Thinking Man's Zoning," *New York Times*, March 7, 1971, p. D22; Louis Calta, "Broadway Enjoying a Profitable Period Despite Recession," *New York Times*, June 15, 1975, p. 1.

50. Sanders, "Adventure Playground," pp. 85–91; Terence Smith, "Filmmakers Will Find a Haven in New York," *New York Times*, June 1, 1966, p. 40; Vincent Canby, "Mayor Renews Filming Pledge," *New York Times*, May 17, 1966, p. 53; Vincent Canby, "12 Unions Here Agree to Relax Rules for Local Film Productions," *New York Times*, March 15, 1967, p. 53.

51. Smith, "Filmmakers Will Find a Haven," p. 40; Sanders, "Adventure Playground," p. 86; "Record Number of Films Shot in City During 1967," *New York Times*, January 24, 1968, p. 37; A. H. Weiler, "Number of Movies Made Here Sets a Record: 26 in 6 Months," *New York Times*, July 28, 1969, p. 23; A. H. Weiler, "New York Is Scene of 45 Movies This Year," *New York Times*, December 9, 1969, p. 9; Robert T. Jones, "New Outdoor Sport: Watching Filmmakers," *New York Times*, May 5, 1969.

52. Boston Consulting Group, "Evaluating NYC Media Sector Development and Setting the Stage for Future Growth: Final Report," May 8, 2012. http://www.nyc.gov/html/film/downloads/pdf/Media_in_ NYC_2012.pdf.

53. Matthew P. Drennan, "The Decline and Rise of the New York Economy," in *Dual City: Restructuring New York*, edited by John Hull Mollenkopf and Manuel Castells (New York: Russell Sage Foundation, 1991), p. 35.

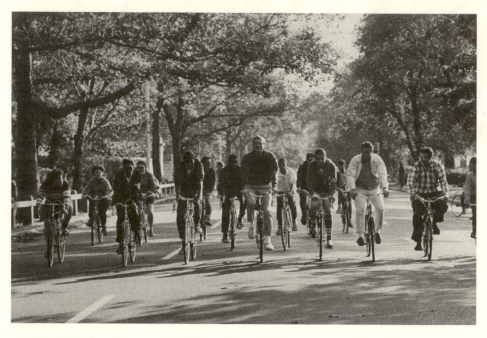

John V. Lindsay bikes in Central Park. Photographer John Dominis. Time & Life Pictures / Getty Images.

CHAPTER EIGHT

Arts as Public Policy

Cultural Spaces for Democracy and Growth

MARIANA MOGILEVICH

As spring arrived in New York City in 1966, Central Park was the site of a notable "happening." "Mr. and Mrs. Average New Yorker and family" were invited
to come and paint on a 105-yard long canvas snaking across the grass behind the
Metropolitan Museum of Art. "Average New Yorkers," young and old, indeed came
and participated in the Parks Department's inaugural "Event in the Open Air." They
painted plants and flowers, abstract patterns, and, in one case, Batman and Robin
on sequential panels of newsprint, and they climbed and poked around sculptures
installed for the occasion. The horizontal scroll painting that resulted may have been
of limited aesthetic appeal, but the event itself was of unmistakable significance,
making several new propositions as to the role of art in the life of the city.

People were free to express themselves, however they wished, in the space of the
public park. Anyone could be an artist. And art could take place anywhere, not
only in the confines of a museum or a studio, but out in open space. The particular
location of this "happening" points as well to the centrality of art to John Lindsay's
urban policy. Indeed, during Lindsay's two terms as mayor, both the role and the
location of the arts in the city expanded dramatically, as Lindsay's administration
employed distinctly spatial strategies both to engage the arts in expanding citizenship, and to cement New York's reputation as an arts capital.

Despite extensive interest in the art of the sixties and its political dimensions,
as well as in New York City's development as a postwar capital of the arts, there
has been no close examination of arts policy in the city in this fertile and tumultuous time. Lindsay brought the arts to the forefront of his vision of urban life by
encouraging their expansion across a new geography. This chapter traces a period in
which the public function and presence of the arts increased dramatically and shows
how Lindsay and his appointees enlisted arts and culture to address demands for
greater democracy in the city. The spatial dimensions of Lindsay's arts policy were

twofold. First, he sought to expand access to the arts to a more diverse citizenry by expanding the locations in which they appeared and occurred, especially in public places. Second, with an eye toward regional, national, and international competition, his administration reinforced the physical presence of arts and artists in the city at key sites. The expansion of citizenship and the development of what has variously been called a symbolic or experience economy proceeded as two highly compatible endeavors.[1]

Lindsay sought to demonstrate New York's value and viability at a time when the city's very future appeared in doubt. Riding a bicycle or ice skating in Central Park, walking the streets of Harlem or seated in the audience of a Broadway show, Lindsay was a symbol of New York City's promise and a spokesman for its advantages over suburban living. The new suburban lifestyle, for all its appeal, was also suffering from attacks on its conformity and dullness. Lindsay's administrators—key appointees in the city's parks and culture administration and receptive figures in the Department of City Planning—used the arts to illustrate and to shape a city that provided the means for personal expression and allowed everyone—especially poor and minority citizens—to accede fully to public life. The arts were a central vehicle and a metaphor in Lindsay's spatial politics of democratization and decentralization. At the same time, city planners attempted to capitalize on the economic importance of the cultural sector in the context of the city's deindustrializing economy. Making space for new publics and creating the image of a new city served as a response to doubts about the value and future of the city to American society.

New Cultural Centers

The spirit of the Central Park "happening" and other initiatives to be discussed in this chapter was in direct opposition to reigning conceptions of the place of the arts in the city. The fall of 1966 marked a cultural milestone for New York City. Only a few blocks from the free and messy play under way in Central Park, the gilded Metropolitan Opera House at the new Lincoln Center for the Performing Arts hosted its inaugural performance. Under construction since 1959, Lincoln Center represented a dramatic bid to locate cultural life at the heart of the city. The city's principal opera, ballet company, orchestra, and conservatory all relocated to the complex, which assembled four travertine-clad theaters, a performing arts library, and the Juilliard School upon a plinth on Manhattan's West Side. This private institution was championed by New York State Governor Nelson Rockefeller's brother John D. and built thanks to the land use machinations and wholehearted support of the city's urban renewal czar, Robert Moses.

The powerful advocates of the performing arts complex sought to cement New

York's title as a national and even a global capital of the arts. A second goal was to make elite performing arts more accessible to a middle-class urban and suburban public with increasing leisure time and interest in cultural activity. Architecturally speaking, Lincoln Center was a realization of the civic center espoused by postwar architects and planners, who assumed that such a monumental site for the gathering of people in collective cultural activity would foster urban identification and strengthen democracy.

Lincoln Center capped two decades of rapid change in New York's cultural life, a permanent symbol of the privileged role of the arts in the city. In the 1940s and 1950s, the city staked a claim as an international center for the arts. New York painters —championed by institutions like the Museum of Modern Art and a growing roster of commercial art galleries—"stole the idea of Modern Art" from its longtime home in Paris.[2] In a few short years, the city's artists shed an inferiority complex and a regionalist bent for international prominence. Meanwhile, the United States was experiencing a perceived "culture boom" in an age of affluence. Public interest and involvement in the arts were increasing. Attendance of the performing arts was up, and artists like Jackson Pollock were household names. Alvin Toffler, a writer for *Fortune* magazine and not yet the prominent futurologist, wrote in 1964 "in a neutral non-pejorative sense" to call attention to the important new figure of the American "cultural consumer."[3] It was for this consumer, in part, that Lincoln Center was built.

The political status of art also changed. In the early 1960s, direct state patronage of the arts for the direct benefit of the American public became a new priority. The Rockefeller brothers, active in business, politics, and the arts, provided support for art in the service of cultural diplomacy in World War II and the Cold War. Governor Nelson Rockefeller established the New York State Council on the Arts (NYSCA) in 1960; it served as a model for the National Endowment for the Arts (NEA), approved by Congress five years later. The NEA provided financial support for the national diffusion of the fine arts, narrowly defined. The reigning philosophy held that contact with artworks of high aesthetic quality, as determined by experts, would provide an uplifting experience for all Americans. This vision of culture's role in society, emphasizing the universal values of an elite-approved art, was shared by the champions of Lincoln Center. The performing arts complex symbolized, in the Cold War context, the strength and depth of American democracy.[4] It promised formal standards of quality, civic ritual, and a rhetoric of universal cultural experience for a civic public. Yet, before the marble dust had settled, the relevance of this cultural model was already in question in a city that was less and less white, middle class, and equal. In the name of the public good, the Lincoln Center urban renewal project displaced a neighborhood's minority residents to make way for a site that did not represent their culture. For all its rhetoric of democracy, Lincoln Center wasn't for everyone.

If in the 1940s and 1950s New York City was the beneficiary of a geopolitical shift in world art centers, the 1960s and early 1970s—a period coextensive with the two mayoral terms of John Lindsay—saw a powerful shift in the geography of culture within the city itself, one in which the mayor and his appointees were active participants. Building on the city's role as arts capital, the Lindsay administration emphasized the role of the arts as a vehicle of inclusion. New art forms in new locations in the city addressed a wider public—and demands both from the counterculture that there be greater freedom of expression and from the civil rights movement and new social movements that the city and its cultural institutions expand their practices and policies to include and recognize minority artists and audiences. This was an explicitly spatial, as well as cultural, politics. Addressing social and cultural discontent, the new strategies and initiatives also sketched the promise of a better, more inclusive city to come.

The Central Park "art happening" was organized by Thomas Hoving, the most visible—and notoriously publicity savvy—of Mayor Lindsay's early appointments. The principal agent of the mayor's new cultural and spatial politics was a young curator of medieval art at the Metropolitan Museum of Art, with a doctorate in art history from Princeton and patrician pedigree. With events like the happening, Thomas Hoving activated Central Park not just as a green open space or a busy recreational complex but as a new cultural center for the city. With a brief to "put the people back in the parks," Hoving was chief spokesman and sponsor of Lindsay's New York as a "fun city."[5] While the term was derided in light of a slew of strikes and general concern with the city's functioning, "fun" was one form of commitment to New York's survival and a means of including a larger, more heterogeneous public in the life of the city. Hoving brought Lindsay's promises of a reborn city to life through new programs and policies in the city's parks.

Vibrant and inclusive open spaces pointed to the viability of an integrated and democratic city. New York's parks operated as metaphors for the state of the city more generally, standing in for both its quality of life and the quality of its democracy. With regard to the quality of urban life, city parks had become the subject of frequent criticism, widely perceived as poorly maintained havens for criminals. A civic group conducting a survey of park users in 1962 concluded: "People who live in New York City are *afraid to use* their parks."[6] Expressions of fear outpaced even widespread complaints about broken benches and overgrown grass. Crime and disrepair in parks also pointed to city government's responsiveness to citizens.

In 1965, the Lindsay campaign seized on the parks as a major issue. Hoving penned a white paper on city parks charging that the previous administration did not "care very much about parks and with rare exceptions do not understand why parks are necessary for the well-being of the city's citizens."[7] The metaphor of the state of the parks for the state of the city resonated well beyond city limits. Governor George Wallace countered accusations on the state of civil rights in his state in 1963 with this argument: "We don't have any utopia in Alabama. But neither do you have one here in New York City, where you can't walk in Central Park at night without fear of being raped, mugged, or shot."[8]

In its first years, the Lindsay administration used the city's parks as visible proof of its cultural and political distance from the previous regime—the city was more responsive and open to the needs and desires of its citizens. As Hoving set about implementing the "renaissance in usage and pleasure" in parks promised by the Lindsay campaign, Central Park played the role of Florence.[9] The park itself was a valuable social work of art. Hoving appointed an official curator to look after Frederick Law Olmsted and Calvert Vaux's landscape, designated a National Historic Landmark in 1963. But more than a static landscape, Central Park's most important function was as the chief stage for free aesthetic expression and delight in open space.

Hoving commissioned a series of new "adventure playgrounds" along the park's perimeter. Works of sculpture unto themselves, these miniature landscapes allowed children to determine their own experiences rather than have them dictated by standardized slides and swings. The first of these, designed by architect Richard Dattner in 1966 and inaugurated the following year, featured an assemblage of granite, concrete and wooden landforms, water features, and a tunnel on a sandy base. A scaled-down cityscape that children could explore freely, the playground modeled an urban environment that was both exciting and accommodating. More immediately, new activities and participatory events introduced a spirit of free play in the park. New Yorkers could lay claim to the space of the park as an act of citizenship, countering feelings of anomie in a troubled city.

In the spring of 1966, Hoving declared to the press that he planned to "open up Central Park and have . . . a Central Park a Go Go."[10] The park's new season mixed high and low culture with dance contests, magic shows, barbershop quartets, a recital of Faust, and a series of participatory events the press deemed Hoving's "happenings." From kite-flying to costume parties, these official events were loosely inspired by the exploits of New York's avant-garde. In fact, Hoving granted permission to Charlotte Moorman, organizer of the fourth annual New York Avant Garde Festival, to hold her event in Central Park between 6 a.m. and midnight on a Friday in September. Former Parks Commissioner Robert Moses was reported to be filled with horror at the "misuse, disorder and freakish behavior" that took place there, citing the washing of clothes in the Conservatory Lake and the dropping of pages of the *New York Times* into a blender. Hoving, in contrast, declared himself all for "encouraging joie de vivre," so long as the artists eschewed nudity and explicit political content.[11] The "disorder" included chamber music and electronic music performances by artists associated with the Fluxus group, as well as "Towers," a happening that consisted of stacks of used tires covered in plastic sheets amongst which participants could climb and crawl.

"Towers" was the work of the artist Allan Kaprow, who first coined the term "happening." In a book on the topic, Kaprow defined the happening as predicated on the idea that the "line between art and life should be kept as fluid, and perhaps indistinct, as possible." The happening attempted to turn spectators into participants and "replace habit with the spirit of exploration and experiment."[12] For a growing contingent of New York artists in the early 1960s, art was not a special occasion requiring the support of an imposing institution or a commodity to be bought, sold, and appreciated under rarefied circumstances. Art was something rather less refined. Art could be experienced on the street, in everyday life, by anyone and everyone. With the cultural shifts of the 1960s, attempts by avant-garde visual artists, composers, and choreographers to elide the separation of art and everyday life, of artists and audience, gained increasing resonance. The happening, which sought to turn spectators into participants and "replace habit with the spirit of exploration and experiment," resonated outside the admittedly narrow world of the New York downtown art scene. Such unconventional and unbounded activity found official sanction in the city's most hallowed public space.

In addition to projects for the pedestrianization of streets, the conversion of waterfront areas to recreational uses, and new networks of small parks, the presence of the arts in the city's parks was a form of spatial reclamation. Concerts and sculptures, like cyclists and joggers, were the signs of new life in the city—and they offered particular forms of urban culture with which suburbia could not compete. The attempt to use the arts as urban policy benefited from a happy confluence with contemporary artists' attempts to move out of the studio and gallery and into urban space, whether painting a mural on a city wall or performing on a sidewalk. Bureaucratically speaking, the conjunction of arts and open space was also the result of a major administrative reorganization. Lindsay moved the City's Office of Cultural Affairs, established by Mayor Wagner in 1962, to the Parks Department and later turned the office into a full-fledged department within a newly combined Parks, Recreation, and Cultural Affairs Administration (PRCAA). This administrative move gave the Department of Cultural Affairs access to valuable new resources—Parks Department equipment, manpower, and land.

Always a trendsetter, Hoving appointed the Parks Department's very own artist-in-residence, with a desk at the Office of Cultural Affairs. Phyllis Yampolsky presented her work at the Judson Memorial Church in Greenwich Village alongside Allan Kaprow and fellow proponents of participatory happenings and experimental works. As Parks artist-in-residence, she organized a series of "Events in the Open Air," beginning with the Central Park easel painting event, which was subsequently replicated in Prospect Park in Brooklyn and at a park on Manhattan's Lower East Side. Later in 1966, at the evocatively titled "Build Your Own Castle and _____ in it Day," the Parks Department provided styrofoam, cardboard, lumber, string, paint, nails, and magic markers for park-goers to do precisely "_____".[13] Rather than serving as audience at a performance, park-goers were invited to orchestrate it themselves. The indeterminacy of the event, with creative control ceded to participants, acknowledged the antiauthoritarianism and search for meaningful experience of the day. Amidst growing demands for participatory democracy and community control, participation in this work of art—collective and yet accommodating individual desires—was an analogy or symbol of political participation and individual liberation.

The language of the counterculture, emphasizing personal liberation and celebrating the ludic and the nonconformist, found accommodation in Lindsay's transformation of New York into a "fun city." But there were clear limits to free play, starting with physical ones. The adventure playground was a microcosm; it provided freedom only within its borders. The snaking easel where children and adults could paint whatever they wanted was split up into orderly individual panels, and the whole event was cordoned off by police barricades. The presence of police officers, one imagines, might have inhibited totally free painterly expression. The experiment was controlled, and the situation clearly delineated. Order could be disrupted only within such guidelines.

Public Art

Thomas Hoving's tenure at the helm of the Parks Department was as short as it was groundbreaking. He quickly parlayed his tremendous visibility into the directorship of the Metropolitan Museum of Art and was succeeded at the Parks Department by August Heckscher. Like Lindsay, Heckscher was a graduate of St. Paul's School and Yale, but he came from wealthier stock—prominent New York industrialists and philanthropists. An editorial writer for the *Herald Tribune* and then director of a liberal think tank, Heckscher was an early supporter of government involvement in the arts. Heckscher and Lindsay worked together on cultural policy under John F. Kennedy, who appointed Heckscher his "special consultant" for the arts in 1962. As congressman, Lindsay made the arts (a major industry of his district) a legislative focus, championing the creation of a federal arts agency from 1961. Eighteen years older than Hoving, Heckscher was more experienced—and less exciting. Heckscher's relationship to the radical cultural practices of the day was more tolerant bemusement than aggressive promotion. His cultural policies emphasized the enlightening effects of the fine arts. In contrast to Hoving's happenings, Heckscher promised cultural "occurrences." He explained later that the term reflected his desire to implement events that could be repeated and developed over time and would be "related to the life of the city rather than to the intense inner life of men and women."[14] Heckscher's civic vision called for more official, less offbeat events, and in that spirit he sponsored festivals in city parks featuring dance, music, and kinetic art.

Doris Freedman, Heckscher's director of Cultural Affairs, had a lasting impact on the city's cultural life, going on to head the Municipal Arts Society and establish the Public Art Fund. Before becoming a pioneer of New York's public art scene, Freedman—daughter of prominent architect and real estate developer Irwin Chanin—was an amateur enamelist and Upper West Side activist. Politicized by the civil rights movement, Freedman's first foray into public service stemmed directly from her friendship with August Heckscher's wife, Claude. At the helm of Cultural Affairs, Freedman's particular approach to the new concept of "public art" combined a universalist belief in fine art's function of social uplift with a desire—inspired by the avant-garde—to put art on the street, in the spaces of everyday life.

Such was the mission of City Walls, a hybrid project of art and urban amelioration, high and low culture, that confused many and reflects the contradictory impulses of Lindsay's arts policy. Freedman championed City Walls, which sponsored the painting of abstract murals of brightly colored geometric forms and patterns on exposed building walls. The earliest murals were commissioned for a program of new city parks on vacant lots in deteriorating neighborhoods, including Bushwick in Brooklyn and Manhattan's Lower East Side. City Walls artists spoke with enthusiasm about their work on the street, emphasizing its public and ephemeral qualities. Like the happening, mural painting freed the painters from the production of art as commodity. City Walls murals, however, still hewed to the visual conventions of painting. Allan D'Arcangelo, one of the first participants in the program, painted a Pop landscape of oversized blades of grass and deconstructed road signs on the side of a tenement building on Ninth Street between First and Second Avenues in 1966. For D'Arcangelo, the impermanence of the murals demonstrated that "art is not the activity of creating static objects but . . . that the activity of art is not a rarity . . . it's a process that is available to everybody."[15] Despite this rhetoric of participation, the murals, designed by professional artists and installed by professional billboard painters, were quite unlike the aleatory happening or the community murals with realist styles and political messages that developed distinctly in the early 1970s.

City Walls served an instrumental function. In drab and decaying areas, Freedman claimed the murals were a "new kind of instantaneous urban renewal, upgrading architecture and uplifting human spirits."[16] These beautification effects could be achieved at a low price and without the contentious process of relocating residents for renovations or new construction. In retrospect, Freedman would claim that the new public art she espoused served as aesthetic recompense for New Yorkers' oppressive daily existence, writing that, "by 1967, the Lindsay administration, confronted with . . . social and political upheaval, was casting about for a way to shed some positive light on its crumbling city."[17] The City Walls program—privately funded, with the exception of the murals in city parks—was a winning proposition for both the Lindsay administration and for artists less radical than the avant-garde but still seeking to engage with daily life. "Cities are the natural home of the artist," Freedman explained, "and it is natural that many should want to 'neutralize a brutalized environment' to give a place an identity and make people proud of where they live."[18] To outside observers, the value of the murals was less clear. Art critics despised City Walls, and as the program branched out to more neighborhoods, existing community groups felt sidestepped by the outside professionals who arrived to decorate their area. Such were the vagaries of art in public, as social groups previously subsumed in the ideal of a homogeneous civic public now demanded art in their own idiom and of their own hand.

Freedman's first major project at the Department of Cultural Affairs, the October 1967 exhibition *Sculpture in Environment*, involved liberating large sculpture from art institutions and displaying it around Manhattan. The exhibition's scale was unprecedented—so many works of art installed out in public, dispersed throughout urban space. Most of the work, with which organizers and catalogue writers promised the birth of a new public art, was large-scale, abstract, geometric sculpture. In metal and plywood, works like Tony Smith's black-painted steel *Snake* (installed in Lincoln Center) or Bernard Rosenthal's *Cube* (still at Astor Place today) represented a new approach to monumentality that insisted on art's autonomy. The works on display were neither figurative and heroic sculptures nor dematerialized events. Far from the spirit of the happening, and save the lights of some kinetic sculpture, nothing in the exhibition could be said to be alive or acting on the environment. This display prefigured the installation of Alexander Calder's *Grande Vitesse* in the postwar civic center of Grand Rapids, Michigan. The forty-three-foot tall, five lobed, red-painted steel creature was harbinger of the federally sponsored public sculpture that would come to be known as "plop art," whose aspirations to universality would be critiqued as a lack of specificity.[19] What site, and what public, were being addressed by such a sculpture?

Swedish-born, New York–based sculptor Claes Oldenburg had previously sent up the idea of a postwar monumental sculpture with universal, noncommercial weight with his proposals for colossal monuments at choice New York City locations—an inverted Good Humor ice cream bar on Park Avenue or a half-peeled banana astride 42nd Street. Installed in Central Park for *Sculpture in Environment,* Oldenburg's *Hole,* or *Placid Monument,* similarly rejected the project of social transformation implied in Freedman's public art. Oldenburg hired professional gravediggers to make a hole in the ground behind the Metropolitan Museum of Art, in a piece that challenged the idea of monumentality, befuddled the public, and prefigured earthworks and other dematerializing tendencies in sculpture. The piece was variously read as a critique of the American war in Vietnam, a reference to the assassination of John F. Kennedy, and an indictment of the aspirations of late liberalism, whose values the more conventional public sculpture on display in this exhibition were seen to endorse. Indeed, Doris Freedman's programs, while partaking of the avant-garde impulse to move art out into urban space, followed Lincoln Center's model of a unitary civic culture; they did not address or even conceive of the city's publics as multiple and diverse. In a place and time rife with division, they were out of sync with social reality. The following year, Freedman staged an exhibit of oversized, round, and brightly colored fiberglass sculptures by Niki de Saint Phalle and metal constructions by Jean Tinguely. The innovation, this time, was the exhibit's location in Central Park's Conservatory Garden. In contrast to the monumental display of sculptures in Manhattan below 96th Street, this exhibit was at the far northern end of the park, along the border with Harlem. Merely by virtue of its siting, the exhibit introduced a different kind of social concern in public art. The Parks Department secured publicity photographs in which young children of color frolicked about the fantastic, giant sculptures, an image of equal opportunity enjoyment of the arts.

There were two aspects to the connection between art and citizenship in Lindsay's cultural policy. One was individualistic—providing means for personal expression or fulfillment. The second required engaging new and different publics in the city's cultural life. Sometimes, the second goal could be achieved at a central location. Indeed, at this time of heightened racial tension and attention to the city's spatial inequalities, Commissioner Heckscher described Central Park as an ecumenical space, "a kind of hyphen between affluent downtown and the poor ghetto area at the north end . . . a kind of joint big-city common."[20] Heckscher stressed that for this to happen, "events had to be programmed in the park that would bring down the ghetto residents from the north, and the ever popular bicycling and other events brought north the more affluent residents of the south."[21] But to directly address cultural divisions and inequality in the city, the redistribution of artworks and programs also had to happen across urban space.

Decentralization

Cultural tensions in New York City extended far beyond the confines of its Central Park. By 1968 demands by concerned citizens that the city "do something"—whether about the threat of violence or its causes—reached new heights. In this context, the city employed the arts as a strategy of public relations and as a public service of "corrective socialization," as Doris Freedman once referred to DCA's work.[22] Mayor Lindsay's Urban Action Task Force, whose job was to serve as neighborhood liaison to City Hall, organized summer programs to "keep the city cool." This largely meant arts programs as riot prevention, making sure inner city children and teenagers were entertained and out of trouble when school was out. Mobilizing private funds from "corporate citizens" with an interest in avoiding class and race warfare, the task force acted as a middleman, bringing in private funds and then parsing them out to various programs.

In the summer of 1967, the task force sponsored a Harlem Cultural Festival and outdoor performances of the contemporary Puerto Rican playwright René Marqués' *The Ox Cart*, the tale of a poor Puerto Rican family's journey to New York and its disillusion with life there. The following summer, the task force funneled private funds to the Parks Department to sponsor a series of mobile units. The Cinemobile was a traveling movie theater in a converted school bus that screened abstract films and conducted workshops for audiences of young children. A Jazzmobile and a Dancemobile (both run by the Harlem Cultural Council), the Bread and Puppet Theater, which put on political theater with oversized papier-mâché puppets, and the new Puerto Rican Traveling Theater all brought performances to city streets closed off for the occasion in places like Harlem, Bedford-Stuyvesant, Brownsville, and the South Bronx. Such gatherings of performers and audiences mixed together in public space sublimated the energy of the street in a powerful counterimage to ghetto residents lighting garbage cans on fire and clashing with the police.

The contrast between the mobile arts programs and the city's public sculpture ventures went beyond their physical location. The various mobile units and street theater programs presented culture that was topical and that reflected the lives of their audience in a way that the Metropolitan Opera did not. "Task Force was not trying to fund Lincoln Center in the streets," Barry Gottehrer, its chairman, told an interviewer in 1974, "we were interacting with the community to know what they wanted."[23] "Task Force" programs promoted involvement beyond spectatorship and emphasized local, nondominant cultural forms. In addition to sponsoring Shakespeare and opera performances in the city's parks, DCA's mobile programs brought jazz and Latin musicians and Spanish-language and participatory theater to city streets. The Dancemobile presented modern dance by black choreographers, performed by black dancers, to audiences in the five boroughs. The Jazzmobile, established by Harlem musician and educator Billy Taylor, brought musicians like Duke Ellington, who normally played in downtown establishments out of reach of Harlem audiences, back uptown to their music's home. The Jazzmobile also organized educational programs to form new young music makers, not just to create new audience members.

The Department of Cultural Affairs sponsored neighborhood workshops where children and teenagers could participate in art, theater, and filmmaking, rather than just appreciating it. Participants in a filmmaking program for teenagers produced films based on their own experiences, depicting gangs, roaches, and interracial romance. The resulting films were then screened for other teenagers all around the city on projection equipment transported by a roving Moviebus. The integration of other voices into official city culture was an important act of recognition. Inasmuch as these programs built skills and strengthened the capacities of local institutions, they were more than a mere palliative.

Critics dismissed the inner city arts initiatives common to urban antipoverty programs in this period as middle-class paternalism and social control through passive entertainments. Indeed, Thomas Hoving would later cop to dabbling in "bread and circuses" at the Parks Department.[24] All the same, Junius Eddy, an arts education specialist at the Ford Foundation, specifically praised New York City's arts programs and their support for community organized endeavors like the Jazzmobile and Dancemobile as vast improvements on the "cultural enrichment model" in which municipalities brought in opera companies or, for that matter, Aretha Franklin, to play for free to inner city audiences.[25] The DCA redistributed city funds and facilities to encourage and integrate new artistic voices and audiences situated far beyond Lincoln Center or Central Park. The shift in the distribution of funding for the arts from a few elite institutions corresponding to a narrow definition of the performing arts to a panoply of people and programs stands as a major achievement of Lindsay's Department of Cultural Affairs.

Before Lindsay became mayor, New York City's cultural spending took two tacks. Historically, the city provided capital and operating support for a small number of privately endowed institutions located on city property (these numbered thirteen in 1966, including the Metropolitan Museum of Art and American Museum of Natural History). In 1962, the city began allocating funds for free public performances by a handful of performing arts groups. Through an arcane budget appropriation (Code 998), the Office of Cultural Affairs provided funds for eight prominent organizations—the Metropolitan Opera, New York Philharmonic and New York State Theater (all neighbors at Lincoln Center), and Joseph Papp's Shakespeare in the Park among them—that presented largely high culture music and theater performances in city parks.

Doris Freedman expanded Code 998 spending to sponsor outdoor performing arts in more places and events programmed by several smaller arts organizations. Freedman reorganized this line of funding to provide support for additional forms of cultural activity, including dance, visual and literary arts, and community arts programs. From $1.2 million granted to ten organizations in fiscal year 1966-1967, Code 998 allocations expanded to $2.8 million for distribution among almost thirty organizations in 1973. The city also began to provide funding to five borough arts councils. These followed the lead of the Harlem Cultural Council and the Bronx Council on the Arts, established in 1964 and 1966, respectively, to encourage the arts in and serve the needs of their particular communities. The new borough councils were supported by, but existed uneasily with, the Department of Cultural Affairs. They provided a degree of true cultural decentralization, acting somewhat autonomously in their boroughs, but as in other realms, administrative decentralization was not equivalent to community control. Irma Fleck, leader of the Bronx council, called it a "grudging kind of relationship": DCA funded the borough councils, but it also approved their proposals.[26]

Decentralization brought not only temporary cultural activity at new sites but also new permanent institutions outside the centers of cultural power. Between 1968 and 1973, a number of new art museums were established outside central Manhattan with the city's support. Like city streets, New York's museums were sites of contention. Artists and their allies picketed the sidewalks of the Metropolitan Museum, the Whitney Museum of American Art, and the Museum of Modern Art, protesting racist exhibition strategies and demanding that they display the work of African American and Puerto Rican artists.[27] Finding museums resistant to changing their collections, exhibitions, and education and outreach programs, artists achieved better results by establishing new institutions. In this endeavor, the museums found an ally in the Lindsay administration. City agencies provided arts producers with funds and with space. Alternative art spaces proliferated in this period. Alana Heiss, who would go on to establish the P.S. 1 gallery in an abandoned schoolhouse, secured numerous spaces from the city for the activities of the Institute for Art and Urban Resources.[28] In 1973, the Housing and Development Administration found vacant or leftover space in city-owned buildings for seventy-five cultural groups.

Some new institutions found semipermanent space for creating and displaying avant-garde work. Others focused on specific neighborhoods or ethnic publics, either bringing cultural offerings available elsewhere in the city closer to home or providing spaces for art and artists underrepresented in the city's principal institutions. MUSE was an experimental community museum in a renovated auto showroom in Bedford-Stuyvesant. A satellite institution for the Brooklyn Children's Museum, then closed for renovation, MUSE sponsored free workshops for children and adults and was open from 10 a.m. to 10 p.m., five days a week. MUSE circulated a loan collection to public schools. Taking decentralization to its logical conclusion, its "Take Home Collection" allowed children in Bedford-Stuyvesant to borrow items from the museum, just like Mayor Lindsay could borrow a Picasso etching from MoMA to decorate his office at City Hall.[29]

MUSE ceased operations after the Children's Museum reopened, but other museums that began life in temporary quarters have become major institutions. The Studio Museum in Harlem, a private endeavor established in 1969 to support contemporary artists and to display work by African Americans artists, would receive funds from the Department of Cultural Affairs beginning in 1973. Dedicated to Puerto Rican arts and culture, El Museo del Barrio came into being following demands from East Harlem parents for more culturally relevant education. The Board of Education provided space and funding to founding director Rafael Ortiz, an artist and educator.[30] The museum initially presented temporary exhibits at P.S. 206 on East 120th Street; it sits today in a city-owned building on Fifth Avenue's Museum Mile. In the longer view, decentralization would pose complex new difficulties, as cultural visibility and the transformation of power relations were clearly not equivalent. An expanded cultural footprint for the city was nonetheless geographically differentiated, as even the official names of these new institutions shows. The Studio Museum in Harlem, established with the support of MoMA trustees, also freed the Museum of Modern Art from hanging more work by African American artists on West 53rd Street. El Museo del Barrio has been criticized for simultaneously serving as a "vehicle of empowerment and of containment of difference," yet it was an important site for Puerto Rican New Yorkers' accession to cultural citizenship.[31]

A Metropolitan Museum?

The new Bronx Museum of the Arts and the Queens Museum of Art were both established in city-owned properties and supported with city funds. Their program

Soprano Maria Callas enjoys a light moment with Mayor John Lindsay, Met manager Rudolph Bing (*left*), and former UN Ambassador Arthur Goldberg (*second from left*). September 17, 1968. © Daily News, L.P. (New York). Used with permission.

was concerned not with cultural recognition but with spatial equity, bringing art where it was not. The Bronx Museum of the Arts began life in 1971 in the rotunda of the Bronx County Courthouse, with support from the Bronx Council on the Arts. Paintings by Vincent van Gogh, Romare Bearden, and Robert Motherwell, among others in the inaugural exhibition, were all on loan from the permanent collection of the Metropolitan Museum of Art. The Metropolitan Museum loaned work to the Bronx Museum, as well as to a number of libraries in Queens, as one response to an active debate regarding access to its collection and possible measures of decentralization. The museum had a long and complex relationship with the city of New York. Located on city-owned parkland, it received capital and operating funds from the city, but the Met supplemented these funds with private donations, and the institution was privately run. The public and private missions of the museum were perpetually intertwined.

As its centennial approached, the Metropolitan Museum of Art played a fundamental role in the city's cultural life, both material and symbolic. The museum's encyclopedic collection operated on a logic of concentration, bringing all the treasures of the world, from Greece to New Guinea, to a site on the edge of Central Park. But people questioned this logic, voicing demands for expanding both the scope of the art displayed in New York City and for relocating the cultural institutions that displayed it in a more equitable distribution throughout urban space. The Metropolitan Museum's social relevance and accessibility to the public and the city's development as a cultural capital would prove to be very different goals, and the relative strength of each commitment—by the museum and by the city—were brought into question.

In March 1967, Thomas Hoving exchanged control of the city's open spaces and cultural and recreational programs for the Metropolitan Museum's collection of paintings and sculptures. During his eleven-year tenure at the helm of the museum, Hoving, ever the showman, would become best known for scandalous acquisitions and blockbuster exhibitions. Initially, however, Hoving's concern was for the social "relevance" of the museum. In Hoving's telling, he immediately regretted the decision to leave city government for the art world, ruing his retreat from public administration to a dissatisfyingly smaller domain.[32] So at first, Hoving treated the museum like he had the parks, increasing access and information to make the Metropolitan more public. He kept the museum's doors open until 10 p.m. on Tuesday nights and began the practice of hanging banners across the museum's facade to announce current exhibitions.[33] Most controversial, Hoving attempted to bring the social concerns troubling the city into the institution of the museum with the exhibition *Harlem on My Mind*, inaugurated in early 1969. Seeking to address some of the complaints of exclusion and exclusivity in elite art institutions, *Harlem on My Mind* managed to please almost no one, infuriating both the stodgy art critics who did not find any art on display in the vast multimedia environment exploring Harlem's culture and history and the Harlem-based artists who decried the absence of any works of art by black painters in the show. In the wake of the bitter 1968 school strike and the deteriorating state of race relations in the city, the Harlem Cultural Council disavowed the project, and liberals and Mayor Lindsay himself turned against the exhibition after a misunderstanding over a perceived anti-Semitic statement in the exhibition catalogue. Widely dismissed as a fiasco, the exhibition can be credited with the discovery of the work of the great Harlem photographer James Van Der Zee, for bringing new audiences to the museum, and claiming a greater stake for the museum in the city's public sphere.[34]

If *Harlem on My Mind* brought Harlem to the Met, the museum's leadership also explored bringing the Met to Harlem and other neighborhoods. A 1967 proposal envisioned a program of temporary exhibits housed in a geodesic dome that could hang from a helicopter and be flown to different sites around the city. This characteristically late-sixties fantasy was realized, with significant modifications. The Met sent a mobile exhibition housed inside an inflatable structure out on a flatbed truck to visit sites in all five boroughs in 1970 and 1971. The Eye Opener, as it was called, cosponsored by the city's Department of Cultural Affairs, brought formalist art appreciation to the outer boroughs, with an exhibit focusing on spiral forms in art, nature, and everyday life and workshops in which children could make spiral-based op-art and designs for spiral-embellished fences.[35]

The museum's efforts in decentralization were but a spiral-shaped microorganism next to the large-scale efforts of its second century expansion. As parks commissioner, Hoving authored and defended Mayor Lindsay's policy against encroachments in Central Park, preventing construction of a two-story café at its southeast corner.[36] But immediately upon assuming his new post in March 1967, Hoving began aggressively investigating expansion plans for the Metropolitan Museum of Art. With public funds, Hoving commissioned a new master plan by the architectural firm of Kevin Roche and John Dinkeloo. The plan called for the construction of three new wings to house a series of important gifts—a series of glass pavilions that would expand the museum's footprint into Central Park. This alleged encroachment sparked a virulent backlash from parks advocates and infuriated those with other priorities for the development of culture in the city. Carter Burden, an early champion of the Studio Museum in Harlem and city councilman for the Metropolitan's district, wrote to Mayor Lindsay charging that the museum's expansion plan reflected the "Lincoln Center syndrome," by which we must assume he meant a hyperconcentration of cultural resources in the city center.[37] Indeed, the Lindsay administration's efforts at transforming the city's cultural footprint pale in comparison to its support for the Metropolitan Museum. Between 1966 and 1974, New York City's contribution to the museum's operating budget increased from $1.5 to 2.7 million. In fiscal year 1969-1970, whereas the budget for DCA's Code 998 allocations was $1.3 million in toto, with just $35,000 set aside for programs proposed by the five Borough Arts Councils, the city allocated $1.3 million for the construction of a glass pavilion to enclose and display the museum's prized new acquisition, the ancient Egyptian Temple of Dendur.

The acquisition of the temple illustrates the cultural geography in which the city was newly situated. Beyond networks of international relations, New York was engaged in new economic competition with other American cities. When the Temple of Dendur, which would have disappeared under water in the construction of the Aswan Dam, was donated to the United States by Egypt, twenty institutions competed to bring home the carved sandstone temple. Hoving acquired Dendur for the Met with lobbying help from his friend John Lindsay, promising to preserve and display it in a sleek, climate controlled glass pavilion, dramatically illuminated at night. The temple was the centerpiece of the museum's expansion—and as such it drew criticism as an act of imperialism both international and metropolitan. New Yorkers asked whether the cultural asset should not rather go instead to Harlem or Bedford-Stuyvesant, neighborhoods with strong ties to African culture and a need for economic investment. But the Temple of Dendur was too valuable to sacrifice to decentralization. Culture was an important sector of the new "symbolic economy" emerging in the wake of deindustrialization, and cities were competing for their share of the arts.[38] New York won the competition for Dendur, but the beneficiaries were not the same citizens engaged by cultural projects in the city's parks or other public spaces. More than a generator of civic identification, the temple would surely be a magnet for visitors to the city and contribute to an image of an arts capital that could yield fiscal benefits.[39]

Whereas its efforts at cultural decentralization aimed to increase connections between the museum and citizens, the Metropolitan conceived its expansion plans with a different public in mind. In 1973, Thomas Hoving declared that the Met was "no longer a local museum."[40] In direct opposition to the institution's public mission, Hoving also implemented a suggested admission policy at the formerly free museum, adapting the language of participation in city parks to introduce barriers to entry for museumgoers. The Museum's "pay what you wish (but you must pay something)" policy began as an "experiment" in 1970. The suggested donation, one dollar for adults and fifty cents for students, was hardly in the spirit of open access to all, an intriguing development one year after the city's public university system adopted an open admissions policy. When Mayor Lindsay wrote Hoving to say that he "fully endorsed" the new policy, he raised only the question of "a large segment of New York citizens . . . who would find any admission charge a strain on their limited incomes." He was referring specifically to senior citizens.[41]

While restricting public access to the museum, Hoving continued to engage the city strategically to ensure its continuing fiscal and political support. One of Hoving's tactics was to introduce the threat of mobility familiar to the fight to retain corporate headquarters to another crucial industry: the city's arts and culture. To win the city's approval of the Metropolitan Museum's expansion plans, Hoving threatened that, if he could not build a new wing for it, a large promised gift by Charles Lehman would instead go to the National Gallery of Art in Washington, D.C.[42] The argument that the arts were critical to the city's economy in a difficult transition from an industrial to a service economy was one Hoving made frequently. In 1971, the museum director wrote Mayor Lindsay to update him on the Met's activities, concluding and underlining "when the City *gives* us money, it gets it *back*. Yeah!"[43] The following year, justifying staff layoffs and reduced hours at the museum, the director described the potential repercussions of the Met's financial troubles as "analogous to the failure of a major industry or its moving out of the city."[44]

Art Appreciation

In the early 1960s, optimistic city, state, and federal governments increased their financial support for the arts. This was in part a reaction to a perceived arts "crisis." As cost increases fast outpaced productivity gains, the live performing arts in particular were unable to pay for themselves. Art was a public good whose meaningful presence in Americans' lives was not ensured. To that end, expert panels and reports advocated for new public, foundation, and corporate funding for the arts.[45] In turn, Lindsay's cultural policies, with their wider conception of art's public, sought to redistribute this good in urban space. In 1966, city arts spending was principally concerned with promoting inclusion and public happiness. However, as the 1969 economic downturn impacted New York City's budget, deindustrialization continued apace, and fears of losing corporate headquarters proved prescient, New York City would increasingly look to the arts as a solution to its own financial troubles. The author of an internal history of the Department of Cultural Affairs highlighted the relatively small scale of city spending on cultural institutions and activities in 1969—just one-tenth of one percent of the city budget—considering that the "arts contribute more than two and one-half billion dollars to the economy of New York City, a city that is recognized as the cultural capital of the world."[46] By the time Lindsay's successor Abraham Beame commissioned a new report on New York's cultural policy, the language of economic value eclipsed arguments for democracy, urban identification, or uplift in art. "Cultural activity constitutes a fundamental aspect of city life; it is integral to the needs and interests of a vast majority of the city's residents," the introduction to the 1974 report begins, continuing, "It is a magnet for millions of visitors from across the country and abroad; it is an indispensable element in the city's economy."[47]

The Lindsay administration pursued this tack all along. In strengthening the city's culture industries, as in efforts to redistribute access to the arts, space played a critical role. Physical planning initiatives used tools and policies beyond those at the disposal of the Department of Cultural Affairs to direct the locations of cultural life in the city. Early in his first year as mayor, Lindsay appointed a Cultural Committee to review the city's funding and administration of the arts, exploring "ways in which New York City could maintain and enhance its position as a leading cultural center of the world."[48] As noted by Lizabeth Cohen and Brian Goldstein in chapter 7, Lindsay was a great advocate of the theater, both as a politician and as a private citizen. In a public capacity, he promoted a critical local industry that not only attracted out-of-town visitors but also was an important source of employment. In private, the mayor was something of an actor manqué, with college theater and an appearance in an off-Broadway play to his credit. In his wife's own words, Lindsay had a "bit of the ham in him." He delighted in his close relationship with the theater world and its stars and the cameo opportunities they afforded him, just as Joseph Papp, Richard Rogers, Woody Allen, Christopher Plummer, Liza Minnelli, Harold Prince, Rita Moreno, and others would fête the mayor when he stepped down in 1973, thanking him for all he had done to support their art and their livelihood.[49]

In Lindsay's quest to save the legitimate theater, location was the key. His administration funded new theatrical productions on far-flung streets, but on a larger-scale, the decentralization of dramatic activity was a threat to the city's economy. Broadway, a report commissioned by the Rockefeller Brothers Fund in 1966 claimed, "has been the center for which our finest playwrights have written, in which our greatest performing talents have flourished, from which our American stage has taken its creative direction."[50] Yet, as profits declined and other theaters and the cinema challenged its supremacy, Broadway's output dwindled from an average of 142 theatrical productions a year in the 1930s to a mere thirty-four in the 1963-1964 season. For landowners, commercial redevelopment made more economic sense than keeping legitimate theaters on valuable sites. When theaters closed, it was not just the survival of Broadway that was threatened but also that of the many businesses so closely interwoven with it. Broadway's status as a major tourist attraction and as a symbol for the city was of increasing value to New York's economy. The Lindsay administration's creation of a special zoning district resulted in the construction of four new theaters by 1974. This indirect subsidy to the performing arts inaugurated the Lindsay administration's use of urban design and incentive zoning as an economic and cultural tool, as well as one of physical planning.

Lindsay's determined promotion of filmmaking in New York City similarly leveraged the arts to create jobs, with lasting effects on the city's economy. Declaring "Movie Month" in October 1966, the mayor announced that "this administration is determined to do everything in its power to assist the [film] industry and increase production in our city." Since the film industry boosted economic activity, "the public interest is being served," Lindsay claimed, when the city provides public facilities for filming.[51] Lindsay established a new Office of Television, Broadcasting and Film to streamline film production in the city. The administration's efforts to increase film production were an indisputable success—366 movies were filmed in the city in Lindsay's eight years as mayor, or an average of forty-six movies per year, in contrast to thirteen films made in New York in 1965.[52] In this case, the opening up of public spaces to the arts did not contribute to a more positive image for the city. The cultural policies of the Parks Department sought to turn open spaces into festivals and educational opportunities and nurture an image of the city as a place of fun and personal fulfillment. The mayor's engagement in cultural politics took a step back with regard to film content. Lindsay put city facilities at filmmakers' disposal, denying individual departments the ability to reject scripts they felt represented them in a negative light. In the fruits of Lindsay's film policy—films like *Panic in Needle Park* or *Serpico*—New York is portrayed as a gritty urban jungle, not an international cultural capital inhabited by dancers, actors, and visual artists.

Ensuring the presence of artists and other cultural producers in the city was the final component of Lindsay's cultural policy. Not content with helping artists to find places to display their work, the Lindsay administration also attempted to give artists a place to live and to make their work within city limits. The mayor was directly involved in and receptive to demands to solidify and expand the legal status of live-work loft spaces, an issue artists began to raise in the early 1960s. While New York artists sought to secure their status as tenants, urbanists saw early on the value their presence had for the city's continued economic survival. Pondering the future of cities then seen as places of "decay, crime, of fouled streets, and of people who are poor or foreign or odd," urbanist William H. Whyte pointed to the important role that "the Bohemians"—sculptors, artists, and musicians among them—could play in maintaining a demand for residential real estate downtown.[53] While it seemed that everyone was fleeing to the suburbs, artists—along with the young and childless, empty nesters, academics, and busy professionals—could be expected to remain in or return to the inner city. Thus, in addition to producing culture, artists in residence provided twenty-four-hour vitality and tax revenues for the city. They were the generators of economic activity that included a growing number of commercial galleries, auction houses, and art book publishing and sales.[54]

Much like encouraging the presence of the city's commercial theaters on Broadway, keeping artists living and working in lower Manhattan was a question of land use. SoHo—the downtown light manufacturing district south of Houston Street that was transitioning to art world epicenter as loft buildings and units were converted into artists' studios, homes, and new galleries—was the principal battleground in this regard. Artists lived in about six hundred loft units in buildings zoned and used for small-scale manufacturing. Large spaces and low rents appealed to the artists who settled there. The area's industrial character, too, appealed to those who wished to situate the making of art in less-than-rarefied precincts. In a few years, artists had turned SoHo into a thriving cultural center, their lofts home to free jazz and dance performances. In addition to Trisha Brown and Ornette Coleman, SoHo counted many of the artists involved in the city's cultural programs discussed here among its residents, including Claes Oldenburg, several of the participants in the 1966 Avant Garde Festival, and Jason Crum, a City Walls painter.[55]

The city had informally agreed not to evict any of them from their lofts, but artists, having been pushed out of other neighborhoods as property values increased, demanded security. At the Department of Cultural Affairs, Doris Freedman worked to legalize artists' housing in SoHo and to relax the procedure for granting artist-in-residence permits. Freedman characterized the plight of the artist tenants of SoHo as a "critical situation" that threatened "mass exodus of our creative artists, which would in turn undermine the cultural health of the City and jeopardize our prestigious status as the major art center of the world."[56] But the City Planning Commission was worried about opening the doors to deindustrialization in an area where some twenty-seven thousand blue-collar workers still went to work. Sharon Zukin has described how artists captured Mayor Lindsay's interest and secured his support for their demands. By cooperating with reporters who disseminated articles on their lifestyles and homes, they provided free publicity for the city as arts capital in the country and abroad, publicity the mayor was anxious to see circulate. After much lobbying by artist tenants groups, and with Lindsay's support, the City Planning Commission approved a rezoning plan to allow artist housing in a forty-three-block area between Houston and Canal Streets.[57]

The intent of the 1971 plan was to maintain a delicate balance of industry in the area, old and new. But change came rapidly to SoHo. Although the new zoning allowed artists to live only in lofts too small to be used for commercial purposes, the plan accelerated the pace of landlords' evictions of SoHo manufacturers in the hopes of replacing them with more lucrative residential tenants. At the same time, commercial galleries, another growing component of the city's culture industry, moved to SoHo in droves. Paula Cooper was the pioneer, establishing a gallery on Prince Street in 1968. Three years later, even the prominent art dealer Leo Castelli and his uptown neighbors wanted a foot in the neighborhood and opened satellite galleries in an old paper warehouse on West Broadway in SoHo. The "upgrading" of the area was aided by its new historic status. Preservationists had long been agitating to landmark the area, also known as the Cast Iron District. The Landmarks Preservation Commission designated SoHo a historic district in 1973, protecting its nineteenth-century industrial architecture from demolition and clearing the way for the area's increasing appeal to affluent professionals and gallery-goers.

Indeed, by 1974, area landlords were seeking to legalize all residential use of SoHo buildings (artist-in-residence laws remain on the books today in name only), and a new report to Mayor Beame on the value of the arts to the city made crystal clear the primacy of the connection between the arts and urban development: "Of all the tangible and intangible economic contributions of the city's cultural institutions and organizations, none is more impressive than their impact on real estate values and tax revenues."[58] Cultural organizations paid rent and, more important, "they almost always produce a positive spin-off in terms of the quality and desirability of their neighborhoods, and consequently raise the tax base."[59] The nature of this relationship between art and the life of the city was a far cry from the happening's promise of collective participation or personal liberation. Rather than engaging citizens in claiming city spaces as their own, whether as spectators or participants, art contributed to the public good by priming neighborhoods for reinvestment and by contributing to the tax revenues that could continue to finance the city's provision of basic services.

Arts Capital

In the late 1960s, Lincoln Center was a model to be rejected. Its elite vision of cultural democracy was too far removed from the reality and the aspirations of New York City's many publics. At the beginning of Lindsay's mayoral administration, Lincoln Center, with its separation of art from daily life at a rarefied location, was a foil to the promise of new forms of city life. Yet Lincoln Center was deeply entrenched in the city's economic life, and in this it proved an important prototype. Real estate studies in the 1960s already demonstrated the cultural complex's effects on the development of the surrounding area. "The downward trend of value and character experienced prior to the development of the Center, now appears to be arrested and dramatically reversed," a realty firm's 1966 study declared, noting the "beneficial influence of Lincoln Center on West Side properties directly and as a catalyst."[60] Following a summary of the changes generated by Lincoln Center, the Mayor's Commission on Cultural Policy noted in its 1974 report that SoHo had similarly stimulated financial activity and contributed to the "quality of life" in the area. The report's authors described how the "recent 'in-migration' of artists to the vacant industrial and commercial buildings in SoHo has had an interesting and widely noted renewal effect on that area." Artists, in addition to bringing in thirty-six galleries and new supporting businesses, had turned a "formerly declining neighborhood" into a "living community and major center for the arts" that "provided new sources of revenue for the City."[61]

There was a direct path, then, from Lincoln Center to SoHo (it went down Broadway and through the Theater District). From 1966 to 1974, the city solidified its position as a national, even a global, arts capital. Indeed, this was a major goal of Lindsay's cultural policy. The cultural and economic roles of the arts in New York

City were cemented precisely by cementing their claims on city space. Manhattan would become a global cultural center, and its cultural activity would help ensure the city's competitive status and fortune. As a result, in subsequent years the arts have come to play an even greater role in the city's spatial politics. But rather than contributing to the expansion of citizenship, critics have argued that, beginning in the 1970s, the arts neutralized spaces of conflict and contributed to processes of privatization and exclusion. There would be more art—and less democracy.

The role of the arts in the city's development as an exclusive precinct for the rich and powerful in the decades that followed Lindsay's administration is well known. That the arts could be mobilized by the city in an attempt to acknowledge the diversity of the city's publics and emphasize the status of members of excluded groups as full citizens is a less familiar story. In this respect, the new geography of culture discussed above was a distinct development of the Lindsay administration, and one that carved an exceptional path. Using the arts as an instrument of spatial reclamation and cultural recognition in the city's public spaces—its parks, streets, and neighborhoods, even its museums—Lindsay's cultural administrators experimented with new modes and spaces of citizenship. The democratic expansion of the arts in space may not have matched the scale of the city's support for major institutions, but neither did it make real the visions of social transformation of artists of the period. At the very least, Lindsay's cultural policies responded sympathetically to popular demands for a freer and more inclusive city. They illustrated a city where all citizens were recognized to have a claim on space and for whom urban life offered joys beyond the challenge of mere survival. If the gulf between such aspirations and their realization was wide, no mayor since has attempted to close it. The need for such an effort, meanwhile, has hardly diminished.

NOTES

1. Rosalyn Deutsche and Sharon Zukin, examining the spatial politics of the arts in New York City and the relationships between art, economy, and the city's publics subsequent to this period, have highlighted art's complicity and instrumentality in urban development that excludes large portions of the city's public. In this period, just prior to their investigations, new arts policy helped lay the groundwork for the driving role of culture in the city's economy, yet I argue it did so with a different, and more democratic, intent. See Rosalyn Deutsche, *Evictions: Art and Spatial Politics* (Cambridge, MA: MIT Press, 1996), and Sharon Zukin, *The Cultures of Cities* (Cambridge, MA: Blackwell, 1995).

2. Serge Guilbaut, *How New York Stole the Idea of Modern Art* (Chicago: University of Chicago Press, 1985).

3. Alvin Toffler, *The Culture Consumers: A Study of Art and Affluence in America* (New York: St. Martin's Press, 1964), p. 9.

4. On the National Endowment for the Art's model of cultural democracy, see Casey Blake, "Between Civics and Politics: The Modernist Moment in Federal Public Art," and Michael Kammen, "Culture and the State in America," both in *The Arts of Democracy: Art, Public Culture, and the State*, edited by Casey Blake (Philadelphia: University of Pennsylvania Press, 2007). On Lincoln Center, see Samuel Zipp, *Manhattan Projects: The Rise and Fall of Urban Renewal in Cold War New York* (New York: Oxford University Press, 2010), chapter 4, and Julia Foulkes, "Streets and Stages: Urban Renewal and the Arts after World War II," *Journal of Social History* 44, no. 2 (Dec. 2010): 413–434. On the origins and policies of NYSCA and the NEA, see Kevin V. Mulcahy and C. Richard Swaim, eds., *Public Policy and the Arts* (Boulder, CO: Westview Press, 1982); Dick Netzer, *The Subsidized Muse: Public Support for the Arts in the United States* (Cambridge: Cambridge University Press, 1978).

5. "Hoving Is a 'Happening' in the Parks," *Life*, September 9, 1966, p. 4.

6. "Citizens View Their Parks: Citizen Attitudes about New York City's Parks Disclosed by a Survey of Sitting Park Users," December 1962, p. 2, box K, folder 1, Parks Council Records, Avery Archives, Columbia University. Emphasis in original.

7. *Parks and Recreation*, campaign white paper issued by John V. Lindsay (New York: n.p., 1965), p. 2.

8. Quoted in Maurice Isserman and Michael Kazin, *America Divided: The Civil War of the 1960's* (New York: Oxford University Press, 2000), p. 218.

9. 1966 Annual Report to the Mayor, Recreation and Cultural Affairs Administration. Park History: Hoving folder, Arsenal Library, New York City Department of Parks (hereafter NYCDPR).

10. "Outdoorsman of the Big City," *Life*, April 29, 1966.

11. Maurice Carroll, "Moses Scores Park 'Happening,' But City Says More Are Planned," *New York Times*, September 21, 1966. On the history of the Avant Garde Festival, see Peter Frank, "The Avant Garde Festival: And Now, Shea Stadium," *Art in America* 62 (Nov.–Dec. 1974): 102–106.

12. Allan Kaprow, *Assemblage, Environments & Happenings* (New York: Abrams, 1966), p. 188.

13. "P.Y.A.I.R. (Phyllis Yampolsky Artist in Residence)," *Leaflet* 2, no. 2 (Feb. 1967), NYCDPR. Yampolsky was in fact the first to designate any Parks Department events as "happenings," a designation that Hoving adopted only after the press had latched onto it.

14. August Heckscher, *Alive in the City: Memoir of an Ex-Commissioner* (New York: Scribner, 1974), 160. On the politics of the establishment of the NEA, see Milton C. Cummings Jr., "To Change a Nation's Cultural Policy: The Kennedy Administration and the Arts in the United States, 1961–1963," in *Public Policy and the Arts*, edited by Kevin V. Mulcahy and C. Richard Swaim (Boulder, CO: Westview Press, 1982).

15. Doris Freedman, untitled manuscript, box 3, folder "Notes for Book," Doris C. Freedman Papers (hereafter DCF). Since being reviewed by the author, these papers have been transferred to the Fales Library, New York University, as part of the Public Art Fund Archive and boxes have been renumbered.

16. Ibid.

17. Doris Freedman, draft of article for *New York* magazine, box 3, folder 4: "Essays 1969–1975," DCF.

18. Doris Freedman, untitled, undated manuscript, box 3, folder "Notes for Book," DCF.

19. *Sculpture in Environment* (New York: Cultural Affairs Foundation, 1967). On the history of the new public art, *La Grande Vitesse*, and changing conceptions of audience and site

specificity for public art at this time, see Blake, "Between Civics and Politics," and Miwon Kwon, *One Place after Another: Site-Specific Art and Locational Identity* (Cambridge, MA: MIT Press, 2004).

20. August Heckscher, "The Urban Park in the Urban Crisis," speech before the National Recreation and Park Association, December 1967, Parks History: Heckscher File, NYCDPR.

21. Ibid.

22. Freedman quoted in Ryna Appleton Segal, *The New York City Department of Cultural Affairs, 1962 to 1973: A Record of Government's Involvement in the Arts* (New York: n.p., 1976), p. 29. Freedman's writings frequently betray a degree of tone deafness to the situations in which she found herself but also show a willingness to learn from others and correct liberal biases when these were pointed out to her.

23. Gottehrer, interviewed in Segal, *New York City Department of Cultural Affairs*, p. 20.

24. Thomas Hoving, "Artful Tom, A Memoir," 2009, http://www.artnet.com/magazine us/authors/artfultom.asp.

25. Junius Eddy, "Government, the Arts, and Ghetto Youth" *Public Administration Review* (July/Aug. 1970): 400.

26. Segal, *New York City Department of Cultural Affairs*, p. 19.

27. On activism among artists in New York at this time, see Julia Bryan-Wilson, *Art Workers: Radical Practice in the Vietnam War Era* (Berkeley: University of California Press, 2009). Bryan-Wilson, who focuses on the activities of the Art Workers Coalition and artists' identification as laborers and opposition to the Vietnam War, barely scratches the surface of debates over race within the AWC and the city's art world.

28. *Report of the Mayor's Committee on Cultural Policy* (New York: Mayor's Committee on Cultural Policy, 1974), p. 19. On the rise of alternative spaces, see Phil Patton, "Other Voices, Other Rooms: The Rise of the Alternative Space," *Art in America* (July/Aug. 1977): 80–89.

29. Untitled 1975 brochure, box 33, folder "Grants Files, 1973, the Brooklyn Children's Museum," Vincent Astor Foundation Records. Manuscripts and Archives Division, Humanities and Social Sciences Library, the New York Public Library.

30. Various versions of the story of the founding of El Museo give more or less agency to Ortiz, School District 4 Superintendent Martin Frey, and East Harlem parents and activists. See Fatima Bercht and Deborah Cullen, eds., *Voces y Visiones: Highlights from el Museo del Barrio's Permanent Collection* (New York: El Museo del Barrio, 2003); Grace Glueck, "Barrio Museum: Hope Si, Home No," *New York Times*, July 30, 1970.

31. Arlene Dávila, "Culture in the Battlefield: From Nationalist to Pan-Latino Projects," in *Mambo Montage: The Latinization of New York*, edited by Agustín Laó-Montes and Arlene Dávila (New York: Columbia University Press, 2001), p. 161.

32. Hoving, "Artful Tom, A Memoir."

33. Richard F. Shepard, "Later Hours Set by Metropolitan," *New York Times*, May 24, 1967; Thomas Hoving, *Making the Mummies Dance: Inside the Metropolitan Museum of Art* (New York: Simon & Schuster, 1993), p. 55.

34. See contributions by Hoving and exhibition curator Allon Schoener to *Harlem on my Mind: Cultural Capital of Black America, 1900–1968* (New York: New Press, 1995); Grace Glueck, "Harlem Cultural Council Drops Support for Metropolitan Show," *New York Times*, November 23, 1968; Murray Schumach, "Harlem Exhibition Opens to Crowds at Metropolitan Museum," *New York Times*, January 19, 1969; Hoving, *Making the Mummies Dance*, pp. 164–180.

35. Victor Chen, "Museum Extension," August 30, 1967, box 356, folder 336, John Vliet Lindsay Papers (Yale University; hereafter JVL Yale); Jane Norman, "How to Look at Art," *The Metropolitan Museum of Art Bulletin*, 28, no. 5 (Jan. 1970): 192.

36. In this Hoving was in fact defending the business interests of his father, Walter. The Chairman of Tiffany & Co., Walter Hoving feared the effects of a *déclassé* establishment on the shopping district in which his luxury goods emporium was situated.

37. Carter Burden, letter to Mayor Lindsay, February 4, 1971, box 6, folder 106, Accession 1998-M-094, JVL Yale. Burden, with his wife, Amanda, was among those skewered in Tom Wolfe's 1968 essay "Radical Chic," which adds another layer to the cultural politics of the period, the melding of elite and radical cultural priorities.

38. Miriam Greenberg, *Branding New York: How a City in Crisis Was Sold to the World* (New York: Routledge, 2008), p. 9.

39. Sharon Zukin identifies the late 1960s and early 1970s as the origins of the focus on culture as an engine of growth in New York City, describing a "synergy between art, finance, and politics," which, she writes "benefits high cultural institutions and the tourist industry," Zukin, *Cultures of Cities*, p. 111. "Dendur-in-New-York," *New York Times*, November 23, 1967. On Dendur and its enclosure, see David Gissen, "The Architectural Production of Nature, Dendur/New York," *Grey Room* 34 (winter 2009): 58–79.

40. Thomas Hoving, "Report of the Director," *Annual Report of the Trustees of the Metropolitan Museum of Art*, 103 (July 1, 1972–June 30, 1973): 8. Greenberg argues: "it was in the 1970s that the standpoint of the out-of-towner and the imagination of the average tourist became overwhelming preoccupations for the established and emerging leadership of New York City; *Branding New York*, p. 8.

41. Grace Glueck, "Metropolitan Museum to Institute Admissions Charge," *New York Times* , October 9, 1970; John V. Lindsay, letter to Thomas Hoving, January 29, 1971, box 68, folder 1314 "Metropolitan Museum of Art, 1966–1973," Mayor Lindsay Papers (New York City Municipal Archives; hereafter JVL NYC).

42. Murray Kempton, "The Agony in the Garden," *The New York Review of Books*, September 24, 1970.

43. Thomas Hoving, letter to Mayor Lindsay, September 15, 1971. Box 68, folder 1314 "Metropolitan Museum of Art, 1966–1973," JVL NYC. Underlining (by hand) in original. "Yeah!" is handwritten.

44. Douglas Dillon and Thomas Hoving, "Report of the President and the Director," *Annual Report of the Trustees of the Metropolitan Museum of Art* 102 (July 1, 1971–June 30, 1972): 7.

45. See Rockefeller Brothers Fund, *The Performing Arts: Problems and Prospects* (New York: McGraw Hill, 1965); William J. Baumol and William G. Bowen, *Performing Arts—The Economic Dilemma* (New York: The Twentieth Century Fund, 1966).

46. Richard Shapiro, "Brief History of the Department of Cultural Affairs," August 1969, box 1, folder 1 "Department of Cultural Affairs 1968–71," DCF.

47. Mayor's Committee on Cultural Policy Report 1974, p. 1.

48. Eugene R. Black Jr., *Report of the Mayor's Cultural Committee* (New York: n.p., 1966), p. 1.

49. Louis Calta, "Showmen Praise Mayor's Stand-In," *New York Times*, October 7, 1966; Murray Schumach, "Broadway Gives Regards to Lindsay," *New York Times*, December 27, 1973.

50. Rockefeller Brothers Fund, *Performing Arts*, 33.

51. Remarks by John V. Lindsay at the Opening Luncheon for the 1966 Convention of the National Association of Theater Owners, September 28, 1966, box 363, folder 440, JVL Yale.

52. Greenberg, *Branding New York*, 54.

53. William H. Whyte, "Are Cities Un-American?" in his book *The Exploding Metropolis* (Garden City, NY: Doubleday, 1958), pp. 23, 32. Whyte and subsequent housing policy anticipated contemporary enthusiasts of the "creative class" as the engine of urban economic vitality.

54. In *The Transformation of the Avant-Garde: The New York Art World, 1940–1985* (Chicago: University of Chicago Press, 1987), Diana Crane details the growth of the business of art in New York in this period and illustrates how the role of the artist in the city ceased to be that of an avant-garde with its concomitant overtones of alienation from popular culture and middle-class values.

55. See Richard Kostelanetz, *SoHo: The Rise and Fall of an Artist's Colony* (New York: Routledge, 2003).

56. Doris Freedman, *Department of Cultural Affairs Annual Report 1969–70* (New York: Department of Cultural Affairs, 1970), p. 6.

57. Sharon Zukin, *Loft Living: Culture and Capital in Urban Change* (New Brunswick, NJ: Rutgers University Press, 1989), p. 117.

58. *Report of the Mayor's Committee on Cultural Policy* (New York: Mayor's Committee on Cultural Policy, 1974), p. 8.

59. Ibid.

60. Appraisal Department, Brown, Harris, Stevens, letter to Lincoln Center Fund, November 22, 1966, box 62, folder 1161 "Lincoln Center 1966–1971," JVL NYC.

61. *Report of the Mayor's Committee on Cultural Policy*, p. 8.

Mayor John Lindsay strolls through the Bedford-Stuyvesant section of Brooklyn, after apparently serious death threats against him were made barely a week after the assassination of Robert F. Kennedy. June 11, 1968. © Daily News, L.P. (New York). Used with permission.

CHAPTER NINE

After the Fall

John Lindsay, New York, and the American Dream

JOSEPH P. VITERITTI

John Lindsay will always be controversial. He was mayor during one of the most explosive decades in American history, and he did not shy away from conflict. He was both principled and moralistic. He could have a soothing effect on the most troubled communities and enrage those who were better off. He had a deep sensitivity for people who were in pain but could not always understand the anxieties of those who were just getting by. Vincent Cannato has argued in his magisterial book that Lindsay cannot be separated from the liberal policy agenda of the 1960s and all that went wrong with it.[1] Fred Siegel is even less forgiving. Recalling the collaboration between Franklin Roosevelt and Fiorello LaGuardia, Siegel calls New York the ultimate "New Deal City;" which, under the auspices of Lindsay and the Great Society, got swept up in a spirit of "dependent individualism," where people felt they could do whatever they pleased, have as many children as they wanted, and expect the government to pay for it.[2] By the time Cannato and Siegel wrote their epitaphs for New York at the end of the twentieth century, many Americans had moved on. They had lost faith in government, abandoned their cities, and heeded Ronald Reagan's advice to rely on unencumbered private markets to distribute the benefits of a new prosperity.

Could Lindsay be blamed for what was happening in New York? Any assessment of leadership must be mindful of historical context. The choices that political actors make are limited by their options. Existing alternatives can be less than optimal, frequently a choice between two or more terrible courses of action. Then there are the complex moral questions that confound when deciding on the direction of public policy.

Evaluating mayors is further complicated by the fact that they have relatively little power to address the problems facing their cities. Most laws that affect their jurisdictions are made in the state capitol, where legislative leaders can be antagonistic to cities. Local policy is also shaped by federal spending priorities. Even when Washington tries to help, it sets cumbersome rules and creates financial obligations. Lindsay was well aware of these limitations. Like most mayors, he complained about them regularly and cried out for greater home rule and support. Yet, these obstacles are not an alibi. As Gotham wise man and former Lindsay advisor Peter Goldmark observes, "The powers of the office may be limited, but the demands have no bounds, and the mayor must respond."[3] An effective mayor needs to navigate around the institutional encumbrances. They are the fixed challenges he needs to overcome in order to succeed. But what is success? How is it measured? Is it marked by reelection? Fiscal health? Improving the general welfare? Helping those most in need? In the harshest of times, is it simply preventing things from getting worse? The passage of time grants us the benefit of hindsight to examine old priorities in the context of new realities. The first decade of the new century presents us with a new metropolitan tableau that can add further insights on the past.

New York had already begun to deteriorate by 1965. The economy was being restructured, more dependent populations were replacing less dependent populations, and cities were experiencing a frightening crime wave that would only worsen in the coming decades. New York was not the only city suffering from such decline; nor was it any worse than most other urban centers.[4] But New York had magnitude. Observing it was like putting all of urban America under a giant microscope. It had a provocative charismatic mayor who drew the world's attention and an international press corps ready to follow his every move. During his time in office, Lindsay's ever photographic face appeared on the covers of *Time, Life,* and *Newsweek* no fewer than eight times.[5] The Big Apple became a case study of the tensions surrounding massive social change, a prime exhibit for those prepared to argue for a new paradigm of government. And today it remains a showcase for all that is right and wrong with the American experiment that, perhaps with the benefit of retrospection, can help us chart a better future.

The Roads Taken

The storied New York City fiscal crisis of 1975 was not just about money. To critics of American liberalism, it was indicative of a city that had spun out of control, of governmental excess, of a political system that had relied on shady dealing to survive. It was a final reckoning that imposed discipline and exacted penalties long overdue. John Lindsay was out of office for more than a year when the city teetered on the brink of bankruptcy. Nevertheless, the controversial Mr. Lindsay, who famously stood by Lyndon Johnson's aggressive social agenda as both a congressman and mayor, was a shiny target for historians sounding the death knell of big government.

Lindsay was one of the many players who contributed to the apocalyptic fiscal drama that nearly brought New York down, but he was not alone. Mayor Wagner had concocted the financial instruments that allowed the City Council and Board of Estimate to imagine revenues that never materialized. He hid operating expenses in the capital budget. City Comptroller Abraham Beame dutifully lent his imprimatur of approval to legitimize the entire charade, only to take these practices to new lengths when he later became mayor himself. The budget games were New York's dirty little secret. Even the bankers knew, and they went along with the schemes so long as it served them well, only to demand more control and compensation when everything fell apart. All the while, Albany, run under the platinum thumb of a Rockefeller, conveniently looked the other way.

Lindsay was not oblivious to the fiscal storm that was on the horizon. He recruited talented managers and launched a pioneering productivity program to confront the arcane bureaucracy whose entrenched overlords treated the revenue side of a budget ledger as a tender curiosity. He got the state to raise taxes and impose new ones. Although the added taxes provided a motive, or at least another excuse, for businesses to leave the city, they also became an important source of revenue. He experimented with incentive zoning wisely before it became a ruse through which politicians rewarded powerful allies. He was prescient in understanding that the arts and culture of the city could be mobilized as a unique financial resource. He fought a tireless uphill battle to retain corporations that could more profitably conduct business elsewhere. And he attempted to launch a countercyclical effort to protect a manufacturing base uprooted by irreversible economic forces. Experts deem the latter effort as futile. Lindsay would not give up on the blue-collar manufacturing base, because he saw it as part of a larger social agenda.

In fact, most of what Lindsay did during his eight years as mayor was driven by his overarching social agenda. Poor people were coming to New York in droves, much as Irish, Italian, and Jewish immigrants had over the previous century. Their only alternative to public assistance was employment. Their only means to a job was their hard labor. Retaining some part of New York's manufacturing base was worth a try; it was a moral obligation to those who came here seeking a better life. That, after all, was the historical promise of New York that no mayor in good conscience could abandon.

By 1965 that promise became harder to deliver. The political machine that had paved the way for European immigrants was fading away; what was left of it did not embrace black people and Puerto Ricans cheerfully. The machine's crucial role of producing votes for Democratic Party regulars had been taken over by newly empowered municipal unions determined to preserve the ethnic villages that flourished in city agencies. So, if John Lindsay sounded moralistic during his early days as mayor when he denounced the president of the striking transit union as a "power broker," he was not far off the mark. Like his union brothers, Transit Workers Union President Michael Quill had eaten at the table of Mayor Robert Wagner, who had made unknown labor bosses into powerhouses.[6] Lindsay and the city would pay for the meal in years to come. Subsequent agreements, more expensive agreements negotiated by more militant labor leaders, would add to future financial woes, although the deals were no more burdensome than bargains struck in other ailing municipalities where the costs of living were lower. The most generous pension deals were cut in Albany by legislators who claimed to represent the city. Lindsay's awkward way of dealing with blue-collar New Yorkers certainly didn't help. The union guys liked to knock him around when they could, and, besides, the money wasn't bad.

The item in the city budget that added the most strain was social services. Again New York was not unique on this score. The spike in city expenditures was replicated in urban centers throughout the country.[7] It was largely driven by policies written in Washington that required states to support the growing welfare rolls. No state passed on a larger portion of that burden to localities than did New York. Lindsay had always argued that poverty was a national problem that should be addressed entirely by the federal government. When Washington did not comply, he accepted responsibility and instructed his Human Resources Administrator to help people get assistance. It was their legal right.

Ronald Reagan would eventually convince Americans in both political parties that welfare was nothing more than a scam. Some applicants abused the system through fraud, and others read the formula as an incentive to have children they could not afford to properly support. But there were also many people in need. Poverty and unemployment were high, and the economy was not producing the jobs to put unskilled people to work. It was right for the government to step in and provide support for distressed families. There was no real choice but for the city to assume a share of the burden, even in the face of fiscal calamity. In the end poverty rates came tumbling down, and the city survived. The banks and the unions and the power brokers figured out a way to keep the city and themselves solvent.[8] If you were one of the parents whose children were saved from hunger, indecent housing, or poor health care made possible by the Great Society and its local composites, you might think it was a good bet. In the great schoolroom of American government, Lindsay may have failed accounting, but he excelled in philosophy. He offered lessons. He had the right priorities, even if his idealism and naïveté about the hard edges of city politics occasionally could poke him in the eye.

Richard Aurelio, who served as a key Lindsay strategist and deputy mayor, explains, "Lindsay had an obsessive interest in racial justice and civil liberties going back to his time in Congress. It was hard to get him off the subject. He was very tough on President Kennedy. He felt that JFK was slow on picking up on civil rights issues and that he was too concerned about Southern Democrats." Aurelio continues, "As mayor, Lindsay could have a blind spot towards the white middle class. He thought they would realize that giving blacks a piece of the pie would eventually benefit everybody."[9]

Lindsay was confrontational right out of the gate. Taking on the civilian review board issue and the powerful Patrolmen's Benevolent Association in his first campaign speech in 1965 invited controversy. But what were the choices for a candidate who had decided to take the side of the people who were underrepresented in politics? What should he have expected from a political system in which entrenched interests had never been asked to make the compromises that were needed to create a more just city? The Police Department at the time was pervasively corrupt. Street justice was often administered at the end of a nightstick, especially in black and Puerto Rican neighborhoods.

Even though Senator Robert Kennedy eventually agreed to serve as honorary co-chair of the committee to install a review board, he had been reluctant to move ahead with the idea. Kennedy was more pragmatic; he was concerned about losing support in the Catholic parishes that sent their boys to the Police Academy and thoroughly convinced that this was a losing fight in a city overwhelmed by crime.[10] But during the 1960s politicians needed to take unpopular positions if a corner was to be turned on civil rights long denied. That is leadership. Lindsay showed no reluctance, and he pushed Kennedy along, willing to accept the risk of defeat. Lindsay displayed the same backbone a few years later when he stood up for women and gays before most politicians took notice of the need.

Lindsay had also taken a principled position on integrated housing in Forest Hill, Queens. Concerned about the growing tensions between the black and Jewish communities, he eventually enlisted the assistance of a young Mario Cuomo to craft a compromise. His position on housing integration was especially notable in light of his prior reluctance to support school integration as a congressman. School segregation after all is a function of housing segregation. Focusing on the latter over the former places the burden of change and its commensurate conflict on the shoulders of adults rather than children. It makes sense. And, by the way, housing discrimination had recently become illegal.

Lindsay's instinct to make the school system more responsive to the concerns of African American and Puerto Rican parents also was well founded, given how out of touch Livingston Street was with the communities it was supposed to serve. The governance arrangement of the school system ensured that key decision makers were physically and psychically remote from the schools. Lindsay, however, made a strategic error when, in the midst of heated debates over school decentralization, he allowed all three experimental districts to be placed in minority neighborhoods. In so doing he racialized the issue and lost the support of parents in white communities who also wanted a voice in their children's education. It was a mistake he owned up to in a book published in 1969 during his reelection campaign.[11] Lindsay also should have intervened more quickly when the school board in Ocean Hill–Brownsville reassigned Jewish teachers and administrators without abiding by due process protections to which the educators were entitled.[12]

Notwithstanding strategic and tactical errors, Lindsay's larger agenda was both honorable and courageous. Like Lyndon Johnson, he understood that democracy is fragile. He knew that in order for democracy to succeed, people had to trust government. In order for people to trust government, they had to believe that it would treat them fairly and appreciate their concerns. He understood the importance of personal gestures, like a walk down a street that had been forgotten by those in power. He applied that sensitivity most effectively with people who needed it the most. He understood that for democracy to function all citizens must have a meaningful voice. Like the architects of the Great Society agenda, he was overly optimistic about the efficacy of altering institutional structures, when the most substantial barriers to effective participation in governing are social and economic. Decentralization alone was not sufficient if citizens were not prepared to participate. It would take time before African Americans and Latinos would be able to exercise real strength at the ballot box and in the halls of government. But it had to start somewhere. Localized institutions were more accessible to those who lacked influence.

Lindsay saw it as his responsibility to jumpstart the process of involvement; he may not have fully understood the strength of resistance that stood in the way. He used his power of appointment to make city government more representative; he not did recognize the resentment harbored by those who would be pushed aside, however unjustified their reactions might have been. Like Lyndon Johnson, Lindsay eventually tempered his approach to participatory local government. Johnson did it when he moved away from the "maximum feasible participation" requirement of the Community Action Program and found a way to involve elected officials in the Model Cities Program alongside new participants. Lindsay did it by backing off from the confrontational politics that defined Ocean Hill–Brownsville and by becoming more reliant on forms of administrative decentralization like the Office of Neighborhood Government (ONG) that kept government officials in charge but

required them to heed the advice of community residents. He located the ONG offices throughout the city, not just in minority neighborhoods. More than any other
city in the country, New York during the 1960s was democracy on training wheels,
involving people who had never been given a chance. There had to be falls and
scrapes. Lindsay assumed the role of the watchful father, running alongside, hoping
to lend a helping hand. Sometimes his own strong reach would disrupt the ride.

Lindsay's vision of the city was grand and inclusive. If cities were the center of
civilization, New York had to be the epicenter. In an almost classical Athenian way,
he believed that the greatest contribution the city can make to civilization is the gift
of democracy. It was a gift to be shared by all. It went beyond politics, embracing
every aspect of daily life. New York could boast world-class opera companies, dance
troupes, and symphonic orchestras, but every citizen had to be given an opportunity to engage in the arts. The mayor's office would seek the expertise of celebrity
architects to give the city a physical form that was worthy of its unique status, but
planners were expected to be mindful of what ordinary people thought. Even as the
city headed toward fiscal disaster, John Lindsay had an abiding faith in its future as
a place that would continue to thrive, as a place that would continue to offer opportunities to the humble.

The Prosperous City

New York has come back. Or, a large part of it has. The subways have been washed
of graffiti; the murder rate is down from its all-time high in 1990; and Wall Street
is generating unfathomable earnings. Yet, the poverty and unemployment rates are
higher now than they were in the 1960s.[13] Almost half the population is categorized
as "near poor" by the Center for Economic Opportunity.[14] The homeless rate is the
highest it has been since the Great Depression.[15] The city has learned to live within
its means in a manner of speaking. It continues to borrow and run deficits, but
there is no evident danger of impending default. It could actually be doing better.
The commuter tax that Lindsay won from Albany was eliminated in 1999, costing
the city billions of dollars in revenue, saving a lot of money for investment bankers
living in Connecticut.[16] Property taxes remain low compared with those throughout
the New York metropolitan region.

Many of the changes Governor Hugh Carey imposed on the city after the 1975
fiscal crisis were for the better. Financial management systems are now in place.
There is better performance information. The state assumed financial responsibility for senior colleges at the City University and a larger share of the expenses for
hospitals, social services, and the courts. There were also massive cutbacks that fell
especially hard on poor and working people, such as an increase in transit fares,

tuition charges at the once-free City University, a 20 percent reduction in the work-force, and the closing of five city hospitals.[17]

In the aftermath of the crisis, urban scholars argued, much as Lindsay had, that the federal government should assume responsibility for redistributive services like health and welfare.[18] The argument made sense. New York and other cities had demonstrated that local governments lacked the fiscal capacity to sustain the redistributive burden. Laying it on them set one against the other and put those with more generous social agendas at a competitive disadvantage in attracting and retaining revenue-producing businesses. After all, it wasn't just the weather that was making firms move from the Rust Belt to the Sunbelt. Because of its greater taxing power, the federal government was better situated to redistribute wealth. It was able to impose progressive tax policies across the entire country, and businesses had nowhere to flee. Or so it was thought.

The idea worked better in theory than in practice. Major companies began to set up shop on other continents. Although the federal government demonstrated its unique capacity to redistribute wealth through imaginative tax policies, it reallocated wealth in the wrong direction. The financial catastrophe of the past three decades has been a growing disparity in wealth and income that has been ushered in by tax loopholes and deregulation. The great shift was not the result of a hidden hand sorting out the inefficiencies of the economy. It was the product of effective lobbying by financial institutions that used their wealth to manipulate the legislative process in their own favor. Campaign donors with huge bundles of money had their way with Republicans and Democrats alike.[19] It is not surprising that New York, the home of Wall Street, saw the worst effects of the shift, experiencing greater income polarization than any other city.[20] After the economy crashed in 2008, Washington bailed out the banks that caused the wreckage, while middle-class and working people lost their jobs and homes with little relief from the government. One can only imagine what influence the bankers carry in their own town, if they could so bully the White House and the Congress.

New York City has never fully recovered from the psychological damage it suffered from the fiscal crisis of 1975. Like a weary old man who had managed to scrape through the worst years of the Great Depression, New York can't get over the fear of being poor again. No matter what the issue of the day—be it crime, schools, or the threat of natural disaster—money, or the lack of it, continues to haunt us. No mayor more honestly reflected that sentiment than Edward Koch. A transitional figure, Koch had lived through the 1929 crisis as a young child, and he was the first chief executive to rule after the 1975 crisis.[21] Rather than being cowed by state control mechanisms that Governor Carey put in place, he was emboldened by them.

The Emergency Financial Control Board and the Municipal Assistance Corporation enabled him to say "no" when the usual array of interest groups pressured him to spend money the city did not have. In an odd way the new state mechanisms, so long as they lasted, centralized power under the mayor.[22]

Power was permanently centralized in 1989 when the U.S. Supreme Court affirmed two lower federal court decisions declaring that the city Board of Estimate violated the one-person, one-vote standard of the Fourteenth Amendment, requiring a significant makeover of the municipal government. The board, on which the five borough presidents had more votes than the mayor, was a last remnant of power for the county political bosses. It had formidable authority regarding the budget and land use and in its own way gave voice to communities throughout the city. Architects of the 1989 City Charter had hoped that with the demise of the board, the City Council, enlarged from thirty-five to fifty-one members, would serve as a more democratic check on the power of the mayor.[23] We are still waiting for that to happen.

While Mayor David Dinkins, elected on the same day the new charter was approved by voters, felt his way cautiously through the new constitutional arrangement, his successors Rudolph Giuliani and Michael Bloomberg treated the council as a pestering nuisance that encumbered their worthy agendas. After all was said and done, the council proved to be quite compliant. It was the council itself that handed Bloomberg a third term when it amended the City Charter to overturn term limits that had twice been approved in popular referenda. Bloomberg had already centralized the power of the mayor further when, immediately after coming to office in 2002, he got the state legislature to give him control of the city schools—a final blow to the dwindled power of the borough presidents.

Michael Bloomberg inherited a very different city from the one that John Lindsay left behind. With more immigrants arriving from different parts of Asia, the city is more racially and ethnically diverse. Many of the Asians are professionals or have the means to start small businesses. The Latino population is also more ethnically diverse, with more Spanish speakers coming from South America and the Dominican Republic than Puerto Rico. A large number of immigrants are actually bypassing New York City for more affordable suburbs. Blacks are moving back to the South. Blacks and Latinos still suffer from higher rates of poverty and unemployment. New York is becoming less affordable.[24]

As a result of national welfare reforms implemented by President Bill Clinton, the public assistance rolls decreased from 1.2 million in 1996 to 350,000 in 2010.[25] It is better for people to work than to be dependent on the government to survive. Unfortunately, as the income share for the top 1 percent (those making more than

$580,000) doubled between 1990 and 2007, the median hourly wage fell 8.6 percent.[26] What good is a job if it doesn't allow you to support yourself or your family? How many jobs should mothers and fathers have to hold to make ends meet? With all of its accumulated wealth, poverty and unemployment rates in New York surpass those that persist in most of the country.[27]

By the time Michael Bloomberg was elected mayor, the finance, insurance, and real estate (FIRE) industries had begun to assume a more dominant role in the city economy and its politics, following a pattern that began during the fiscal crisis.[28] More than a quarter century had passed, yet the public dialogue kept a close eye on fiscal solvency and growth. Mayors Giuliani's and Bloomberg's attention to crime and schools could reasonably be expected to benefit residents in the most depressed neighborhoods. Their efforts could also be seen as part of a larger strategy to retain the middle class and promote economic development. Since 1975 politicians have had an instinctual aversion to new taxes, claiming that such levies are bad for business. The tax abatements they gave out to corporations and developers would make Boss Tweed blush.[29] Such discounts, common among cities competing for businesses, do not always reap the rewards intended, and they can be a sham.[30]

While Bloomberg denounced corporate welfare and had the good sense to raise real estate taxes, he was widely recognized as a product and friend of the FIRE sectors.[31] In a generally favorable review of his mayoralty, biographer Joyce Purnick called Bloomberg the most development minded mayor in history, having rezoned 18 percent of the city during his first two terms.[32] If John Lindsay became indelibly identified with the progressive politics of a city that was not entirely of his making, Michael Bloomberg became emblematic of the new millennium's business friendly city that was already emerging before he came to office.

Like Lindsay, Bloomberg did much to verify his acquired image. He resisted a new state tax on hedge fund managers saying that legislative leaders were "trying to kill the golden goose."[33] He opposed "living wage" and "prevailing wage" laws passed over his veto that raised the salaries of janitors, security guards, and other service workers employed by companies receiving subsidies or leasing space from the city.[34] He opposed a law passed by the city council that required small businesses to provide sick leave for food service workers and other laborers, claiming that it would be prohibitively expensive. He has referred to New York City as a "luxury product."[35]

The city that was once an engine for democracy is now an engine for prosperity. The city that once transformed European peasants into American citizens with hopeful futures is more inclined to welcome immigrants who can help with the bottom line—those with technical qualifications as scientists or engineers, those fortunate enough to become entrepreneurs, the ones who can make it on their own. We might as well replace the Lady in the Harbor with a statue of Alan Greenspan. The civic project has been downsized. Between 1965 and 2009, the actual number of people participating in municipal elections has declined 55.6 percent;[36] the number voting in municipal elections as a percentage of those voting in the previous presidential election (1964 and 2008 respectively) has declined from 86.2 percent to 44.6 percent, the lowest ratio in fifty years.[37]

The entire political process has been retooled since the days of John Lindsay. Participation rates are down all over the country at all levels of government.[38] Here in New York we opted for centralization over decentralization. We don't elect people the way we used to. The armies of volunteers that Tammany and the unions recruited to produce votes have been replaced by finance committees. Elections are no longer just ground wars fought door-to-door by volunteers; they are media campaigns that cost money. Even volunteers get paid. Ironically, John Lindsay and his magical handler David Garth were among the first to prove the power of television, which eventually raised the price of politics. Campaign spending is at an all-time high. According to the City Campaign Finance Board, between 1989 and 2009 spending on City Council races has increased from $2.8 million to $24.7 million, for the comptroller's office it has risen from $4.2 million to $19.4 million, and with billionaire Michael Bloomberg entering politics, spending on the mayoralty leaped from $24.1 million to $120.1 million.[39]

Unions still ferry voters to the polls, but they also fund candidates. With a few exceptions, neither they nor the municipal agencies they staff remain the ethnic fortresses they were back in the day. They can still defend work rules that are obsolete and demand pensions that are unaffordable; but they are not as powerful as they were when they went to war with John Lindsay. For the past twenty years, New York City has been run by mayors who were easily dismissive of the unions, though not as belligerent toward them as the governors of Indiana and Wisconsin who tried to abolish collective bargaining altogether. Public service unions still matter in New York. How much remains to be seen.

There is a lot happening now that would take John Lindsay by surprise. The son of a banking family who died with modest means in 2000, Lindsay could not have imagined the money-making machines designed by hedge fund managers that have contributed to the growing inequality. And though the unions are weaker than they used to be, they remain one of the most significant forces for progressive politics at a time when economic disparity is so undermining the democratic promise. Once antagonists in the battles over race that tormented Lindsay and his city, it is the unions that must be counted on to fight for wages that enable workers and their families to live respectable lives. Like most Americans, New Yorkers are fearful about their economic futures; unlike previous generations who entered the city, they can no longer make the secure assumption that their children will live better than they have.[40]

There is also much that Lindsay would find familiar. The Police Department remains at odds with minority communities over street tactics that threaten their civil rights.[41] The firefighters were recently involved in a court battle over a civil service examination that has allowed the department to remain 90 percent white in a majority minority city.[42] Housing is still segregated.[43] The education department has a glittering new headquarters named after a crooked politician that is more remote from the schools than Livingston Street was. While few want to return to the elected school boards that existed prior to mayoral control, and much has changed for the better, the system lacks an effective mechanism for meaningful parental and community participation.[44]

Future mayors must restore the civic project that historically made New York the major port of entry for those in search of the American dream. They can tinker with the shape of institutions, but that will never be enough. Elections must be more accessible, schools more reliable, housing more affordable, health care more available, wages more gainful, and taxes more equitable. The next mayor can take a page from the book of John Lindsay, but it won't be easy. He can turn to Washington for help but can no longer count on it. It is a dark season for American democracy. The larger inequality that undermines good government today may have been instigated on Wall Street, but it was Washington's doing. It makes the bookkeeping antics that led to the fiscal crisis of 1975 look like child's play. The motives were kinder then. The old excesses were committed to ease poverty; the latest, to enhance privilege.

The next mayor should do what he thinks is right, but not always assume that he is. He should stand firm on principles that are dear, but be prepared to lose. And he should draw strength from knowing that history has a long memory.

NOTES

1. Vincent J. Cannato, *The Ungovernable City: John Lindsay and His Struggle to Save New York* (New York: Basic Books, 2001), p. ix.

2. Fred Siegel, *The Future Once Happened Here: New York, D.C., L.A. and the Fate of America's Big Cities* (San Francisco: Encounter Books, 1997), p. xi. For a more positive assessment of the Roosevelt-LaGuardia alignment, see Mason B. Williams, *City of Ambition: FDR, LaGuardia, and the Making of Modern New York* (New York: Norton, 2013.)

3. Peter Goldmark, interview with the author, February 28, 2012.

4. Cannato, *Ungovernable City,* pp. 525–553.

5. These included *Life*, May 28, 1965, December 12, 1965, May 24, 1968; *Newsweek*, No-

vember 15, 1965, November 3, 1969, August 23, 1971; *Time*, November 12, 1965, November 1, 1968.

6. Quill and his union had longer standing than the other municipal unions, since the Transit Workers Union was established back when the subways were run by private operators.

7. Cannato, *Ungovernable City*, pp. 525–533.

8. William K. Tabb, *The Long Default: New York City and the Urban Fiscal Crisis* (New York: Monthly Review Press, 1982).

9. Author interview with Richard Aurelio, February 20, 2012.

10. Author interview with Jay Kriegel, February 8, 2012.

11. John Lindsay, *The City* (New York: W.W. Norton, 1969), p. 21.

12. There had originally been nineteen, one of whom was black and removed in error, who was later reinstated, according to Richard Kahlenberg, *Tough Liberal: Albert Shanker and the Battles over Schools, Unions, Race, and Democracy* (New York: Columbia University Press, 2007), page 93.

13. According to U.S. Census published data, the unemployment rate went from 5.2 percent in 1960, to 4.9 percent in 1970, to 8.6 percent in 1980, to 9.0 percent in 1990, to 9.6 percent in 2000, to 10.5 percent in 2010; the poverty rate went from 13.8 percent in 1960, to 11.9 percent in 1970, to 17.5 percent in 1980, to 17.5 percent in 1990 (again); to 21.0 in 2000, to 20.1 percent in 2010. See generally, Mark K. Levitan and Susan S. Weiler, "Poverty in New York City, 1969–1999: The Influence of Demographic Change, Income Growth, and Income Inequality," *Economic Policy Review* (July 2008), pp. 13–30 (tracing the growth of poverty and its relationship to income inequality).

14. "The CEO Poverty Measure, 2005–2011," an annual report by the New York City Center for Economic Opportunity, April, 2013, p. 13.

15. According to the Coalition for the Homeless, the number of people in homeless shelters surpassed 50,000 in 2013, an historic high, with the number of homeless families rising by 73 percent since 2002 alone. "State of Homelessness 2013." Coalition for the Homeless, March 5, 2013, p. 2.

16. The Independent Budget Office (IBO) estimated that, if it were in effect, the commuter tax would have brought in $814 million in revenue for 2013. "Budget Options for New York City," New York City Independent Budget Office, April 2012, p. 41. In the same report (p. 42), the IBO estimated that imposing a proportionate progressive commuter tax that is only one-third the rate applied to city residents would have brought in $1.4 billion in revenue for 2013.

17. Kim Moody, *From Welfare State to Real Estate: Regime Change in New York City* (New York: New Press, 2007), p. 73.

18. See, for example, Paul E. Peterson, *City Limits* (Chicago: University of Chicago Press, 1981).

19. See Jacob S. Hacker and Paul Pierson, *Winner-Take-All Politics: How Washington Made the Rich Richer—And Turned its Back on the Middle Class* (New York: Simon & Shuster, 2010); Joseph Stiglitz, *The Price of Inequality* (New York: Norton, 2012).

20. "Pulling Apart: The Continuing Impact of Income Polarization in New York City." A Fiscal Policy Institute Report, November 15, 2012, p. 12.

21. Jonathan Soffer, *Ed Koch and the Rebuilding of New York City* (New York: Columbia University Press, 2010).

22. Robert Bailey, *The Crisis Regime: The MAC, The EFCB, and the Political Impact of the New York City Fiscal Crisis* (Albany: SUNY Press, 1984).

23. Joseph P. Viteritti, "The New Charter: Will It Make a Difference?" in *Urban Politics, New York Style* edited by Jewel Bellush and Dick Netzer (Armonk, NY: M.E. Sharpe, 1990), pp. 413–428.

24. Comparing the cost of living in the nation's ten most expensive metropolitan areas, Manhattan, Brooklyn, and Queens rank one, two, and five, respectively. See "The Middle Class Squeeze: A Report on the State of the City's Middle Class." The City Council of New York, February 2010, p. 13.

25. "Welfare Reform at 15: No *Mission Accomplished* Banner, Please," *City Limits,* 35 (July–Aug. 2011): 23.

26. James Parrott, "As Income Gap Widens, New York Grows Apart," *Gotham Gazette,* January 18, 2011.

27. Sam Roberts, "Income Data Shows Widening Gap between New York's Richest and Poorest," *New York Times,* September 20, 2012; Sam Roberts, "As Effects of Recession Linger, Growth in City's Poverty Rate Outpaces Nation's," *New York Times,* September 22, 2011.

28. Tom Angotti, *New York for Sale: Community Planning Confronts Global Real Estate* (Cambridge, MA: MIT Press, 2008).

29. See Mike Wallace, *A New Deal for New York* (New York: Bell and Weiland, 2002), pp. 16–22, describing corporate giveaways that took place in New York during the 1980s and 1990s.

30. See Louise Story, "The Empty Promise of Tax Incentives," *New York Times,* December 2, 2012, p. 1.

31. Joyce Purnick, *Mike Bloomberg: Money, Power, and Politics* (New York: Public Affairs, 2009), p. 129.

32. Ibid., p. 208.

33. David Seifman, Kaya Witehouse, and Jennifer Gould Kiel, "Bloomie Blitz Aims to Halt Hedge Clippers," *New York Post,* January 23, 2010.

34. Michael M. Grynbaum, "Bloomberg Sues City Council to Overturn Two Laws Raising Wages," *New York Times,* July 28, 2012, p. A20.

35. Diane Cardwell, "Mayor Says New York Is Worth the Cost," *New York Times,* January 8, 2003.

36. According to data compiled by Lorraine C. Minnite, the total number of votes cast in municipal elections in New York City declined every year from highs in 1965 (2,652,454) and 1969 (2,445,467) to 1,170,904 in 1985. It spiked to 1,899,845 in 1985 with the election of David Dinkins, the first black mayor, then dropped to 1,889,003 in 1993 when he was defeated. By 2005 the number of votes cast was down to 1,315,360, before it finally dropped to 1,178,057 in 2009. See generally, Lorraine C. Minnite, "How to Think about Voter Participation," Report prepared for the New York City Charter Revision Commission, July 2010.

37. As Minnite explains in a memo prepared for the author on February 13, 2013, these ratios measure interest in local elections compared with national elections. The decline is dramatic from a ratio of 86.2 percent in 1965 (as a percentage of 1964), to 89.9 percent in 1969 (as a percentage of 1968), to 53.5 percent in 2005 (as a percentage of 2004), to 44.6 percent in 2009 (as a percentage of 2008).

38. Kay Lehman Schlozman, Sidney Verba, and Henry E. Brady, *The Unheavenly Chorus: Unequal Political Voice and the Broken Promise of American Democracy* (Princeton: Princeton University Press, 2012).

39. "Campaign Finance Summary: 1989 Citywide Elections," and "Campaign Finance

Summary: 2009 Citywide Elections," New York City Campaign Finance Board, http://www .nyccfb.info/.

40. Jacob Hacker, Philip Rehm, and Mark Schlessinger, "The Insecure American: Economic Experience, Financial Worries, and Policy Attitudes," *Perspectives on Politics,* 11 (March 2013): 23–49.

41. Joseph Goldstein, "Trial to Start in Class-Action Suit on Constitutionality of Stop-and-Frisk Tactic," *New York Times,* March 18, 2013, p. A15.

42. Mosi Secret, "A Day to Speak Out on Fire Department Bias Case," *New York Times,* October 2, 2012, p. A 26; Mosi Secret, "Judge Approves New Entrance Exam for City Firefighters, *New York Times,* September 29, 2012, p. A21.

43. Angotti, *New York for Sale,* pp. 47–48.

44. Joseph P. Viteritti, ed., *When Mayors Take Charge: School Governance in the City* (Washington, DC: Brookings Institution Press, 2007), pp. 206–234.

The Lindsay Years*

1921–1963

November 24, 1921   John Vliet Lindsay (JVL) and twin brother, David, born in New York City. Educated at Buckley School, Manhattan, then St. Paul's, Concord, New Hampshire.

November 7, 1922   Democrat Al Smith, who had served as governor of New York State from 1918–20 (the terms were then two years) and lost reelection in 1920, returned to Albany as governor in 1922 by defeating Republican Nathan Miller; reelected in 1924 and 1926.

November 4, 1924   Calvin Coolidge (Republican) defeats John W. Davis (Democrat) for President.

November 3, 1925   James "Gentleman Jimmy" Walker defeats incumbent New York City Mayor John Hylan in the Democratic primary, then Frank Waterman (Republican) to become mayor; reelected over Fiorello LaGuardia in 1928.

November 6, 1928   Herbert Hoover (Republican) defeats NYS Governor Al Smith (Democrat) for president.
Franklin D. Roosevelt (Democrat) elected New York State governor over Republican Arthur Ottinger; reelected in 1930.

October 29, 1929   Stock market crash begins the Great Depression.

August 26, 1930   Judge Samuel Seabury appointed to investigate corruption of police and courts, then New York City government. A thousand citizens testify at hearings. Results in reform of lower courts and resignation of Mayor Walker on January 1, 1932 (succeeded by Joseph McKee as mayor).

November 8, 1932   New York State Governor Franklin D. Roosevelt (Democrat) defeats incumbent Herbert Hoover (Republican) for president; reelected in 1936, 1940, and 1944.
Herbert Lehman (Democrat) elected New York State governor

*This chronology is based on research conducted by Steven H. Jaffe, who was guest curator of the Museum of the City of New York 2010 exhibition *America's Mayor: John Lindsay and the reinvention of New York*, with additional contributions by Warren Wechsler.

to succeed FDR, defeating William J. Donovan (Republican); reelected in 1934, 1936, and 1938 (first four-year term).

November 7, 1933   Fiorello La Guardia (Republican) defeats Democratic incumbent John O'Brien to become New York City mayor; reelected in 1937 and 1941.

April 30, 1939   1939 World's Fair opens in Flushing Meadows, Queens, with the park newly planned and rebuilt by Robert Moses. Forty-four million attend over two years.

June 24–28, 1940   JVL and his twin brother work as pages at the Republican National Convention in Philadelphia, where Wendell L. Willkie secures the party's nomination.

May 19, 1941   President FDR appoints Mayor LaGuardia director of the Office of Civilian Defense while he is still serving as NYC mayor.

November 3, 1942   Thomas Dewey (Republican) elected NYS governor over John Bennett (Democrat); reelected in 1946 and 1950.

June 6, 1943   JVL graduates early from Yale, receives commission in U.S. Navy.

1943–1946   JVL serves as gunnery officer on USS *Swanson* during Allied invasion of Sicily; after *Swanson* is transferred to Pacific, takes part in several landings including invasion of Philippines. In March 1946 leaves navy as a lieutenant and *Swanson's* executive officer.

November 6, 1945   William O'Dwyer (Democrat) elected mayor over Jonah Goldstein (Republican); reelected in 1949.

June 20, 1948   JVL graduates from Yale Law School.

June 18, 1949   JVL marries Mary Anne Harrison of Greenwich, Connecticut, and begins a law career at Webster, Sheffield, Fleischmann, Hitchcock & Chrystie in NYC. They rent an apartment in Stuyvesant Town.

August 31, 1950   Under investigation, Mayor O'Dwyer resigns and is appointed ambassador to Mexico by the president; succeeded by Vincent Impellitteri as acting mayor.

November 7, 1950   Mayor Impellitteri is denied the Democratic nomination but wins a special election as an independent over Ferdinand Pecora (Democrat) and Edward Corsi (Republican), the first time a mayor wins without running on one of the two major party tickets.

1951   JVL becomes active in Republican politics; with brother David, helps found Youth for Eisenhower. Visits Paris to urge General Dwight D. Eisenhower to run for president; volunteers in Ike's campaign.

November 4, 1952   Eisenhower elected president (Republican), defeating Democrat Adlai Stevenson; reelected in 1956.

JVL becomes president of New York Young Republicans.

November 3, 1953   Robert Wagner, Jr. (Democrat) defeats Harold Riegelman

(Republican) to become mayor; reelected in 1957 and 1961, when he breaks with the Democratic Party bosses (Tammany Hall) and defeats their candidate, State Comptroller Arthur Levitt, in the Democratic primary.

May 17, 1954	Chief Justice Earl Warren delivers unanimous Supreme Court ruling in *Brown v. Board of Education*, outlawing segregation in public schools.
November 2, 1954	W. Averell Harriman (Democrat) elected governor of New York, defeating Irving Ives (Republican) by only 11,000 votes out of more than 5 million.
January 14, 1955	JVL is appointed executive assistant to Eisenhower's attorney general, Herbert Brownell; works on civil rights, immigration issues for Hungarian refugees in 1956, and the 1957 Civil Rights Act.
September 24, 1957	Brooklyn Dodgers play last game at Ebbets Field before moving to Los Angeles, as New York Giants move to San Francisco.
October 4, 1957	Soviet Union launches *Sputnik*, the first space satellite, initiating the Space Race with the United States and generating a sense of crisis regarding America's scientific and technological capacity and fear of Soviet supremacy in space.
September 2, 1958	In response to *Sputnik* crisis, President Eisenhower signs the National Defense Education Act providing massive funding of technology, science, and languages.
November 4, 1958	JVL elected to Congress from 17th ("Silk Stocking") District on East Side; defeats Democrat Tony Akers after winning Republican primary in August over Elliot Goodwin. Nelson Rockefeller (Republican) defeats incumbent Governor Averell Harriman (Democrat) to become NYS governor; reelected in 1962, 1966, and 1970.
May 14, 1959	President Eisenhower and John D. Rockefeller III break ground for Lincoln Center for the Performing Arts.
1959–1965	JVL serves seven years in the House, after defeating Democrat William vanden Heuvel (1960), Democrat Martin Dworkis (1962), and Democrat Eleanor C. French and Conservative Kieran O'Doherty (1964). He works closely with the Democratic administration on creation of a federal Department of Urban Affairs and on passage of 1964 Civil Rights Act, 1965 Voting Rights Act, and 1965 immigration reform.
November 8, 1960	John F. Kennedy (Democrat) elected president over Vice President Richard M. Nixon (Republican).
January 17, 1961	President Eisenhower gives farewell address warning of the influence of the military-industrial complex.
January 20, 1961	JFK inaugurated, "Ask not what your country can do for you, ask what you can do for your country."

September 13, 1961	Jane Jacobs publishes *The Life and Death of Great American Cities,* challenging the "rationalism" of professional city planners.
April 16, 1962	CBS starts first daily national half-hour television news broadcast anchored by Walter Cronkite.
October 15, 1962	Cuban Missile Crisis begins thirteen days of international tension that seemingly brings the world to the brink of nuclear disaster until Kennedy and Khrushchev reach secret agreement to remove missiles from Cuba.
February 19, 1963	Betty Friedan publishes *The Feminine Mystique.*
April 16, 1963	Martin Luther King Jr., arrested during the campaign to desegregate Birmingham, Alabama, issues his "Letter from Birmingham Jail" making the argument for nonviolent resistance to racism.
June 10, 1963	Alabama Governor George Wallace symbolically stands in the doorway to block black students from entering the University of Alabama, seeking to live up to his inaugural declaration, "segregation now, segregation tomorrow, segregation forever," but steps aside when confronted by U.S. Department of Justice and federalized National Guard.
June 26, 1963	President Kennedy speaks in front of the Berlin Wall two years after its construction, saying "Ich bin ein Berliner" ("I am a Berliner").
August 28, 1963	March on Washington: Martin Luther King Jr. delivers "I Have a Dream" speech from Lincoln Memorial.
October 18, 1963	Demolition of Penn Station begins, to be replaced by Madison Square Garden; spurs landmark preservation movement.
October 26, 1963	Bob Dylan performs "The Times They Are a-Changin'" at Carnegie Hall; released in January 1964 as the title song for his third album, it evokes a deep sense of social unrest that pervades the country.
November 22, 1963	President Kennedy killed in Dallas; Vice President Lyndon B. Johnson becomes president.

1964

February 9	The Beatles appear on the *Ed Sullivan Show.*
March 6	After defeating Sonny Liston for the World Heavyweight Championship, Black Muslim Cassius Clay becomes Muhammad Ali.
June 12	Nelson Mandela sentenced to life in prison in South Africa. He is released after twenty-seven years.
June 14	The *New York Times* first uses the term "hippie," referring to denizens of a Greenwich Village coffee house.
June 22	Civil rights workers Andrew Goodman, Michael Schwerner, and James Chaney murdered by the Ku Klux Klan in Philadelphia, Mississippi, during "Freedom Summer" campaign to register

black voters in Mississippi. Following national outrage, the FBI launches a massive investigation (called "Mississippi Burning") and finds bodies 44 days later.

June 24	Palestine Liberation Organization (PLO) formed.
July 2	President Lyndon B. Johnson signs the comprehensive Civil Rights Act of 1964 into law, with its key provision prohibiting discrimination in "public accommodations."
July 15	Senator Barry Goldwater (AZ), who defeated Governor Nelson Rockefeller (NY) in the California Republican primary, accepts nomination in San Francisco and declares "extremism in the defense of liberty is no vice and moderation in the pursuit of justice is no virtue." JVL and a few other moderate Republicans refuse to endorse Goldwater.
July 16	An off-duty white policeman fatally shoots a 15-year-old black youth, setting off riots in Harlem and Bedford-Stuyvesant for four days.
August 7	Gulf of Tonkin Resolution passed by Congress, beginning full-fledged U.S. involvement in Vietnam War.
September 22	*Fiddler on the Roof*—produced by Hal Prince, choreographed by Jerome Robbins, and starring Zero Mostel—opens on Broadway at the Imperial Theatre.
November 3	President Johnson (Democrat) wins landslide reelection (61 percent of vote) over Republican Senator Barry Goldwater. Robert F. Kennedy elected senator from New York State.

1965

January 25	*New York Herald Tribune* starts "New York City in Crisis" series documenting the city's ills under three-term Mayor Robert F. Wagner Jr.
February 21	Malcolm X assassinated in Audubon Ballroom in the neighborhood of Washington Heights, Manhattan.
March 7	"Bloody Sunday" in Selma, Alabama: State troopers attack 600 peaceful civil rights marchers led by John Lewis, which prompts President Johnson to propose the Voting Rights Act.
April 24	In a speech at Oakland University in Michigan, JVL calls for an international commission to seek an immediate cease-fire in Vietnam. Lindsay is only the third member of Congress to speak in opposition to the war, after Senators Ernest Gruening (D-AK) and Wayne Morse (D-OR).
May 7	"Stand-in" by 200 students protesting Vietnam War disrupts Naval Reserve ceremony at Columbia University.
May 13	JVL declares he will run as Republican candidate for mayor, with endorsements from Republicans Governor Nelson Rockefeller and U.S. Senator Jacob K. Javits.

May 21	In his first major campaign speech, JVL calls for the creation of a Civilian Complaint Review Board to examine allegations of police misconduct.
June 6	Rolling Stones release "(I Can't Get No) Satisfaction" written by Mick Jagger and Keith Richards.
June 10	Mayor Wagner announces he will not run for a fourth term.
June 28	JVL endorsed by Liberal Party, creating a fusion ticket with Liberal Timothy Costello as candidate for City Council President and Democrat Milton Mollen for Comptroller.
June 29	Five thousand off-duty police officers picket City Hall to protest proposed civilian review board.
July 28	President Johnson announces the deployment of 50,000 troops to Vietnam, followed the next day by antiwar demonstration at New York's Whitehall Street Army Induction Center, with burning of draft cards; and a rally two days later of antiwar demonstrators (and counterdemonstrators) in Times Square.
August 6	President Johnson signs Voting Rights Act.
August 11–17	Riots break out in Watts district of Los Angeles, California. Becomes worst race riot since 1943 in Detroit.
October 3	President Johnson signs Immigration Reform Act into law, opening up immigration beyond favored Northern Europe to Asians, Africans, South Americans, and Southern Europeans.
October 31	Democratic District Leader Edward I. Koch endorses Lindsay, front page coverage in *New York Post* and *New York Daily News*.
November 2	JVL elected mayor on the Republican and Liberal tickets, with 43.3 percent; over Democrat Abraham D. Beame (39.5 percent) and Conservative William F. Buckley Jr. (12.9 percent).
November 22	*Man of La Mancha,* starring Richard Kiley, opens at ANTA Washington Square Theatre.
November 23	JVL's first cabinet appointment: Robert O. Lowery as the city's first black fire commissioner.
December 31	Report of mayor-elect's Law Enforcement Task Force recommends modernization of police records and systems, court reform and efficiencies, and a Civilian Complaint Review Board. U.S. now has 180,000 troops in Vietnam.

1966

January 1	JVL delivers first inaugural address from steps of City Hall. Transit Workers' Union (TWU) strikes, shutting down subways and buses for two weeks. Massive traffic jams start at 4 a.m.; millions walk to work. TWU leader Mike Quill, in a gesture of contempt, intentionally garbles Lindsay's name, calling him "Mr. Lindsley."

	Simon and Garfunkel's "The Sound of Silence" becomes number one on the pop record charts.
January 4	Quill and eight other TWU strike leaders are sent to the Civil Jail on West 37th Street for leading an illegal work stoppage by public employees; Quill collapses, is taken to Bellevue Hospital, and dies of heart attack on January 28.
January 23	Indira Gandhi becomes the third prime minister of India.
	Lindsay hosts dinner at Lincoln Center on March 30, signaling a move of celebratory events from hotel ballrooms to cultural institutions.
February 1	I.S. 201 opens in Harlem and becomes the focal point for the emerging movement for community control of schools.
February 12	JVL proposes state legislation to combine the Triborough Bridge and Tunnel Authority with the Transit Authority so that car tolls could be used to finance the subways, an attack on the long-standing pro-auto, anti–mass transit policy of Robert Moses. It failed but the concept becomes the basis for the MTA enacted in 1968.
February 16	JVL appoints Howard Leary from Philadelphia as police commissioner.
February 25	Police Commissioner Leary appoints Lloyd Sealy as assistant chief inspector, the first black officer to attain such a senior rank. This is rapidly followed by the appointment of two other blacks to senior command positions, Eldridge Waithe and Arthur Hill.
March 21	JVL creates NYC Urban Corps, modeled after JFK's Peace Corps.
March 26	Pacifist A. J. Muste leads antiwar rally in Central Park.
	To stem loss of businesses and jobs, JVL creates Public Development Corporation (PDC) to assist businesses locating in New York. In 1991 PDC made part of Economic Development Corporation.
May 13	In testimony before a U.S. Senate subcommittee, Timothy Leary estimates that one-third of American college students are "experimenting" with LSD.
May 17	Police Commissioner Leary creates a seven-member (four civilians, three police officials) Civilian Complaint Review Board (CCRB).
May 31	JVL issues Executive Order No. 10, creating the Mayor's Film Office and streamlining red tape for movie making, which leads to significant increase in movies shot in NYC. The same procedures remain in effect today.
June 1	JVL launches pilot project on Bowery with the Vera Institute of Justice, with police bringing alcoholics to a detox center rather

than jail. This becomes Manhattan Bowery Project in 1967 and continues today as Project Renewal.

June 5   JVL and Parks Commissioner Thomas Hoving close Central Park to automobiles on weekends, soon repeated in other parks around the boroughs and eventually around the country.

June 19   Student Nonviolent Coordinating Committee (SNCC) leader Stokely Carmichael and others first use the term "Black Power" in Mississippi and suggest that nonviolence is no longer the answer to racism and discrimination; Southern Christian Leadership Conference head Martin Luther King Jr. deplores their statements.

June 25   U.S. Government closes Brooklyn Navy Yard; nine thousand jobs lost.

June 30   U.S. Army leaves Governors Island after 150 years, turns it over to the U.S. Coast Guard.

          National Organization for Women (NOW) formed in Washington, D.C. by Betty Friedan, Pauli Murray, Shirley Chisholm, and twenty-five others.

July 1   NY State Legislature and Governor Nelson Rockefeller, after much political dispute, approve JVL's proposed city income tax and a historic commuter tax.

July 5   To finance the settlement of the transit strike, subway and bus fares increase from 15 cents to 20 cents.

July 7   The Patrolman's Benevolent Association (PBA) and the Conservative Party deliver 51,000 signatures to the City Clerk to place a referendum challenging the CCRB on the November ballot.

July 19   Racial tensions erupt in East New York (Brooklyn). JVL visits area, meets with black and white youths. Lindsay begins walks in minority neighborhoods to create a visible presence.

July 21   A young black boy, Eric Dean, is shot in East New York. Police move 1,000 officers into the area, keep the peace, and fire no shots, the first test of the new policy of police restraint.

August   "Summer in the City," sung by John Sebastian and the Lovin' Spoonful, holds the number one spot on the Billboard Hot 100 List for three consecutive weeks.

August 1 JVL appoints Frederick Hayes, who comes from federal government with extensive federal experience in budgeting and information systems, budget director. This begins a new era of modern municipal management.

August 5 Groundbreaking for the World Trade Center.

August 13 Chairman Mao Zedong launches Cultural Revolution in China.

August 23 Beatles perform concert at Shea Stadium.

September 16 New Metropolitan Opera House opens at Lincoln Center.

September 22	JVL initiates meeting of the state's six biggest cities—Albany, Buffalo, Rochester, Syracuse, Yonkers, and New York—to form the Big Six Mayors to fight jointly for more state aid.
October 10	The *New York Times* first reports on Hare Krishnas in the East Village.
October 15	Black Panthers founded in Oakland, California.
November 8	Lindsay suffers major electoral defeat as voters reject the controversial CCRB by an overwhelming 63-to-37 percent margin.
	Governor Nelson Rockefeller elected to third term.
November 15	JVL announces his plan for consolidating fifty-three city agencies into 10 superagencies.
November 20	*Cabaret* by John Kander and Fred Ebb opens at Broadhurst Theatre, starring Joel Grey and directed by Hal Prince.
November 28	Truman Capote hosts Black and White Ball at Plaza Hotel.
December 14	JVL halts construction of Richmond Expressway route chosen by Robert Moses, which cuts through wooded areas; selects alternative route that preserves the Staten Island Greenbelt, which today includes 2,800 acres of forested hills and wetlands.
December 20	JVL proposes Waterside Housing Complex on a platform in the East River at East 23rd Street.
December 31	United States now has 385,000 troops in Vietnam.

1967

January 4	JVL proposes bill to create a network of Little City Halls to bring services to neighborhoods across the city. Democrats in City Council refuse to approve.
January 27	Three astronauts die in flash fire of *Apollo* rocket on launch pad.
February 7	City takes ownership of Brooklyn Navy Yard.
	Task Force on Urban Design releases "The Threatened City," or Paley report as it was more generally known, which details the quality of the city's architecture and design. Results in creation of Urban Design Group and appointment of development offices reporting to the mayor for Midtown, Downtown, Downtown Brooklyn, Staten Island, and Jamaica, Queens.
March 27	In response to president's Crime Commission report, JVL creates nation's first Criminal Justice Coordinating Council, bringing together police, prosecutors, judges, correction officers and others, with agencies sharing data and sponsoring joint programs.
April 15	Rev. Martin Luther King Jr., Dr. Benjamin Spock, and Harry Belafonte lead 100,000 people in an antiwar march from Central Park to the UN.
April 27	In advance of long hot summer, JVL announces Citizens Summer Committee, led by Andrew Haskel, chair of Time Inc.,

	and Tom Hoving, which raises private funds for summer youth programs.
April 29	JVL appoints McGeorge Bundy of the Ford Foundation to advise him on school decentralization.
May 2	Phoenix House is launched under Dr. Mitchell Rosenthal, which becomes one of the largest drug addiction treatment programs in the nation.
May 13	"Support Our Boys in Vietnam" march down Fifth Avenue draws 70,000.
May 23	Paley Park opens on East 53rd Street as the first privately funded vest pocket park.
June	Aretha Franklin's "Respect" reaches the top of record charts, making a song originally written and recorded by Otis Redding in 1965 into an anthem for women.
June 5	Six Day War begins with preemptive Israeli attack under General Moshe Dayan.
June 17	Barbra Streisand holds a concert in Central Park before a crowd of 150,000.
June 24	*La Bohème* becomes the first opera performed for free in Central Park by the Metropolitan Opera.
June 27	Electric Circus opens in the East Village with flashing strobe lights, videos, music—a precursor of the discotheque scene.
July 6	The Ford Foundation grants $135,000 to three school districts to experiment with "community control" in East Harlem, the Lower East Side, and Ocean Hill–Brownsville in Brooklyn.
July 12	City Council approves Lindsay's first superagency, the Human Resources Administration (HRA).
July 12–16	Large-scale riots in Newark with looting and fires, state police and National Guard called in.
July 19	At the mayor's insistence, the first air-conditioned subway train is put into service on the F line. It would take twenty-five years to convert the entire fleet.
July 22–25	Disturbances begin in East Harlem after a policeman shoots a youth. Brief outbreaks follow the next week in Bedford-Stuyvesant; disorders flare up again during early September in Brownsville.
July 23–30	Devastating riots in Detroit, with U.S. Army paratroopers finally called in to support exhausted police and National Guard.
July 27	President Johnson appoints the eleven-member National Advisory Commission on Civil Disorders (the Kerner Commission) to investigate the causes of urban riots. JVL chosen as vice chairman.

August 3–5   Ocean Hill–Brownsville holds election for governing board for experimental community-controlled school district.

August 21   In Washington, D.C., a mass anti–Vietnam War march ends at the door of the Pentagon; many New Yorkers take part.

September 25   *Bonnie and Clyde* opens, starring Warren Beatty and Faye Dunaway, directed by Arthur Penn.

October 2   Thurgood Marshall becomes the first black justice on the U.S. Supreme Court.

October 17   *Hair* opens at Joe Papp's new Public Theater, moves six months later to Broadway at the Biltmore Theatre; inaugurates the rock musical and heralds the "Age of Aquarius."

December 2   Francis Cardinal Spellman dies after twenty-eight years as archbishop of New York, longest tenure ever; replaced by Terrence Cardinal Cooke.

December 4   During a weeklong antiwar protest at Whitehall Street Army Induction Center, City Hall aides guide protesters from Whitehall to Union Square. Some elected officials criticize the role of City Hall in "interfering" with the police and call for firing of Lindsay aides Barry Gottehrer and Sid Davidoff.

December 7   Special Theater Zoning District adopted, with incentives that produce three new theaters, first in 40 years, and 54-story One Astor Place, hoping to spur the rebirth of Times Square.

December 13   City Council approves second superagency, Health Services Administration (HSA).

December 18   Water Commissioner James Marcus indicted by District Attorney Frank Hogan for accepting a $40,000 bribe for a contract to clean the Jerome Park Reservoir.

December 21   *The Graduate,* starring Dustin Hoffman and Anne Bancroft and directed by Mike Nichols, released to theaters.

December 31   United States now has 485,000 troops in Vietnam.

1968

January 8   JVL signs a bill creating the nation's first Environmental Protection Administration (EPA), his third superagency. Additional superagencies created include Economic Development Administration (EDA), Housing and Development (HDA), Parks, Recreation and Cultural Affairs (PRCA), and Municipal Services Administration (MSA).

January 30   Tet Offensive is launched as surprise attack by North Vietnamese and the Vietcong, shocking the American public by the capacity of the enemy to mount a major campaign and dashing hopes that the United States can achieve its goals in Vietnam anytime soon.

February 2–10	The Uniformed Sanitationmen Association strikes. Governor Nelson Rockefeller resists Lindsay's request that the National Guard be deployed to help collect accumulating garbage, sparking a conflict between the two Republicans that will continue through their careers. Sanitation union leader John DeLury goes to jail for violating the Taylor Law, enacted in 1967 after the transit strike.
February 27	Following a visit to Vietnam, Walter Cronkite reports that the war is unwinnable and that "the bloody expense of Vietnam is to end in a stalemate;" this has major impact on turning public opinion against the war.
February 29	The Kerner Commission report is released condemning excessive police force and calling for police restraint and massive investment in cities. Declares "our nation is moving towards two societies, one Black and one White—separate and unequal."
March 1	Metropolitan Transportation Authority (MTA) created by the state as a regional transportation agency that combines subway, bus, commuter rail, and bridges and adopts concept of using road tolls for mass transit. This marks the end of Robert Moses' long dominance of regional transportation with his emphasis on cars and roads instead of rail.
March 8	Fillmore East opens in the East Village, becomes premier rock concert venue on East Coast.
March 12	Senator Eugene McCarthy wins the New Hampshire Democratic presidential primary over incumbent President Johnson with a startling 42 percent to 29 percent victory.
March 18	Senator Robert Kennedy announces his candidacy for the Democratic presidential nomination.
March 19	JVL denounces the Vietnam War in a speech at Queens College.
March 22	Abbie Hoffman's Yip-In in Grand Central Station; 3,000–6,000 Yippies and Hippies converge; the station is cleared by police.
March 31	President Johnson makes surprise announcement that he will not run for reelection. Democratic contest is now between senators Kennedy and McCarthy and Vice President Hubert Humphrey.
April 4	Reverend Martin Luther King Jr. assassinated in Memphis; rioting occurs in minority communities across the nation, including Harlem; JVL goes to Harlem where he calms crowds. Robert Kennedy, in Indiana to campaign for the Democratic primary, addresses grieving crowd.
April 8	First issue of *New York* magazine published.
April 22	JVL insists that York College be located in Jamaica, Queens, business district to spur development of deteriorated area.

April 23–30	Columbia University students begin protests over construction of gym in nearby Harlem park, expressing racial concerns and opposition to Vietnam War. Thousands of students occupy multiple buildings and disrupt the university. On April 30, 120 students injured when NYPD clears occupied buildings.
April 25	JVL and Governor Rockefeller announce memorandum of understanding to allow Battery Park City to be built on landfill.
April 27	Massive antiwar demonstration in Sheep Meadow in Central Park and Loyalty Day Parade supporting the troops on Fifth Avenue; JVL appears at both.
May 6–13	Parisian students begin massive protest, clash with riot police at the Sorbonne; joined by all major French trade unions in a general strike on May 13, signaling growing worldwide youth dissatisfaction and protest.
May 8	Ocean Hill–Brownsville governing board dismisses thirteen teachers and six administrators; on May 22, union teachers walk out in sympathy.
May 23	City launches "Give a Damn" advertising campaign and establishes Urban Action Task Force under mayoral aide Barry Gottehrer to work in unstable communities.
June 5	Senator Robert F. Kennedy assassinated in Los Angeles moments after declaring victory in the California Democratic primary.
June 21	JVL breaks ground for Westbeth, nation's largest affordable live-work space for artists in reused industrial buildings in Greenwich Village, first project by architect Richard Meier. Opens in 1970.
July 1	NYC introduces the nation's first "911" police emergency number supported by advanced computerized communication center; every officer on patrol to be equipped with miniature walkie-talkie.
July 10	Fifteen hundred youth protest at City Hall for summer jobs; some jump on car of a Queens councilman, who accuses mayor of ordering police not to act.
August 5	First Jewish Defense League (JDL) demonstration at NYU. JDL leader Meir Kahane becomes a public figure and, eventually, a Lindsay antagonist.
	Republican Convention in Miami Beach nominates former Vice President Richard Nixon. JVL seconds the nomination of Maryland Governor Spiro Agnew for vice president, citing blacks, cities, and opposition to the war.
August 21	The USSR and four other Warsaw Pact nations invade Czechoslovakia, ending the reform excitement of the "Prague

Spring." Three die in Prague after being fired on by Bulgarian tanks.

August 26–29   In Chicago, the Democratic National Convention nominates Vice President Hubert Humphrey, splitting the party over the Vietnam War. Chicago police club and tear gas protestors and demonstrators in Grant Park; "police riot" is nationally televised. Some dissident leaders—the "Chicago Seven"—are later tried and convicted in federal court in a heavily publicized and politicized trial.

September 6   The United Federation of Teachers (UFT) calls a citywide teachers strike, as union president Albert Shanker demands reinstatement of the thirteen Ocean Hill-Brownsville teachers. Strike lasts two days. The teachers strike again three days later, this time for six days. A third strike begins on October 14, lasting five weeks.

September 10   After three months of jockeying between Governor Rockefeller and Mayor Lindsay, Rockefeller appoints upstate congressman Charles Goodell to fill the Senate seat of the late Robert F. Kennedy.

JVL establishes nation's first Department of Consumer Affairs; appoints former Miss America, Bronx-born Bess Myerson, commissioner on February 2, 1969.

September 26   The Studio Museum opens in a rented loft on 125th Street, Harlem, the first black fine arts museum in America.

September 28   Placido Domingo debuts at Metropolitan Opera in *Adriana Lecouvreur.*

October 15   During the third teachers strike, JVL speaks at the East Midwood Jewish Center (Brooklyn) to urge understanding on school decentralization. He is unable to finish speech over angry crowd and is forced to leave.

October 16   At Olympic Games in Mexico City, two black American runners give the Black Power salute from the medal stand.

October 29   South Street Seaport given landmark protection. In 1972 Lindsay creates special South Street District to foster targeted development.

November 5   Republican Richard Nixon defeats Vice President Hubert Humphrey with only 43 percent of the vote, as third-party candidate Alabama Governor George Wallace receives 13 percent.

November 28   Luciano Pavarotti makes debut at Metropolitan Opera in *La Bohème.*

December 24   Colonel Frank Borman, Major William Anders, and Captain James A. Lovell fly around the moon.

December 31   U.S. Troops in Vietnam peak at 536,000.

1969

January 6	Black and Puerto Rican Coalition demonstrates at Queens College, demanding control over the SEEK program for minority students; college closed next day; students ransack college offices on January 13 and Feb 5; college agrees to appoint protesters' choice as director of the program.
January 12	New York Jets, led by quarterback "Broadway Joe" Namath, defeat the heavily favored Baltimore Colts in Super Bowl III, 16–7.
January 18	*Harlem on My Mind* exhibition opens at Metropolitan Museum of Art, evokes public discussion of the city's long-standing racial divide.
February 1	Under new legislation, the city launches pilot work release program for inmates on Rikers Island.
February 2	Six-volume *Plan for New York City* that was produced under the City Charter is released.
February 3	Yasser Arafat elected head of the PLO.
February 9	The Great Snowstorm: with an unexpected 15 inches of snow, streets in Queens remain impassable for four days. JVL is confronted by enraged residents when he walks through Queens on Februrary 12.
February 13	Black and Puerto Rican students briefly occupy offices at City College; vandalism occurs on February 17; the college is closed temporarily.
March 18	JVL announces run for reelection as mayor on the Republican ticket; endorsed by the Liberal Party on April 16. U.S. bombing of Cambodia provokes national protests.
March 31	Lindsay wins major victory over police union when state legislature reverses 1911 law and allows police to be assigned to new Fourth Platoon from 6 p.m. to 2 a.m. during hours of greatest need.
April 24	Lincoln Square Zoning District enacted so that future development complements new Lincoln Center.
April 27	State legislature approves Lindsay plan to create an independent Health and Hospitals Corporation to manage city's hospital system.
April 29	Students protest for preferential minority admissions policies and studies programs at Queens, City, and Brooklyn colleges and at Manhattan Community College. Clashes between white and black students at City College shut down school on May 7.
April 30	State legislature passes the School Decentralization Act, which divides the city school system into thirty-one (later thirty-two) districts with elected community boards.
May 6	Lindsay's Rent Stabilization Law enacted by City Council places

more than one million apartments under rent regulation that is still in effect.

May 14   JVL announces agreement with federal government for creation of Gateway, including Jamaica Bay and Rockaway Beaches, the first urban National Park; begins major federal investment in New York City harbor's recreational and nature site and facilities.

May 17   Leonard Bernstein leads last concert as conductor of the New York Philharmonic after a record 939 concerts.

May 25   *Midnight Cowboy,* directed by John Schlessinger and starring Dustin Hoffman and John Voight, released, depicting a seedy side of New York.

June 17   Mayoral primaries: State Senator John Marchi (113,000 votes) defeats JVL (107,000) for the Republican nomination; Comptroller Mario Procaccino (255,000 votes) beats former Mayor Robert Wagner (224,000), Bronx Borough President Herman Badillo (217,000), author Norman Mailer (41,000), and Congressman James Scheuer (39,000) for the Democratic nod.

June 18   Deprived of the Republican nomination, JVL forms an Independent Party and runs as the Liberal-Independent candidate, describing New York's mayoralty as "the second toughest job in America."

June 27–28   The "Stonewall Riot," where police raid a private gay club on Christopher Street in early morning hours and club patrons fight back.

June 30   Museo del Barrio opens as the city's first Puerto Rican art museum.

July 9   City University (CUNY) announces open admissions for all city high school graduates beginning September 1970.

July 16   JVL kills Robert Moses' plan for the Lower Manhattan Expressway through SoHo.

July 20   Neil Armstrong becomes the first person to walk on the moon. The three astronauts are later celebrated with a tickertape parade up Lower Broadway's "Canyon of Heroes."

August 16–19   Woodstock: The "counterculture" music festival is held on a farm in rural New York State.

August 18   The Young Lords protest inadequate sanitation service in East Harlem by dumping and burning garbage, attracting their first press coverage.

September 29–
October 1   A visit by Israeli Prime Minister Golda Meir, American-born and enormously popular, helps JVL's reelection bid with the Jewish community, including attending a 1,100 guest dinner at the Brooklyn Museum and a ceremony on the steps of City Hall.

October 15	The Vietnam Moratorium, a nationwide protest against the war in Southeast Asia, is endorsed by JVL and observed throughout New York.
October 16	The "Miracle Mets" win the World Series by beating the Baltimore Orioles at Shea Stadium; news photos of JVL being doused with champagne in Mets locker room help his reelection bid.
November 4	JVL wins reelection, with (41.1 percent); Democrat Mario Procaccino gets (33.8 percent); Republican John Marchi (22.1 percent); Norman Mailer 3 percent (running with Jimmy Breslin). Lindsay is the second mayor since 1898 (along with Vincent Impelleteri in 1950) to be elected without the support of one of the two major parties.
November 10	*Sesame Street* first broadcast on public television.
November 12	Journalist Seymour Hersh breaks the story of the My Lai massacre of at least 347 South Vietnamese civilians; "My Lai" becomes the symbol of American military abuses in Vietnam.
November 24	Construction begins on 63rd Street Tunnel under East River, a Lindsay and Rockefeller joint project with two subway tracks to Queens and two LIRR tracks for future use as East Side Access to Grand Central Station.
December 13	Carmine De Sapio, the last Boss of Tammany Hall, is convicted of conspiracy; serves two years in federal prison.
December 28	Young Lords occupy First Spanish Methodist Church in East Harlem as part of demonstration for free-breakfast program.
December 31	JVL sworn in and delivers second inaugural address.

1970

January 1	Subway fare increases from 20 cents to 30 cents.
January 5	JVL appoints Gordon Chase as health services administrator and directs him to launch attack on lead poisoning.
January 12	JVL approves start of Third Water Tunnel, the largest construction project in the city's history, now scheduled for completion in 2020.
January 14	Leonard Bernstein hosts cocktail party fundraiser for Black Panthers, a symbol of "radical chic."
March 6	Weathermen "bomb lab" on West 11th Street in Greenwich Village blows up, killing three.
March 12	Series of bombings by an unknown group at the Manhattan corporate offices of IBM, General Telephone and Electronics, and Mobil. No one is hurt because police were tipped by an anonymous call a half hour before.
March 20	United Nations Development District approved.
April 2	JVL speaks at University of California, Berkeley, criticizing

	Nixon and Agnew for violating basic rights by calling their actions "repression in a business suit."
	Patton starring George C. Scott opens.
April 10	The Beatles break up.
April 11	New York State law legalizing abortions up to the twenty-fourth week of pregnancy is signed by Governor Rockefeller, replacing 1830 statute permitting abortions only to save the mother's life.
April 22	The nation's first Earth Day; thousands committed to the environment converge on Union Square; a supportive Mayor Lindsay closes Fifth Avenue to vehicular traffic.
April 23	JVL announces creation of a five-man panel, headed by Corporation Counsel J. Lee Rankin, to investigate police corruption in advance of *New York Times* series based on allegations of Detective Frank Serpico that begins on April 25.
May 4	Four students killed by National Guardsmen during an antiwar protest at Kent State University in Ohio. More than eighty universities across the country close during May in response to antiwar protests.
May 6–8	"Hard Hat Riot" with construction workers in Lower Manhattan, including those building the World Trade Center, attacking antiwar demonstrators; culminates in May 8 "Bloody Friday" melee on Wall Street and at City Hall.
May 8	The New York Knicks win their first championship by defeating the L.A. Lakers at Madison Square Garden, 113–99, following the dramatic entrance of injured captain Willis Reed.
May 20	Construction workers and others lead pro–Vietnam War and pro-Nixon march of a 100,000 from City Hall down Broadway.
May 21	20,000 antiwar demonstrators rally at City Hall.
	JVL appoints an independent five-member commission to investigate police corruption chaired by P. Whitman Knapp, replacing the Rankin Panel; public hearings begin October 1971.
June 4	JVL creates Office of Neighborhood Government (ONG), launching demonstration projects in eight neighborhoods, creating a local service cabinet with representatives of city agencies for each, coordinated by a full-time district manager.
June 9	A bomb planted by the Weather Underground explodes inside Police Headquarters.
June 25	Federal judge orders McSorley's Old Ale House to admit women, following a suit filed by NOW (National Organization of Women).
June 29	First Gay Pride Parade on the anniversary of the Stonewall Riots.
August 8–11	Prisoners at the Manhattan House of Detention (the "Tombs") stage uprisings and take three guards hostage to protest overcrowding and poor conditions. Hostages are released when

Correction Commissioner George McGrath agrees to meet with inmates and to commit no reprisals.

August 10   JVL signs City Council bill prohibiting discrimination against women; McSorley's opens its doors to women.

August 26   More than ten thousand people, mostly women, march down Fifth Avenue in Women's Strike for Equality, marking the fiftieth anniversary of women obtaining the right to vote under the Nineteenth Amendment.

September 13   First NYC Marathon.

October 1–5   Prison inmates riot and take three hostages in Queens; rioting spreads the next day to the Tombs, where seventeen hostages are taken, then in Brooklyn, three hostages taken (though guards there quickly retake control). On October 4, JVL addresses the inmates at the Tombs by radio, who release their hostages and then meet with the mayor. The next day, Queens inmates release their three hostages and then meet with JVL.

October 11   Patrick Murphy becomes Police Commissioner after Howard Leary retires.

November 3   Governor Rockefeller elected to fourth term after JVL endorses Democratic challenger Arthur Goldberg.

1971

January 12   *All in the Family* premiers on CBS, starring Carroll O'Connor as Archie Bunker and produced by Norman Lear.

January 14   A six-day wildcat strike by 85 percent of police begins over the issues of pay and other grievances.

January 22   Lindsay's proposed Taxi and Limousine Commission (TLC) approved by City Council to regulate yellow medallion taxis and black cars; ends oversight by Police Department Hack Bureau.

January 28   After Lower Manhattan Expressway proposed by Robert Moses is rejected, city amends zoning to allow certified artists to live-work in SoHo. Later (1973) landmarked as SoHo Cast Iron Historic District.

February 9   City adopts Fifth Avenue Special Zoning District to restrict retail uses at street level and to enable mixed use above Olympic Tower next to St. Patrick's Cathedral as nation's first building combining retail, commercial, and residential space.

March 2   After considering a move to New Jersey, Yankees agree to remain in the Bronx and sign long-term lease with the city.
Yankee Stadium is acquired from Rice University and begins major physical reconstruction.

March 8   Joe Frazier beats Muhammad Ali for the heavyweight title at Madison Square Garden.

March 25   JVL has the city purchase historic Astor Theater and leases it

	back to Joseph Papp and the Public Theater for an annual rent of one dollar.
April 8	NYC becomes second jurisdiction in the nation (after Nevada) to authorize off-track betting (OTB) when state legislature passes Lindsay's OTB bill. OTB Chair Howard Samuels begins opening of 140 parlors.
May 17	JVL endorses City Council bill to eliminate discrimination against homosexuals in New York City; bill is defeated on January 27, 1972.
May 21	Marvin Gaye releases album *What's Going On?*
	The Black Liberation Army (BLA) kills two police officers on patrol in the 32nd Precinct in Harlem: Waverly Jones and Joseph Piagentini.
June 6	Conductor James Levine makes his Metropolitan Opera debut.
June 28	Mobster Joseph Columbo killed at Italian American Unity Day at Columbus Circle.
July 1	Twenty-Sixth Amendment of the U.S. Constitution ratified, giving 18-year-olds the right to vote.
	The U.S. Supreme Court upholds the *Washington Post*'s and the *New York Times*'s right to publish the Pentagon Papers, the secret report of the United States' military involvement in Southeast Asia, affirming the First Amendment's broad protection against most prior restraints in journalism.
August 2	Governor Nelson Rockefeller, after a public dispute with Lindsay over state aid, appoints Temporary State Commission to Make a Study of Governmental Operation of the City of New York, chaired by Stuart Scott; Stephen Berger serves as executive director. In response, Lindsay appoints City Commission on State-City Relations, chaired by William vanden Heuvel; Professor Jewel Bellush of Hunter College serves as executive director.
August 11	JVL switches party enrollment from Republican to Democratic, signaling a probable presidential bid in 1972.
September 9	Attica prison riot by a thousand prisoners, who take thirty-three hostages. After four days, Governor Rockefeller orders state police to retake control of the facility, resulting in thirty-nine deaths (twenty-nine inmates and ten prison employees).
October 7	*The French Connection* premiers, starring Gene Hackman.
November 1	Groundbreaking for a passenger ship terminal to be created through the renovation of four Hudson River piers.
November 19	The Forest Hills Residents Association, led by Jerry Birbach, pickets the site of proposed city-sponsored high-rise scatter-site housing for low-income residents. Lawyer Mario Cuomo helps negotiate a compromise.

November 21	JVL initiates massive expansion of city's methadone maintenance program for heroin addicts, which grows to forty clinics treating 8,000 addicts.
December 1	Association for Better New York (ABNY) formed by business community, led by real estate executive Lewis Rudin.
December 14	Detective Frank Serpico testifies at Knapp Commission hearings, alleging widespread corruption in the Police Department. Serpico was later the subject of a book by Peter Mass and a movie directed by Stanley Lumet, starring Al Pacino.
December 28	In Miami, JVL announces his candidacy for the Democratic presidential nomination; plans to enter Florida and Wisconsin primaries.

1972

January 1	Subway fare increases from 30 cents to 35 cents.
January 27	Members of Black Liberation Army assassinate two police officers on patrol in Ninth Precinct on Lower East Side, Rocco Laurie and Gregory Foster.
January 29	JVL finishes a surprising second in the Democratic caucuses in Arizona, gaining 23.6 percent of the delegates.
January 30	Bloody Sunday in Northern Ireland as British soldiers attack Catholic protestors, killing thirteen, including seven teenagers.
Feb 7	JVL issues the first executive order by government prohibiting discrimination against gays in public sector hiring.
February 21	Nixon arrives in China for meetings with Chairman Mao and Zhou Enlai, ending twenty-five years of hostility.
March 7	In the New Hampshire Democratic Primary, antiwar candidate Senator George McGovern, with 37 percent of the vote, comes close to defeating front runner Senator Edmund Muskie, with 46 percent. Muskie's candidacy later falters, and McGovern goes on to become the nominee.
March 14	JVL finishes fifth, with 7 percent of the vote, in the Florida Democratic primary.
March 15	*The Godfather*, based on book by Mario Puzo (1969), released as movie, directed by Francis Ford Coppola and starring Marlon Brando and Al Pacino.
April 5	JVL finishes sixth, with 7 percent of the vote, in the Wisconsin Democratic primary; ends his presidential campaign. Celebrated gangster "Crazy" Joe Gallo gunned down at Umberto's Clam House in Little Italy.
April 12	JVL and Chase Bank Chair David Rockefeller announce plan for Manhattan Landing housing development on a platform in the East River south of the Brooklyn Bridge.
April 14	Police officer Phillip Cardillo is fatally shot in Nation of Islam

	Mosque No. 7 on West 116th Street; there is controversy over police handling of the incident.
May 9	President Nixon orders the mining of North Vietnam ports to pressure Hanoi to release prisoners of war and to agree to an internationally supervised cease-fire.
May 27	Nixon and Soviet Communist Party chief Leonid Brezhnev sign two agreements limiting the growth of their nations' nuclear arsenals.
June 9	Elvis Presley gives last New York City concert at Madison Square Garden.
June 17	The Watergate break-in occurs at Democratic Party campaign headquarters in Washington, D.C.
June 29	U.S. Supreme Court rules the death penalty unconstitutional as "cruel and unusual punishment." President Nixon objects to the decision.
August 10	Deputy Mayor Edward Hamilton launches Productivity Program to develop management information systems and upgrade agency performance, forming basis for current Mayor's Management Report.
September 5	At the Munich Olympics, Palestinian terrorists take Israeli Olympic Team members hostage, resulting in the death of all eleven athletes.
October 20	Federal revenue sharing adopted after JVL leads a group of seventeen mayors to Washington to lobby for it.
October 24	Brooklyn Dodger great Jackie Robinson dies at age 53.
October 27	Groundbreaking for the Second Avenue Subway. Construction is twice suspended and eventually restarts in 2007 on one section from 63rd to 96th Streets.
November 7	President Richard Nixon (Republican) defeats Senator George McGovern (Democrat), winning 60 percent of the vote.
December 27	Knapp Commission issues final report finding widespread police corruption, recommends command accountability and other internal interventions.

1973

January 3	George Steinbrenner leads group that buys the Yankees from CBS for $10 million.
January 22	U.S. Supreme Court decides *Roe v. Wade*, upholding a woman's right to an abortion.
January 27	The Vietnam Peace Accord is signed; in Paris by Henry Kissinger and Le Duc Tho of North Vietnam; both awarded 1973 Nobel Peace Prize. United States has 45,948 combat deaths and 303,000 injured.
March 7	JVL announces he will not run for a third term as mayor.

April 4	World Trade Center opens, with the Twin Towers now the two tallest buildings in the world.
April 30	JVL announces $160 million Portman Hotel to begin revitalization of Times Square. Opens as Marriot Marquis in 1985.
May 3–10	JVL visits Moscow and meets with leading Soviet Jewish "Refuseniks"; issues detailed report upon return on the treatment of Soviet Jews seeking to emigrate.
May 10	The Knicks win their second NBA championship by beating the L.A. Lakers, 102–93.
May 17	Senate Watergate Committee hearings begin.
June 9	Secretariat wins the Triple Crown at Belmont.
June 25	JVL opens TKTS discount theater ticket booth in Times Square over opposition by theater owners.
July 11	JVL's plan to create the Madison Avenue Mall by closing Madison Avenue to car traffic (bus and taxi only) and widening sidewalks with cafes and pedestrian amenities defeated by the Board of Estimate in a 12–10 vote.
August 30	Federal Judge John Sirica orders President Nixon to surrender tape recordings of White House conversations as evidence in the Watergate investigation; the president refuses.
September 24	JVL renames Welfare Island as Roosevelt Island in honor of FDR.
October 5	City approves purchase of 197-acre Howland Hook Containership Terminal as part of effort to revive port.
October 6	Yom Kippur War with surprise attack on Israel lasts three weeks.
October 10	Spiro Agnew resigns the vice-presidency, admitting to tax evasion in 1967.
October 12	Representative Gerald Ford is appointed vice president by President Nixon.
October 13	Arab oil embargo begins in retaliation for West's support of Israel in the Yom Kippur War.
October 16	After twenty years of planning and delay, Lindsay dedicates modern new police headquarters at One Police Plaza.
November 6	Democratic Party candidate Abraham Beame elected mayor, defeating Republican John Marchi.
November 15	Board of Estimate approves JVL's plans for Convention Center on Hudson River at 44th Street, following state legislative approval. Project is halted during fiscal crisis in 1975; Javits Center opens at 34th Street in 1986.
December 15	Dump truck falls through elevated West Side Highway, which never reopens.
December 18	Governor Nelson Rockefeller resigns to head Commission on Critical Choices for Americans. Lieutenant Governor Malcolm Wilson becomes Governor.
December 31	JVL's last day as mayor.

1974

August 8   Nixon resigns as president, succeeded by Gerald Ford.

November 6   Congressman Hugh Carey (Democrat) defeats incumbent
                    Malcolm Wilson with 58 percent of vote to become governor of
                    New York State; reelected in 1978.

                    JVL returns to law firm of Webster, Sheffield.

December 19   Nelson Rockefeller becomes vice president. Only time in history
                    both president and vice president were appointed under Twenty-
                    Fifth Amendment procedures.

1975–1979

April 19, 1975   Helicopters evacuate U.S. troops and diplomats from the
                    embassy roof in Saigon, Vietnam, as North Vietnamese troops
                    prepare to enter Saigon.

June 10, 1975   After New York City is unable to sell bonds in February and
                    runs out of cash in April, creating the Fiscal Crisis, the state
                    legislature acts on Governor Hugh Carey's proposal to create
                    the Municipal Assistance Corporation (MAC), which refinances
                    short-term city debt. In November, the state creates the
                    Emergency Financial Control Board to oversee city finances and
                    reforms.

October 30, 1975   "Ford to City: Drop Dead" is front page *Daily News* headline,
                    when President Ford refuses federal assistance to help New York
                    City avoid bankruptcy.

April 26, 1977   SEC issues report on the NYC fiscal crisis assailing irresponsible
                    practices and finding that "the Mayor [Beame] and the
                    Comptroller misled public investors" regarding billions of
                    dollars of municipal securities.

November 8, 1977   Congressman Ed Koch (Democrat) elected Mayor, first
                    defeating incumbent Mayor Beame in the Democratic primary,
                    then Mario Cuomo in the primary run-off, then Cuomo
                    (running as a Liberal) and Republican Roy Goodman; reelected
                    in 1981 and 1985.

August 9, 1978   President Carter signs $1.65 billion federal loan guarantee
                    package for New York on the steps of City Hall.

1980–2000

September 9, 1980   JVL loses Democratic primary for U.S. Senate, coming in
                    behind Elizabeth Holtzman and Bess Myerson. Al D'Amato
                    defeats incumbent Senator Jacob Javits in Republican primary
                    and goes on to win the general election in November against
                    Javits and Holtzman.

November 2, 1982   Mario Cuomo (Democrat) elected governor, defeating Mayor

	Ed Koch in the Democratic Primary, then Republican Lewis Lehrman; reelected in 1986 and 1990.
September 7, 1985	JVL becomes chairman of the closed Lincoln Center Theater, which reopens in March 1986 with the revival of John Guare's *House of Blue Leaves*.
November 8, 1988	Vice President George H. W. Bush (Republican) elected president over Massachusetts Governor Michael Dukakis (Democrat).
November 7, 1989	David Dinkins (Democrat) elected city's first black mayor, defeating incumbent Mayor Koch in Democratic Primary, ending Koch's bid for an unprecedented fourth term, then defeating Republican Rudy Giuliani by 47,000 votes out of almost two million. Lindsay endorses Dinkins, his first mayoral endorsement since leaving City Hall.
November 3, 1992	Democrat Bill Clinton elected president, defeating incumbent George H. W. Bush; reelected in 1996.
November 2, 1993	In a rematch, Republican Rudy Giuliani defeats incumbent Mayor Dinkins by 53,000 votes; reelected in 1997.
November 8, 1994	George Pataki (Republican) elected governor, defeating incumbent Mario Cuomo's bid for a fourth term; reelected in 1998 and 2002.
November 1999	John and Mary Lindsay move to Hilton Head, South Carolina.
November 7, 2000	Republican George W. Bush elected president, defeating Vice President Al Gore in controversial Florida recount, ultimately decided by the U.S. Supreme Court; reelected in 2004.
December 19, 2000	JVL dies of complications of pneumonia and Parkinson's disease.

JOSEPH P. VITERITTI, editor, is the Thomas Hunter Professor of Public Policy at Hunter College, City University of New York, where he is also chair of the Urban Affairs and Planning Department. His most recent of ten books is *When Mayors Take Charge: School Governance in the City.* His more than one hundred articles and essays have appeared in social science journals, law reviews, and popular media such as the *New York Times, Washington Post, The Nation,* and *Huffington Post.* His extensive record of public service and consulting in New York has cut across issues of education policy, charter revision, criminal justice, and public management. In 2010 he served as research director for the New York City Charter Revision Commission.

LIZABETH COHEN is the Howard Mumford Jones Professor of American Studies and Dean of the Radcliffe Institute for Advanced Study at Harvard University. Her book *Making a New Deal: Industrial Workers in Chicago, 1919–1939* won the Bancroft Prize in American History and was a finalist for the Pulitzer Prize. She is also author of *A Consumers' Republic: The Politics of Mass Consumption in Postwar America* and is currently writing a book about Ed Logue and urban renewal in the Northeast.

PAUL GOLDBERGER is contributing editor for *Vanity Fair.* He is formerly the architecture critic for the *New Yorker* and holds the Joseph Urban Chair in Architecture and Design at the New School. He received the Pulitzer Prize in 1984 for his work as architecture critic at the *New York Times.* Among his many books are *Why Architecture Matters* and *Up from Zero: Politics, Architecture, and the Rebuilding of New York.*

BRIAN GOLDSTEIN is a Mellon Postdoctoral Fellow at the Center for the Humanities and the Department of History at University of Wisconsin–Madison. He received his PhD in Architecture, Landscape Architecture, and Urban Planning from Harvard University. He is writing a history of urban development in Harlem, New York.

GEOFFREY KABASERVICE is the author of *Rule and Ruin: The Downfall of Moderation and the Destruction of the Republican Party, from Eisenhower to the Tea Party* and *The Guardians: Kingman Brewster, His Circle, and the Rise of the Moderate Establishment*. He has written for numerous national publications and has been an assistant professor of history at Yale University. He is a visiting research fellow at the Roosevelt House Institute for Public Policy at Hunter College.

MARIANA MOGILEVICH is a visiting assistant professor of metropolitan studies at New York University. She received her PhD from Harvard University, with a dissertation *Designing the Urban: Space and Politics in Lindsay's New York*. She was a senior editor at *Next American City Magazine* and has published widely on the history of architecture and urbanism, art, and film.

CHARLES R. MORRIS is recently the author of *The Dawn of Innovation: The First American Industrial Revolution*. Among his ten other books are *The Trillion Dollar Meltdown*, which received the Gerald Loeb Award and was a *New York Times* best seller, and *The Cost of Good Intentions: New York City and the Liberal Experiment*, which was listed as one of the *New York Times* Best Books in 1980. He was assistant budget director for the Lindsay administration.

DAVID ROGERS is emeritus professor of management and sociology at New York University's Stern School of Business where he was chair of the management department. He has published ten books, including *110 Livingston Street: Politics and Bureaucracy in the New York City School System* and *The Management of Big Cities*. He has been a management consultant to federal and city agencies as well as business and labor organizations.

CLARENCE TAYLOR is professor of history at Baruch College and the Graduate Center of the City of New York. He has published six books, including *The Black Churches of Brooklyn* and *Knocking at Our Own Door: Milton A. Galamison and the Struggle to Integrate New York City Schools.*